Onwards to Omdurman

The Anglo-Egyptian Campaign to Reconquer the Sudan, 1896-1898

Keith Surridge

Helion & Company

Helion & Company Limited
Unit 8 Amherst Business Centre
Budbrooke Road
Warwick
CV34 5WE
England
Tel. 01926 499 619
Email: info@helion.co.uk
Website: www.helion.co.uk
Twitter: @helionbooks
Visit our blog at blog.helion.co.uk

Published by Helion & Company 2022
Designed and typeset by Mach 3 Solutions Ltd (www.mach3solutions.co.uk)
Cover designed by Paul Hewitt, Battlefield Design (www.battlefield-design.co.uk)

Text © Keith Surridge 2022
Images © as individually credited
Maps drawn by George Anderson © Helion & Company 2022

Cover: 'Sudanese troops of Hector McDonalds Brigade during the battle
of Omdurman', by Peter Dennis (© Helion & Company 2022)

ISBN 978-1-915070-51-7

British Library Cataloguing-in-Publication Data.
A catalogue record for this book is available from the British Library.

For details of other military history titles published by Helion & Company Limited
contact the above address or visit our website: http://www.helion.co.uk.

We always welcome receiving book proposals from prospective authors.

Contents

List of Illustrations

In Text

In Colour Plate Section

List Of Maps

Abbreviations

AEA	Anglo-Egyptian Army
BL	British Library
EA	Egyptian Army
LHCMA	Liddell Hart Centre for Military Archives
NAM	National Army Museum
QM	Queen Mary, University of London
SAD	Sudan Archives, Durham University
SIR	Sudan Intelligence Reports
SMR	Sudan Military Railway
TNA	The National Archives
WSRO	West Sussex Record Office

Acknowledgements

Thankfully, most of the archival research had been done before the outbreak of the Covid pandemic and I wish to thank the archivists, librarians and staff of the following institutions for their help and support: the Manuscripts Department of the British Library; the Sudan Archive of the University of Durham; Liddell Hart Centre for Military Archives; the London Library; the National Archives; the Templar Centre, National Army Museum; the West Sussex Record Office. Thanks also to Nichola Wood at the Archives and Special Collections held by Queen Mary, University of London.

I would like to thank the Trustees of the Liddell Hart Centre for Military Archives for the use of the Major General Sir J. Frederick Maurice papers.

On the internet, Internet Archive (https://archive.org) and the Haithi Trust were most helpful in gaining access to contemporary publications.

Friends and colleagues at the University of Notre Dame (USA) in England, Faculty Seminar proved to be an enthusiastic and insightful audience. A special mention to my colleague, Hadas Elber-Aviram for her help with picture research and, with Alice Tyrell, for enabling me to gain access to the collection of the *Illustrated London News* at the London Library.

Over the years of research and writing I've discussed the campaign at various lengths with the following friends, scholars all, and would like to thank them for their valuable insights: Rodney Atwood, Ian F. W. Beckett, Peter Boyden and Roger Stearn.

Thanks also to Professor Stephen Miller of the University of Maine – I owe you one – as I do Chris Musk for his earlier help with the maps.

A special mention to all my Walthamstow friends of over forty years' standing, you know who you are, who provided much needed support before, during and after the pandemic.

I would like to thank especially Christopher Brice for inviting me to write about the Sudan campaign in the first place and for his unflagging support throughout the process.

Most of all, I would like to thank Justine Taylor for reading the whole manuscript and for her incisive and constructive editing. Any mistakes that remain are entirely mine.

Preface

'The terrible machinery of scientific war'[1]

The victory of the Anglo-Egyptian army under Sir Horatio Herbert Kitchener at the battle of Omdurman on 2 September 1898, brought an end to the Mahdist state in the Sudan. It was the culmination of a campaign, begun in March 1896, to reconquer the Sudan in the name of the former overlord of Egypt and to avenge the death of the British hero General Charles Gordon at Khartoum in 1885. Furthermore, the local significance of the battle of Omdurman meant that the Sudan would then be governed by what became known as the Anglo-Egyptian Condominium until 1956. The battle was also, in the words of one historian 'the climax of the period of imperialism known as the "scramble for Africa", which enabled Europe to dominate the continent'.[2] The battle's significance also went beyond the valley of the Nile and, as another historian has argued, became 'a major international event in both African and European contexts and was rightly regarded as such by contemporaries'.[3]

The battle of Omdurman (known as Karari by the Sudanese) was for the British one of the most decisive of the Victorian era, and if it had been the last battle of Queen Victoria's 'little wars' it would have been a fitting end to her reign, considering that the first conflict in Afghanistan, between 1839 and 1842, had seen British forces badly defeated. Yet to understand how and why the Anglo-Egyptian Army had advanced hundreds of miles up through the Nile Valley for a final showdown with the Khalifa, this book considers the whole campaign undertaken by Kitchener's forces, constrained only by the demands of concision. There is much more to be said but the book provides a solid grounding for further study. The two-year Sudan campaign, unhurried and well-planned, owed much to Kitchener's foresight and the application of cutting-edge Victorian technology, for not only did the Mahdists have to be defeated, but also nature too. Kitchener's Egyptian and British forces had to master both the desert and the river Nile which both posed severe

---

1   Frederick Woods (ed.), *Young Winston's Wars. The original despatches of Winston Churchill* (London: Sphere Books Ltd., 1972), p.182.

2   'Ismat Hasan Zulfo, *Karari*, London, Frederick Warne (Publishers), 1980), p.xiii

3   Edward Spiers, (ed), *Sudan. The conquest reappraised*, (London: Frank Cass, 1998), p.9

challenges. To help defeat the obstacles of sand, rock and water, Kitchener's army deployed railways, the telegraph, gunboats, breech-loading artillery pieces, Maxim machine guns and breech-loading rifles, alongside camels and sailing craft. The deployment of all that Victorian military science had to offer is testimony to the respect that the British officers felt for their Mahdist enemy. In their account of the campaign, two officers opined that though the Khalifa was not as powerful as he once was 'he was still able to gather round him thousands of fanatical warriors, worthy foemen for the finest troops in the world'.[4] Mahdist forces that tried to block their enemy's advance were brushed aside until in September 1898, Kitchener's combined Anglo-Egyptian army stood outside the Mahdist capital of Omdurman. During the battle Kitchener took few chances and ensured that modern weapons technology was deployed to the utmost advantage. According to one eyewitness, G. W. Steevens, the correspondent of the *Daily Mail*, 'It was not a battle, but an execution', a view supported by another correspondent, Bennet Burleigh of the *Daily Telegraph*, who wrote that 'the battle of Omdurman has the right to be considered from the victor's point of view the safest action ever fought'.[5] If one's knowledge of the battle comes from the two major films that feature it – *The Four Feathers* and *Young Winston* – then one's perception might be that the Mahdists simply threw themselves at the Anglo-Egyptian forces with no consideration given to the power of modern weapons. One might then agree with Steevens that the generalship of the Mahdist leader, the Khalifa Abdallahi, 'was a masterpiece of imbecility'.[6]

Yet Steevens, Burleigh, Churchill, as well as those British officers who took part, suggest that if the Khalifa had given the matter more thought, then the result of the battle might have been closer and might even conceivably have ended in defeat for Kitchener's men. The complete destruction of the Khalifa's army has, however, obscured the fact that the Khalifa did have a plan, that his army did attempt to follow it and manoeuvre in front of the Anglo-Egyptian army.[7] The battle of Omdurman was more nuanced than films and later books would suggest: the Khalifa indeed had a plan for the battle and his generals attempted to follow it.

This book is based on British sources because there is a wealth of diaries, letters and books written by those who were there in British archives, museums and libraries. Even in Sudan, as one historian has recently pointed out, the available contemporary sources held in Khartoum 'were written chiefly by British military and intelligence officers, as well as colonial administrators'.[8] So far, the only major work on the Sudan campaign written by a Sudanese

---

4   Henry S. L. Alford and W. Dennistoun Sword, *The Egyptian Soudan. Its loss and recovery* (London: Macmillan and Co., Ltd., 1898. Reprinted Dallington: Naval & Military Press, 1992), p.35.

5   G. W. Steevens, *With Kitchener to Khartum*, (Edinburgh & London: William Blackwood & Sons, 1898), p.264; Bennet Burleigh, *Khartoum Campaign*, (London: Chapman Hall Ltd., 1899), p.166.

6   Steevens, *With Kitchener*, p.289.

7   Zulfo, *Karrari*, pp.15–16, 137–138.

8   Ronald M. Lamothe, *Slaves of Fortune. Sudanese soldiers and the River War 1896-1898*, (James Currey: Woodbridge, 2011), p.5.

historian that has been translated into English is that by 'Ismat Hasan Zulfo, to which all non-Sudanese historians owe a great debt.[9] Nonetheless, there is plenty in the words of contemporaries to provide a comprehensive appreciation of the actions of the Khalifa's forces and it is the intention of this book to give them their due recognition. What follows, then, is an account of the Anglo-Egyptian conquest of the Sudan between 1896–1898, with a particular focus on the climactic battle of Omdurman.

With regard to the transliteration of Sudanese names, I have followed Philip Ziegler by 'using the version which it seems to me will be most readily recognised by the general reader', thus Osman Digna instead of 'Uthman Diqna; Osman Azrak instead of 'Uthman Azraq.[10] Egyptians and Sudanese with anglicised versions of their names should still be familiar and identifiable to the reader.

---

9   'Ismat Hasan Zulfo, *Karari*, (London: Frederick Warne (Publishers), 1980).
10   Philip Ziegler, *Omdurman* (London: Collins, 1973), p.7.

Chapter 1

Britain, Egypt, and the Sudan

On 13 September 1882, British forces under General Sir Garnet Wolseley decisively defeated Egypt's army at the battle of Tel-el-Kebir. It was the start of a British military presence in the country that was to last for 72 years. The British had invaded Egypt at this point to protect the vital Suez Canal trade route and because the interests of Britain and France, particularly their control over Egypt's economy and finances, had been threatened by a nationalist uprising led by the army and by severe anti-European riots in the port of Alexandria.

Anglo-French dominance of the Egyptian government and economy had been in place since 1876 and had resulted from Egypt's bankruptcy that had endangered the investments and loans provided by European financiers. Egypt had officially been a part of the Ottoman empire since 1517 and had followed an independent path since the French invasion of 1798. An Albanian Muslim named Muhammed Ali Pasha (or Mehmed Ali in Turkish) gradually claimed more power as the Ottoman Sultan's viceroy or governor of Egypt and had soon begun the process of Egypt's modernization and imperial expansion. In a quest for gold and slaves, Egyptian forces had advanced south, up the Nile river valley taking control by 1820 of much of neighbouring Sudan, a region with long economic ties to Egypt. During the hereditary governorship of Muhammad Ali's grandson, Ismail Pasha (1863–1874), the Egyptian advance continued and reached as far south as the modern Ugandan border.

It was under the viceroyalty of Ismail that the modernization of Egypt really took off. Bolstered by record exports of cotton, Ismail borrowed lavishly to fund his schemes, the most spectacular being the building of the Suez Canal, opened in 1869. Ismail's investments in agriculture, railways and telegraphs also cost huge sums, as did the annual tribute to the Ottoman Sultan. In 1867, after paying a huge bribe, Ismail gained recognition from the Ottoman Sultan for his title of Khedive, which in his eyes made him an independent sovereign. Eventually, Egypt had a state debt of £90 million, serviced by inadequate tax revenues of just £8 million.[1]

---

1   Caroline Finkel, *Osman's Dream. The Story of the Ottoman Empire 1300–1923* (London: John Murray, 2006), pp.399, 427–428, 445–446, 472–473. H. L. Wesseling, *Divide and Rule. The Partition of Africa 1880–1914* (Wesport, CT: Praeger Publishers, 1996), pp.31–43.

An Egyptian cotton boom had been created in 1861 by shortages of the commodity caused by the outbreak of the American civil war in that year. With few American supplies reaching Europe, buyers there turned to Egypt. But once that conflict ended in 1865 the boom was over. Not that it mattered to Ismail: he carried on with his large projects, now financed by loans provided by eager European banks and financial houses. To them, Egypt was a good, sound investment, for under Ismail they thought Egypt was now on the path to leaving Africa and becoming fully European. Thus, as one historian has remarked 'foreign cash poured into Egypt like a Nile flood'.[2] Inevitably, the Egyptian economy could not keep up with Ismail's ambitions and so, on 8 April 1876, the country went bankrupt. Egypt's two main creditors, Britain and France were, understandably, not impressed by this turn of events, and after various fits and starts imposed restrictions over the economy, each appointing a controller to ensure Ismail made cuts to government expenditure. For the next three years Ismail wriggled and squirmed trying to avoid losing some of his gains as well as his political authority. In this he failed and lost his throne. On 26 July 1879, he was dismissed by the Ottoman Sultan acting under British and French pressure. Although Egypt still had an empire, Ismail's bid to become an acknowledged sovereign of a flourishing independent state had been shown to be a chimera. Having the distant Sultan as an overlord was one thing, but now Ismail had gifted Egypt to the European powers.

The next khedive was Ismail's son Tewfik and he had little choice but to comply with European demands. Eventually, a revamped system of Anglo-French dual control was established. In July 1880, the Caisse de la Dette, first formed in 1876 and comprising two British, two French and one member each from Austria-Hungary, Italy and Germany, was tasked to oversee Egyptian debt repayments and interest rates. The new Law of Liquidation ensured that money was set aside to meet Egyptian obligations and for domestic purposes. Europe's dominance of Egypt was complete; constrained by the European financial straitjacket, the khedive and his ministers had no choice but to follow the path of financial probity and good housekeeping. Egypt's financial mire meant vassalage, creating a situation which grew ever more intolerable to Egyptians already suffering from the stringent cutbacks.

Already, in 1879, Egypt's army officers had protested against the reduction of the officer corps. Following this, in 1881, disaffected Egyptians began to coalesce into a nationalist movement. In February, protests occurred, but in September, Colonel Ahmed Arabi Pasha led a military coup, forcing the khedive to put the government into the hands of the army and its civilian supporters. Eventually, on 8 January 1882, a warning note sent by Britain and France failed to deter the nationalists who, instead, were invigorated by the threat and made Colonel Arabi the new minister of war. With no improvement in the situation by May, British and French warships appeared off the port of Alexandria, exciting the nationalists still further. By the end of that month, the khedive's authority had vanished: 'The armed power was in

---

2   Dominic Green, *Three Empires on the Nile. The Victorian Jihad 1869–1899* (New York: Free Press, 2007), p.16.

the hands of Arabi, and it had become evident that, whatever Ministers were appointed, they would be virtually puppets.'[3]

In Alexandria, the Egyptian population soon took matters into their own hands. Between 10 and 11 June 1882 rioters killed up to 50 Europeans. Turmoil in French domestic politics meant that Britain would be forced to act alone in dealing with the nationalists. On 11 July 1882, a Royal Navy squadron bombarded Alexandria's defences which led to the retaliatory burning down of the European quarter. The British had since 28 June begun to prepare for a military intervention.[4] With rare speed and efficiency the preparations were completed and so it was on 13 September 1882 that Sir Garnet Wolseley defeated Arabi's forces at Tel-el-Kebir. Arabi was captured and exiled to Ceylon. Britain was now firmly in control of Egypt.

As the desert dust settled in Egypt, the British now had to determine how it was to be governed. The Khedive was restored to his throne and his ministers would continue to govern the country, with the British ready to offer advice. On the recommendation of Lord Dufferin, the ambassador to the Ottoman empire, the dual control with the French was ended – with French agreement. The British would undertake reforms of the legal and governmental systems and the police, while Major General Sir H. Evelyn Wood was appointed Sirdar, or commander-in-chief, of the Egyptian Army. Wood, alongside a group of selected British officers, including Captain Horatio Herbert Kitchener, hoped to turn the Egyptians into a well-trained, disciplined and efficient fighting force.

The British official chosen to oversee Egypt's finances as Consul General was Sir Evelyn Baring, a former soldier and veteran of Egypt's financial affairs, who was recalled from India for the purpose. From 11 September 1883, Baring was to be the effective authority in Egypt until 1907. Nevertheless, the European powers still had to be consulted on any major financial measures through the Caisse de la Dette, and while the British remained in Egypt, the French grew ever more hostile.

The British government under its prime minister William Gladstone had been reluctant to become involved in Egyptian affairs and was keen to find a way out as quickly as possible. But now that Britain was in effective occupation Egypt's problems became its own, a situation that Gladstone refused to acknowledge. Since 1881, a revolt had been underway against Egyptian rule in the Sudan. To the Sudanese, Egyptian rule was known as *al-Turkiyya* – the rule of the Turks. This reflected early Ottoman domination and the language spoken by Egyptian officials, many being of Turkish-Circassian origin.[5] Moreover, by the 1880s, many of the officials working in the Sudan were Europeans and none had been more famous than Charles Gordon, a British soldier, whose appointment by the Khedive as governor general between 1877-1879 has been described as 'unique'. Gordon was

3   Colonel J. F. Maurice, *The Campaign of 1882 in Egypt* (London: J. B. Hayward & Son, 1887. Reprinted: Portsmouth: Eyre & Spottiswood, Grosvenor Press, 1973), p.1.
4   Maurice, *Campaign of 1882*, p.4.
5   Alice Moore–Harell, *Gordon and the Sudan. Prologue to the Mahdiyya 1877–1880* (London: Frank Cass, 2011), pp 4–5.

given latitude to reform Sudan's administration and he appointed several other Europeans as provincial governors, including the Austrian Rudolf Slatin and the Italian Romolo Gessi. At the same time, 'Gordon's friendly attitude and empathy brought him into close contact with the population, an exceptional behaviour as against the arrogance and aloofness his predecessors had displayed.'[6] Gordon brought corrupt and tyrannical officials to book and encouraged trade and agriculture. But in trying and failing to end the slave trade, he caused a revolt of the Sudanese slave traders in 1878. Furthermore, Egypt's demands for revenue meant that tax gathering was brutal, something Gordon was unable to stop. Frustrated by his inability to effect real change, Gordon resigned from his post on 29 July 1879. He was not unpopular and although he had impressed the citizens of Khartoum he had fatally alienated the slave traders. Additionally, Egyptian religious policies that tried to end local Sudanese traditions of worship and the separation of civil law from religious law meant that religious dissent was ready to explode. Gordon had tried to bring something better to a benighted country but failed to end 60 years of Egyptian misrule and oppression. His actions, however, ensured that 'Sudan ceased to be a remote, isolated *terra incognita* and entered the global political arena of the late nineteenth-century.'[7]

The revolt against Egyptian rule in the Sudan was led by Muhammed Ahmed, a religious teacher whose devotion to the Islamic faith soon gained him disciples, including one Abdallahi ibn Muhammad al Ta'aisha, who would become his closest follower. It was he who urged Muhammed Ahmed to tour the countryside, particularly the western region of Kordofan, and 'he was soon convinced that there was a spirit of the most bitter hostility against the authorities on the part of the poor population … who suffered terrible oppression and tyranny at the hands of the self-seeking and unscrupulous tax-gatherers who infested the country'.[8] Muhammed Ahmed's religious devotion and simple, puritanical lifestyle, as well as his ability to preach and inspire soon gained many adherents and a growing reputation. He gradually convinced his followers that he was blessed by visions and divine revelation, that he was in fact the *Mahdi* – the Chosen Guide. Such was his fame by late 1881 that he and his followers had defeated government attempts to arrest him. By the end of the year, the Mahdi's revolt had begun in earnest and he was determined to bring religious reform and renewal to not just the Sudan and Egypt, but also to the rest of the Islamic world and beyond.

Two years later, the Mahdists, also known as the Dervishes, had taken control of large swathes of Kordofan. Success gained followers as well as modern arms from the defeated Egyptian garrisons. The capture of the regional capital, El Obeid, on 19 January 1883 had brought a windfall of Remington rifles and artillery. The British, in a wilful display of legitimism, regarded the revolt as a matter for the Egyptian government. All Egypt could

---

6   Moore–Harell, *Gordon*, p.235.
7   Moore–Harell, *Gordon*, p.7.
8   Colonel Sir R. Slatin Pasha, *Fire and Sword in the Sudan. A Personal Narrative of Fighting and Serving the Dervishes* (London: Edward Arnold, 1896. Reprinted: London: The Long Riders' Guild Press, nd.), pp.54–55.

then do was to send the remnants of Arabi's army to the Sudan, along with some European officers of doubtful quality, and commanded by a retired British officer, William Hicks, or Hicks Pasha as he was known in the Egyptian service. In late 1883, Hicks set out to recapture El Obeid. On 4 November, Hicks and his army of about 9,000 men were attacked and slaughtered at the battle of Shaykan. More weapons fell into the hands of the Mahdists and now 'all looked to this holy man who had performed such wonders, and they eagerly awaited his next move'.[9] This was not long in coming. Mahdist forces moved into Darfur and at Dara, on 23 December 1883, Rudolf Slatin was forced to surrender, his life being spared by his conversion to Islam. For Slatin, this was now the prelude to twelve years of captivity. On 22 November 1883, the British learnt of Hicks' disaster. As far as Baring was concerned Hicks should have remained at Khartoum which could have been defended.[10] Without Hicks's army, however, Khartoum was doomed.

The British were painfully aware that Egypt could do nothing to save the Sudan and that the new Egyptian army being formed would be unable to defend the frontier with the Sudan being bereft of men, money, and weapons. Gladstone's pusillanimous British government now recognised the obvious as Lord Northbrook, the First Lord of the Admiralty conceded: 'We have now been forced into the position of being the protector of Egypt.'[11]

The British were fearful for the security of Egypt and particularly for the safety of the Suez Canal. Baring was concerned that the financial costs of defending the country would be prohibitive. But if Egypt was not defended then it would be conquered by the Mahdists, and then the Ottoman empire might fall to the fanatics next and even the Muslim populations of Britain's Indian empire might become affected by the contagion. Baring advised the British cabinet that the Sudan should be abandoned and that Egypt's government should ensure that this happened. The cabinet's response was supportive stating that 'in matters affecting the administration and safety of Egypt the advice of Her Majesty's Government should be followed as long as the provisional occupation lasts. Ministers and Governors must carry out this advice or forfeit their offices'.[12] Baring, knowing that evacuation was not a popular policy, now gained an Egyptian government more amenable to his views. Many ministers forfeited their offices, including Sharif Pasha, the Khedive's prime minister. Nubar Pasha, a more compliant individual and political veteran, replaced Sharif and acquiesced in the evacuation of the Sudan. The British government was eventually awakening to the fact that the Sudan and Egypt were intimately connected and that events in the south could have serious repercussions well beyond their desert origins. But how to withdraw successfully from the Sudan? Such an action would necessitate the evacuation of thousands of people over vast distances and through hostile territories. Baring had earlier suggested a British officer be sent to oversee such a move, which the British cabinet had

9   Slatin, *Fire and Sword*, p.135.
10   The Earl of Cromer, *Modern Egypt*, (London: Macmillan, 1908), vol. 2, p.31.
11   Northbrook to the Cabinet, 24 December 1883, quoted in R. Robinson & J. Gallagher with Alice Denny, *Africa and the Victorians* (London: Macmillan, 1981), p.134.
12   Quoted in Roger Owen, *Lord Cromer* (Oxford: Oxford University Press, 2004), pp.188–189.

ignored. No Egyptians wanted to go because the Sudan was dangerous and the task a humiliation. One former governor, Abd al Qadir, now the minister of war, had already refused Baring's offer.[13]

In Britain, once the evacuation policy became known one candidate received enormous press and public backing. W. T. Stead of the *Pall Mall Gazette* led the clarion call on 9 January 1884. 'We cannot send a regiment to Khartoum, but we can send a man who on more than one occasion has proved himself more valuable in similar circumstances than an entire army. Why not send … Gordon with full powers to Khartoum, to assume control of the territory, to treat with the Mahdi, to release the garrisons, and to do what he can to save what can be saved from the wreck of the Sudan.'[14] Five days later, Baring recommended sending for Gordon. The British government agreed to give Gordon full powers to evacuate the Sudan but put him under Baring's authority, much to the latter's relief. Baring told Lord Granville, the foreign secretary, 'it is well he should be under my orders, but a man who habitually consults the Prophet Isaiah when he is in difficulty is not apt to obey the orders of anyone.'[15]

The success of Gordon's earlier service was exaggerated by his admirers, while the Mahdi's impact was not taken seriously enough. By sending the pious and devout Gordon back to the Sudan it was as if the British hoped that one religious fanatic could deal with another. But there were no other candidates with Gordon's stature and British knowledge of the Sudan was thin. This lack of expertise was in the process of being remedied by the British army's intelligence department. Acting on a memorandum written by Lieutenant Colonel Sir Charles Wilson, who had been in Egypt during the first months of the occupation, the cabinet, in early 1884, ordered the occupation of the Sudanese port of Suakin on the Red Sea coast.[16]

The occupation of Suakin was timely as the area around it had been raised in support of the Mahdi by Osman Digna, one of the most loyal adherents to the Mahdi's cause thereafter. Apart from offering the British a base for an advance on Berber, a strategic town situated on the Nile north of Khartoum, the possession of Suakin prevented the export of Mahdism to Arabia and Islam's holy cities of Mecca and Medina. The British though had to fight to retain the port. A force under General Gerald Graham managed to inflict two defeats on Osman Digna's forces, at El Teb on 29 February and at Tamai on 13 March. Both battles were hard fought and would provide epic material for contemporary and future accounts of the campaign. Many of the Mahdists were Beja Hadendowa tribesmen, known to the British as 'fuzzy-wuzzies' because of their abundant hair styles and who were later the subjects of an admiring poem by Kipling. Suakin would remain in British hands, becoming a base for a future advance on Berber.

---

13   Owen, *Lord Cromer*, pp.189, 192.
14   Quoted in Green, *Three Empires*, p.155
15   Quoted in Owen, *Lord Cromer*, p.196.
16   William Beaver, *Under Every Leaf* (London: Biteback Publishing, 2012), pp.113–125. Colonel Mike Snook, *Beyond the Reach of Empire. Wolseley's Failed Campaign to Save Gordon and Khartoum* (London: Frontline Books, 2013), pp.10–14.

Meanwhile, General Gordon had reached Khartoum on 18 February 1884. While the evacuation process was underway Gordon tried to bargain with the Mahdi by offering him the sultanate of Kordofan, which was rejected. The Mahdi's forces now began to isolate Khartoum and in May captured Berber, thus providing a link with the remaining forces under Osman Digna. With Gordon now cut off completely, pressure began to build on the British government to extract him from Khartoum. After weeks of dithering, Gladstone's cabinet decided in August 1884 to send a relief force under General Lord Wolseley, who decided to advance up the Nile. This would be a formidable undertaking, requiring troops, boats, camels, horses and supplies to be brought up river at a time when its level was falling owing to the end of the summer rains and the annual Nile flood. This meant that the series of rapids, known as cataracts, were more exposed and their rocks a death trap for river traffic. Some of these cataracts were miles long and presented obstacles that taxed the ingenuity of the British officers. Getting boats over them took time, a luxury that Wolseley did not have. By December 1884, Wolseley's forces had concentrated at Korti, a point where the Nile bends eastwards if advancing upriver. But here there was a shortcut of 174 miles across the Bayuda desert to the town of Metemma, situated on the Nile as it bends south once again. In desperation, Wolseley sent a force of 1,700 men, known as the Desert Column, to take Metemma and await Gordon's river steamers, and the 3,000 men under Major General W. Earle who were following the great bend of the river. The advance of the Desert Column is one of the great epics of the Victorian period. It fought two major battles against numerically superior Mahdist forces and against the odds reached the river and on 21 January 1885 rendezvoused with the steamers. On 24 January, the two boats, packed with 200 loyal Sudanese troops and 22 British soldiers set sail for Khartoum, desperately hoping that the mere presence of the British would undermine Mahdist morale. It was supposed to be a subtle hint that the British were coming! It took the two boats four days to reach Khartoum, having fought their way through massed rifle and artillery fire from the river banks. They found that Khartoum had fallen to the Mahdi two days earlier and that the city was a pillaged ghost town. Gordon was dead and all the little force could do was turn around and fight their way back, which they did, although not before losing the two steamers and having to wait several days on a Nile island to be rescued.

The news of Gordon's death shocked Queen Victoria and the British public. As trouble was brewing with Russia over Afghanistan, Gladstone's embattled government found an excuse to order the evacuation of the Sudan. This was accomplished during the summer months of 1885. The Mahdists eventually followed the British retreat but at the battle of Ginnis on 30 December 1885, on the Egyptian frontier, they were defeated by British forces. Afterwards, the frontier settled down, apart from Mahdist raiding of nearby Egyptian villages. The port of Suakin remained in Anglo-Egyptian hands.

Wolseley would never command in the field again and was posted to the War Office to oversee the reform of the British army. His plan to relieve Gordon, a mixture of forlorn hope and hubris, had fallen apart on the Nile and in the desert. The efforts of Wolseley and his officers revealed plainly that campaigning in the Sudan could not be rushed – timing was everything. The Mahdi's armies were found to be formidable opponents, imbued with a native courage that was now tempered by religious fanaticism. The last thing the British needed was to add nature to their list of opponents.

Horatio Herbert Kitchener, then a major, out in the desert with his loyal band of friendly tribesmen, had been the last British officer in contact with Gordon. He had previously known Gordon, was full of admiration for the general and was greatly affected by his death. Kitchener's exploits had gained him prominence and he was asked to write a report on the fall of Khartoum which would later be incorporated in the campaign's official history.[17] His report is best known for its ending which encapsulates his sense of loss: 'The memorable siege of Khartoum lasted 317 days, and it is not too much to say that such a noble resistance was due to the indomitable resolution and resources of one Englishman. Never was a garrison so nearly rescued, never was a commander so sincerely lamented.'[18]

Four years after their first invasion of Egypt the Mahdists tried again in 1889 with a totally inadequate force of 5,000 men led by Wad el-Nejeumi, the main architect of the 1883 Mahdist victory over Hicks Pasha. Low in numbers but strong in faith, Nejumi's army was destroyed on 3 August 1889 at the battle of Toski, by a reformed Egyptian army under its new Sirdar, Major General Sir Francis Grenfell. Few Mahdists escaped and Wad el-Nejumi himself was killed. 'For the first time since 1885' as one historian has remarked, 'complete tranquillity reigned on the frontier.'[19] But while one Egyptian frontier remained quiet, another, at Suakin, was not. In 1890, Baring, supported by Grenfell, believed that the town of Tokar, 'the granary of the Eastern Sudan', could be taken, a blow which would seriously undermine Osman Digna's position. Grenfell insisted that 'The Dervish force has never been so weak or so discredited at the present time.' But if the British did nothing 'I foresee a dark future for the Eastern Soudan, as the tribes, seeing that the Government will do nothing, must, for very existence throw themselves into the hands of the Dervishes.'[20] The British prime minister, now Lord Salisbury, authorised operations around Suakin. On 19 February 1891, Colonel Holled Smith, commanding Egyptian forces, defeated Osman Digna at the battle of Ajafi, near Tokar. This crushing victory was 'hailed with genuine satisfaction by the population' and 'Tokar did for Eastern Soudan what Toski did for the Nile valley.'[21] Thus from 1891, the two frontier areas of Egypt were quiescent, suiting Lord Salisbury who had no interest in conquering the Sudan. He

---

17   Sir George Arthur, *Life of Lord Kitchener* (London: Macmillan & Co., 1920), vol. 1, p.112, note.

18   Arthur, *Lord Kitchener*, vol. 1, p.124.

19   A. B. Theobald, *The Mahdiya. A History of the Anglo–Egyptian Sudan 1881–1899* (London: Longmans, Green & Co., Ltd., 1951), pp.58–64.

20   Cromer, *Modern Egypt*, vol. 2, p.74; The National Archives (TNA): PRO/30/57: Kitchener Papers, PRO 30/57/12/K7: 'Correspondence Respecting the Re-occupation of Tokar by the Egyptian Government', Memorandum by Major General Sir F. Grenfell, n.d., [1891], to Sir Evelyn Baring.

21   Cromer, *Modern Egypt*, vol. 2, pp.76–77; Field Marshal Lord Grenfell, *Memoirs* (London: Hodder & Stoughton, 1925), pp.106–108.

told Baring that the Mahdists 'were created for the purpose of keeping the bed warm for you till you can occupy it'.[22] Baring, now ennobled as Lord Cromer, supported Salisbury's view in order to get on with the job of repairing Egypt's economy, while the army was reformed and modernised by its British officers.[23]

In July 1895, Lord Salisbury's Conservatives again won the British general election ending three years of Liberal government, with Salisbury also taking over the Foreign Office as well as returning as prime minister. Salisbury had no ambition for involving Britain again with a Mahdist Sudan, nor had Cromer. In Egypt, Cromer already had too much on his plate, particularly in the form of the new khedive, Abbas Hilmi II, who had unexpectedly inherited the throne in 1892. He was proving difficult to work with and Cromer wanted to undermine the Khedive's support for Egyptian nationalism by improving Egypt's agriculture through the building of a dam at Aswan.[24] The hopes of both Salisbury and Cromer, however, were dashed by Italy's ambitious but ill-considered attempts to extend its East African empire.

Sir Evelyn Baring, Lord Cromer.
(*Illustrated London News*)

On 1 March 1896, the Italians were defeated at Adowa by the Abyssinians. The Italian garrison at Kassala, a strategic town, was now under real threat from the Mahdists. Three times the British were asked by Italy to help and finally, on 11 March, Salisbury's government decided something must be done: the Sudan would be invaded. The decision took Cromer by surprise and he later complained that it 'was taken and publicly announced with somewhat excessive haste'. Salisbury was also frustrated that the British had been rushed into their decision: 'I would have wished our Italian friends had less capacity for being beaten … but it would not have been safe either from an African or European point of view'. Salisbury, in fact, supported the decision for reasons that had more to do with European great-power politics but once the government's verdict had been announced the nature of the invasion of Mahdist Sudan had to be worked out.[25]

22   Robinson & Gallagher, Denny *Africa and the Victorians*, pp.304–305.
23   Cromer, *Modern Egypt,* vol. 2, pp.80–81.
24   Owen, *Lord Cromer*, pp.286–287.
25   Cromer, *Modern Egypt*, vol. 2, p.83; Salisbury quoted in Andrew Roberts, *Salisbury. Victorian Titan* (London: Weidenfeld & Nicholson, 1999), p.641; John Gooch, 'Italy, Abyssinia and the Sudan 1885-98', in Edward M. Spiers (ed.), *Sudan. The Reconquest Reappraised* (London: Frank Cass, 1998), p.141.

The next day, 12 March, the cabinet met with its military advisers, including Wolseley, now the British army's Commander-in-Chief. The main questions before the politicians and generals concerned how far the invasion should go and who would undertake it – the Egyptian army alone or with British support – and under whose command – a British general or Kitchener, Sirdar since 1892. The War Office, which from the military point of view meant Wolseley, was keen for Major General C. Knowles, commanding the British garrison in Egypt, to take command of preparations. The secretary of state for war, Lord Lansdowne, dutifully telegraphed Knowles to get things moving and, rather belatedly at the end of the telegram told him to 'consult Sirdar'. Knowles felt that the whole Egyptian army would be required for the advance because 'the time necessary for this operation would allow of the Dervishes to be strongly reinforced.' An advance to Akasha was approved, as well as a prospective raid towards Abu Hamed, although Knowles was warned that the arrangements for the Egyptian army were the responsibility of the Sirdar alone.[26] Although the military authorities were, like Cromer, surprised by the decision to invade the Sudan, the immediacy of the messages to Knowles suggest that the War Office expected to control aspects of the forthcoming campaign, especially as the objectives were clearly laid out – Akasha first, about 90 miles south of the frontier town of Wadi Halfa, followed by Abu Fatmeh, a further 60 miles south. The idea of a raid on Abu Hamed too had been that of the War Office. It has been suggested that this was Wolseley's way of constraining Cromer and Kitchener, whom he feared would try to go all the way to the town of Dongola and even beyond. Moreover, Wolseley, who was not alone in this thought, felt the Egyptian army operating alone was not up to the job.[27]

Cromer was incensed by the War Office's presumption. First, he thought that the plans were for the benefit of Britain's European interests and not those of Egypt and wanted it made plain that Egyptian interests would be at the forefront of Britain's decision. Secondly, he feared that the Egyptian army would be subordinated to the British. On 14 March, he raised objections to his not being consulted about the preparations, about the state of the Egyptian economy and about the limited advance to Akasha. He defended the Sirdar as 'cool and sensible and [who] knows his job thoroughly and is not inclined to be rash.' Cromer's special pleading won over Salisbury who decided that the advance would come under the auspices of the Foreign Office and not the War Office. But there was still to be no advance to Dongola. On 20 March 1896, Lansdowne informed Knowles that 'All orders for advance to AKASHEH [sic] will be given by Baring [sic] to Sirdar who will be responsible for all necessary preparations.'[28]

26   TNA: Kitchener Papers, PRO 30/57/11-J/, Lansdowne to Knowles, 12 March 1896; Knowles to Lansdowne, 13 March 1896; TNA: Kitchener Papers, PRO 30/57/11/J/2, 3, 6, Lansdowne to Knowles, 14 and 16 March 1896.

27   Ian F. W. Beckett, 'Kitchener and the Politics of Command' in Edward M. Spiers (ed.), *Sudan. The Reconquest Reappraised* (London: Frank Cass, 1998), pp.37–41.

28   G. N. Sanderson, *England, Europe and the Upper Nile* (Edinburgh: Edinburgh University Press, 1965), pp.244–248; Cromer quoted in Trevor Royle, *The Kitchener Enigma* (London: Michael Joseph, 1985), p.106; Philip Magnus, *Kitchener. Portrait of an Imperialist* (London:

Nevertheless, anxiety persisted within both the War Office and the Foreign Office that Cromer and Kitchener would go beyond their orders and attempt an advance to Dongola. In a memorandum delivered to the British cabinet on 24 March 1896, Lord Lansdowne outlined the views of the War Office. His military advisers 'are unanimous' that the capture of Dongola, 'cannot be accomplished without severe fighting'. Evidently, Wolseley felt that only the addition of British troops, 'some 6,000 Officers and men' would enable the Egyptian army to complete its task because 'Military opinion … is almost unanimous in its opinion that the ordinary Egyptian troops are not trustworthy for employment against a courageous and fanatical enemy.' For Lansdowne, the occupation of Akasha would be enough to fulfil Britain's pledge to help the Italians retain Kassala and keep Mahdist forces away from the Egyptian frontier, then 'neither Italy nor Egypt will be able to complain of us.'[29] Yet, the following week, following the receipt of telegrams from Cromer, Lansdowne was complaining

Brigadier General, later Major General, Sir Horatio Herbert Kitchener. (*Illustrated London News*)

to Salisbury that Kitchener was concentrating so many troops at Wadi Halfa that 'early movement on Dongola is contemplated.' Lansdowne was being informed by Kitchener's chief-of-staff, Colonel Rundle, who also indicated that far too many camels were being bought 'to meet present requirements'. 'Does Cromer thoroughly understand policy of Cabinet[?]' Lansdowne asked. 'I suggest you should telegraph to him asking information as to Sirdar's plans. Please say nothing to him about Rundle.'[30] Wolseley too was exercised by fears that Cromer and Kitchener were exceeding their instructions telling Lansdowne, 'Cromer ignores the policy desired upon by the Cabinet'. While the build-up at Wadi Halfa 'was a mistake' to Wolseley, in view of the limited advance contemplated, 'Cromer & Kitchener seemed as if acting with a free hand & under little or no restraint from home'. Wolseley was concerned and told Lansdowne that together they 'might force your hands & lead you into war when & where you did not want it'. He urged the cabinet to 'forbid any serious advance beyond Akasheh [*sic*] without the specific order of the

---

John Murray, 1958), pp.90–91; TNA: Kitchener Papers, PRO 30/57/11/J/7, Lansdowne to Knowles, 20 March 1896.

29 TNA: CAB 37: Cabinet Papers, CAB 37/41/21: 'Proposed Advance up the Nile Valley', Memorandum by Lord Lansdowne, 24 March 1896, pp.3–4.

30 British Library (BL): 88906: Lansdowne Papers, 88906/16/21: Lansdowne to Salisbury, 31 March 1896.

Cabinet [and] to prevent any large outlay upon purchase of camels and stores for an early advance to Dongola'.[31]

Officials in the Foreign Office were equally fearful of Kitchener exceeding his orders, and especially his taking troops from Suakin to reinforce his army at Wadi Halfa.[32] But nothing happened to the contrary as Kitchener built up his forces and supplies at Wadi Halfa, telling Eric Barrington, Salisbury's private secretary, that 'I am making a success as safe a thing as it is possible to do in wartime', while endorsing Cromer as 'a splendid man to serve under, he does everything one can possibly want'.[33] Keeping his head down and getting on with the job did not, however, mean that Kitchener could relax. Wolseley continued his campaign to get him superseded by an officer of the British army. Evidently, Salisbury informed Cromer on 1 May that Wolseley still wanted Kitchener replaced, while on 8 May, Wolseley produced another memorandum for the cabinet setting out his views, which in the words of one historian, was 'reeking with innuendo against Kitchener's competence for command.'[34] Wolseley referred to the arrangement whereby Kitchener would command the army, while reporting back to Cromer. 'All that I wish,' he stated, 'is that the effect of this position of affairs be clearly grasped. War is too serious a matter for it to be possible to accept vicarious responsibility.' He wondered whether the Government had 'full confidence' in Kitchener and his plans. He worried too about the Egyptian army and 'stiffened by white troops at present in Egypt, will be equal to the task in front of it.' Then, archly, 'The present plan does not appear to me to embrace all the means that we might combine to ensure success.' In spite of earlier disclaimers in the memorandum, Wolseley reached the point regarding Cromer and Kitchener conducting the forthcoming campaign: 'then I do not think that we can leave them too free, or support them too much in carrying it out according to their own views … It is impossible for a campaign to be conducted by two different people or from two different places, and once the question of general direction is settled, those to whom the direction is entrusted should be backed up in every way.'[35]

Wolseley continued to battle away in vain to obtain some War Office direction for events in the Sudan. With Salisbury's backing, however, Cromer and Kitchener were free of War Office oversight but only success in the field would justify the war in the Sudan as a 'Foreign Office' war. With the railway now reaching as far as Ambigol Wells, close enough to Akasha and a Mahdist force at Firket some sixteen miles away, Kitchener now felt the time was ripe to show the world the fighting qualities of the Egyptian army he had done so much to bring to a peak of fighting efficiency.

---

31 BL: Lansdowne Papers, 88906/19/28, Wolseley to Lansdowne, 31 March and 1 April 1896. See also BL: Lansdowne Papers, 88906/19/17-18, Haliburton to Lansdowne, 2 April 1896.

32 BL: Lansdowne Papers, 88906/19/4, St John Brodrick to Lansdowne, 1 April 1896; BL: Lansdowne Papers, 88906/19/25, Sanderson to Lansdowne, 31 March, 6 and 18 April, 1896.

33 TNA: Kitchener Papers, PRO 30/57/10/I3, Kitchener to Barrington, 21 May 1896.

34 Sanderson, *England, Europe & the Upper Nile*, p.261

35 TNA: Cabinet Papers, CAB 37/41/19, 'Memorandum by the Commander-in-Chief', 8 May 1896. Magnus, *Kitchener*, pp.91–92.

Chapter 2

The Mahdist State

In May 1896, as Kitchener's army prepared to invade the Sudan, there was time enough to consider the challenges that lay ahead and at first glance these appeared formidable. The terrain over which the army would march and sail was utterly hostile and provided a looming test of fitness, character and ingenuity. Indeed, Kitchener's own experience of the region had taught him that 'the real enemy… is not the Dervishes … but the Sudan itself'.[1] Looking south from the Egyptian army's forward position at Akasha all that could be seen was an endless flat expanse of desert, comprising both hard and soft sand variants and full of rocks. The view would look like this all the way to Omdurman, the Mahdist capital. In the summer months the weather was ferociously hot, made worse by a searing wind that blew from the south. Later in the campaign, Kitchener's forces would discover that baking hot days, accompanied by scouring desert dust, would give way in the night to gale-force winds and cold torrential rain. Through this sun tempered, unyielding landscape there ran a huge crack and in it flowed the river Nile.

The Nile begins at Khartoum for here the White Nile, coming north from Lake Victoria (shared by modern Uganda, Tanzania, and Kenya) or even from its tributaries beyond, meets the Blue Nile from Lake Tana (in modern Ethiopia). In fact, most of the flood water of the Nile comes from this tributary and it brings the fertile sediment that is vital to the agriculture of both the Sudan and Egypt. History has long recorded that the Nile is the lifeblood of both countries, especially for irrigation, but it was also the primary means of travel for those wishing to circumvent the desert. To Winston Churchill, the Nile was 'a thread of blue silk' although 'the blue was brown for half of the year'. But such was the importance of the river for the people who lived by it, and for the armies that would utilize it, that the Nile was 'the great motif that recurs throughout the whole opera'. The Nile broke up the desert, dividing it into the western Libyan and the eastern Nubian deserts. Along its banks and immediate hinterlands, including those of its main northern tributary, the Atbara, which it also flooded annually, the population grew dates and arable crops. Away from the cultivated areas, the unwary would

---

1   G. W. Steevens, *With Kitchener to Khartum* (Edinburgh and London: William Blackwood and Sons, 1898), p.111.

find the river banks and land covered with thorn bushes, which 'bristling like hedgehogs ... and with their prickly tangles obstruct or forbid the path'.[2] During the annual flood, which lasted roughly from May until September, it was only then possible to navigate the river fully. As mentioned in the first chapter, the main obstacles to any advance upriver were the cataracts, large swathes of rocks and rapids, five of which lay between Kitchener's army and Omdurman. The first cataract lay in Egypt just before Wadi Halfa and was formidable enough, but the next, known simply as the Second Cataract, was nine miles long.[3] And adding to these difficulties was the Nile's flow which ran from south to north, meaning that any river traffic would have to sail against it to get to Omdurman. During the flood, the flow was at its strongest making the river much more difficult to navigate at the only time of high water. Once the Egyptian army reached the fifth and sixth cataracts, beyond Abu Hamed, it would find them navigable whatever the time of year, but the water ran fast and turbulent. To add to the army's difficulties near Debbeh, (*al Dabba*), just south of Dongola, the Nile bent and turned back towards the north-east for over 200 miles until it reached Abu Hamed, where it turned south once again. This deviation contained the fourth cataract, making navigation extremely problematic. The most straightforward route was overland between Wadi Halfa and Abu Hamed, but that was through over 200 miles of the waterless Nubian Desert. Thus, wherever the Egyptian army looked there were interminable hinderances to its advance, with both the desert and the river providing unique obstacles to movement and progress.

The people who lived in this hostile and unforgiving land were, to various degrees, largely hostile and themselves unforgiving. They were well known to the British and Egyptian authorities, following encounters during the Gordon Relief Expedition in 1884-1885. Along the border resided people deemed 'Arab' on account of their language, culture, and Islamic religion, and some tribes did originate from the Arabian Peninsula centuries beforehand. The Arabs inhabited the Sudan as far south as Omdurman and Khartoum and were divided into tribes and sub-tribes who were usually antagonistic towards their neighbours. These can be divided into two general types: those tribes who were sedentary and who tended to live along the river, and those who were nomadic and who moved around the desert areas.

The sedentary peoples whom Kitchener's army would encounter first were collectively known as Nubians.[4] There were three Nubian sedentary groupings, the first, known as Barabra, inhabited the frontier areas and whose people often sought work in Egypt. To their south, the second Nubian group, the Ja'ali, comprised the people of Dongola province, the *Danaqla*, from whom the Mahdi himself had sprung. These were a fully Arabised tribe who via Ibrahim Ja'al claimed a common Arab ancestor in Abbas, the uncle of the Prophet Muhammad. To their south, however, covering the first bend

---

2   Winston Spencer Churchill, *River War. An Historical Account of the Reconquest of the Soudan* (London: Longmans, Green, And Co., 1899) vol. 1, pp.4, 8.

3   Churchill, *River War*, vol. 1, pp.148–149.

4   P. M. Holt and M. W. Daly, *A History of the Sudan. From the Coming of Islam to the present day* (London: Longman 1988), pp.3–9.

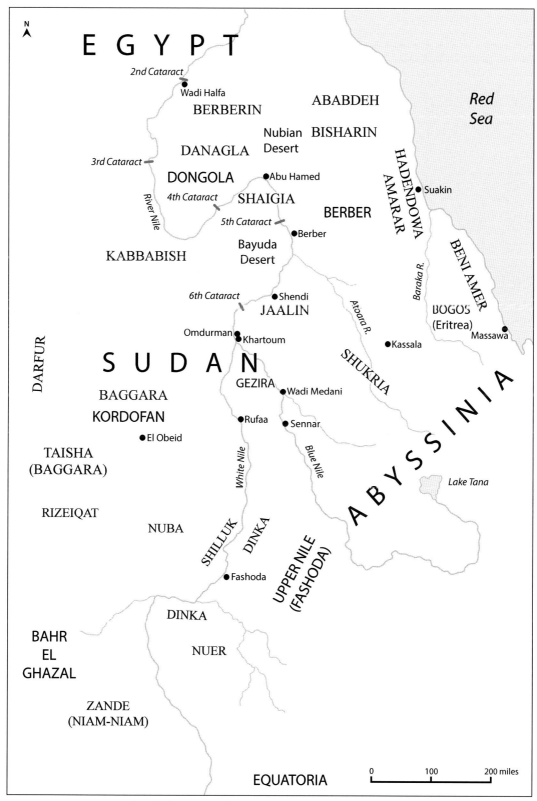

The Nile from Wadi Halfa to Fashoda. Tribes and provinces of Sudan.

in the Nile between Debbeh and the fourth cataract, were the third Nubian grouping known as the Shayqiyya, (or *Shaykia*) who were not popular in the Sudan owing to their earlier work as tax gatherers for the Egyptian government. From then on, as the Nile bent south towards Omdurman but stopping short at the sixth cataract, known as the Shabluka (*Sabaluqa*) gorge, all the tribes claimed to be Ja'ali, who in 1903, were considered to be 'good husbandmen and traders, famous for their boat building, clothmaking, and industries generally'.[5]

In contrast to these settled Nubians, the other general grouping of Sudanese Arabs was the nomadic Juhayna, In the west, the northern portion of the desert was the home of the sheep and camel herding Kababish, 'a fine bold tribe ... They are entirely Nomadic and wander over the great Bayuda and other deserts'. This tribe had been loyal to the Egyptian government during the Gordon Relief Expedition and had 'paid for it after'.[6] South of the Kababish, in Kordofan and Darfur, were the Baggara (or *Baqqara*), who were essentially cattle nomads. This tribe was regarded as 'the most formidable of Dervish tribes...They are bloodthirsty and cruel, but very hardy, and wonderful horsemen. They are very dark skinned and very dirty in their habits and clothes'.[7] One of their sub-tribes, the Ta'aisha would feature prominently after the death of the Mahdi because the Khalifa Abdallahi ibn Muhammad came from this group.[8]

In the Nubian desert, between the Egyptian frontier and Abu Hamed, lived the Ababdeh Arabs, who remained loyal to the Egyptian government throughout the Mahdist revolt and the rule of the Khalifa. Kitchener struck up a good working relationship during the Gordon Relief Expedition with this tribe, and it could be counted on again in 1896. The Ababdeh tribe were part of the Beja peoples and spoke Arabic, while its southern and eastern fellow Beja, who inhabited the Red Sea Littoral, as well as the hills and plains beyond, were less likely to speak Arabic and were less culturally Arab.[9] Among this group were the Hadendowa, Kipling's 'Fuzzy-Wuzzies', against whom the British had previously fought several tough engagements. Since Osman Digna's defeat in 1891, however, the hostility of the southern Beja towards the Anglo-Egyptian presence at Suakin had abated, although a hardcore remained defiant.

These then were some of the peoples, tribes and sub-tribes with whom the Egyptian army was either in friendly contact or with whom it was preparing to fight. The peoples themselves were further riven with inter-tribal animosity and competition and during the campaign these would return to the detriment of the Khalifa's cause and to the benefit of Kitchener's.

---

5   E. A. E. Stanton, 'The Peoples of the Anglo–Egyptian Sudan', *Journal of the Royal African Society*, 2:6 (January, 1903), pp.128–129.

6   Stanton, 'The Peoples', p.127.

7   Stanton, 'The Peoples', p.125.

8   This is my preferred rendering of the Khalifa's name, but in both older and recent works the reader will come across variations such as 'Abdullahi, Abdullahi, Abdullah, or even 'Abd Allahi.

9   Holt & Daly, *History of the Sudan*, pp.7–8.

Many of the tribes had been united with their enemies by the charisma of the Mahdi and their shared hatred of their Egyptian overlords. Following the expulsion of the Egyptian authorities and then the Mahdi's death, the adrenaline rush of religious enthusiasm had largely evaporated and the old antagonisms had begun to resurface. The Khalifa Abdallahi lacked his late master's magnetism and relied heavily on his own people, the Ta'aisha. In 1888, he summoned them and other Baggara and western tribes to Omdurman to join those already gathered there, and they began arriving from their Kordofan homeland during 1889. Once in Omdurman, the Ta'iaisha became a privileged elite as the mainstay of the Khalifa's authority. They took virtually anything they could lay their hands on, especially domesticated animals. Rudolf Slatin recalled that soon, 'Men and women who had the misfortune to cross their path were robbed of their clothing and jewellery'.[10] They swanned around Omdurman, living in quarters taken from the townspeople and eating food brought in by the sedentary tribes. The Khalifa's reliance on his tribal kin became more pronounced by 1896 because almost virtually every provincial governor was a Ta'aisha. To complement the concentration of the Ta'aisha in Omdurman, the Khalifa ordered other tribal chiefs to reside in Omdurman where their authority was 'absolutely powerless'.[11] Yet, in spite of the prodigious problems faced after the Mahdi's death and by his total reliance on his tribal kin, the Khalifa remained firmly in power because no one was left to challenge his authority.

When the Mahdi died, he bequeathed a rudimentary administration based on that used by the Egyptians, but with alterations conforming to his vision of religious renewal. The Mahdi's religious message had been a call to go 'back to basics' in a bid to recreate similar conditions as those in place when the Prophet Muhammad first began his calling. To that end, the Mahdi had named his three main followers 'khalifs' in imitation of those who had been first to follow the Prophet. Apart from Abdallahi, the second follower was Ali Wad Hilu, an early adherent of the Mahdi, pious and totally devoted, and thirdly there was Muhammad al Sharif, a younger man who came from and represented the Mahdi's family, which was known as the *Ashraf*. There should have been a fourth khalif but the candidate, the Libyan religious leader, al Sanusi, declined the offer.[12] Abdallahi, though, had been the Mahdi's principal lieutenant and wanted everyone to know it. According to Slatin, the Mahdi had announced to 'all the followers to implicitly obey the Khalifa Abdullahi, [sic] and to treat him in all respects as the Mahdi's agent in carrying out the will of the Prophet'.[13] It was this sanction that enabled the Khalifa Abdallahi to assume the mantle of the Mahdi's successor and later to deal with his enemies. For instance, the *Ashraf* twice challenged the Khalifa's leadership. Firstly, in 1886 it backed Muhammad Khalid, the

---

10 Colonel Sir R. Slatin Pasha, *Fire & Sword in the Sudan. A Personal Narrative of fighting and serving the Dervishes 1879-1895* (London: F. Arnold, 1897. Reprinted: The Long Riders' Guild Press, 2006), pp.270–271; Babikr Bedri, *The Memoirs of Babikr Bedri* (London: Oxford University Press, 1969), pp.215–218.

11 TNA: Kitchener Papers, PRO 30/57/12/K1, 'Intelligence Report on the Sudan 1890', p.9

12 Holt & Daly, *History of the Sudan*, pp.95–96.

13 Slatin, *Fire & Sword*, p.156.

governor of Darfur, when he marched on Omdurman, but he failed to oust Abdallahi owing to divisions within his army and the superior leadership of the loyal Hamdan Abu 'Anja. Secondly in 1891, the *Ashraf* conspired against the Khalifa and threatened civil war within Omdurman itself and the Khalifa negotiated away this uprising by recognizing the authority of the *Ashraf* figurehead, the khalifa Muhammad al Sharif. The following year, however, Abdallahi struck and had Muhammad al Sharif arrested, imprisoning him for virtually the rest of his reign.

The Khalifa might have been practically illiterate and have little knowledge of his own empire outside Kordofan and Omdurman but he was a cunning operator and used the authority bestowed on him by the Mahdi to good effect. Like the Mahdi, the Khalifa had visions that provided him with divine inspiration and could not be gainsaid. These visions were widely accepted by the people and they 'contained all that was necessary to guide them to a successful issue in their undertakings.'[14] To the British, the Khalifa was one of the era's greatest villains and few had a good word to say about him. The journalist Bennet Burleigh, for example, labelled him as 'ignorant, illiterate and cruel far beyond his dead master'.[15] Slatin, the Khalifa's prisoner for many years, came to know him well and regarded him as an evil, capricious despot and his memoir is laced with accounts of cruel executions and punishments. He described the Khalifa as 'tall and stout' and 'well-versed in every sort of fraud and deception'; he was also 'rash and quick tempered' and 'suspicious', while also 'susceptible to flattery', but 'woe to him who in the slightest degree offends his dignity ... His character is a strange mixture of malice and cruelty'.[16] His brother, Ya'qub, his closest adviser, was described as 'short, stout, very dark and marked by small pox ... He has no great reputation as a warrior but is noted for [his] deceit'. He was the conduit for access to the Khalifa and was in charge of all the arms and ammunition stored in Omdurman. Unlike his brother, Ya'qub was quite literate but like the Khalifa he was very intolerant of those who disagreed with him. Nevertheless, he could exercise some charm and Babikr Bedri described him as a 'wise, sensible and patient man'.[17] Additionally, the Khalifa felt bold enough to designate his eldest son, Osman as his heir apparent, giving him the title of Shaykh al Din. This was another slap in the face to the *Ashraf*, confirming their inferior position within the Mahdist hierarchy.

Other challenges were also dealt with quickly and ruthlessly. The Kababish tribe revolted in 1887 having never accepted Mahdism. Their rebellion was crushed and the head of their leader, Shaikh Salih, was sent to Omdurman. A religious leader, Abu Jammayza, emerged in Darfur in 1889, and gained many desperate adherents who were angry at the depredations of the

---

14   TNA: Kitchener Papers, PRO 30/57/12/K1, 'Intelligence Report on the Sudan 1890', pp.7–8, also p.4.

15   Bennet Burleigh, *Khartoum Campaign 1898 or the Re–Conquest of the Soudan* (London: Chapman & Hall, Limited, 1899. Reprinted: Cambridge: Ken Trotman Ltd, 1989), p.7.

16   TNA: Kitchener Papers, PRO 30/57/12/K1, 'Intelligence Report on the Sudan 1890', pp.5–6; Slatin, *Fire & Sword*, pp.305, 311–313.

17   TNA: Kitchener Papers, PRO 30/57/12/K1, 'Intelligence Report on the Sudan 1890', pp. 11–12; Slatin, *Fire & Sword*, p.164; Bedri, *Memoirs*, p.214.

Mahdist forces. After an initial success, Abu Jammayza fell mortally ill with smallpox and his followers were attacked and annihilated by Osman Adam, a young general related to the Khalifa. Unfortunately for the Mahdist cause, Osman Adam died in 1891 and was succeeded as governor of Darfur and Kordofan by another kinsman, the less effectual Mahmud Ahmad.[18]

Domestic enemies were not the only ones to challenge the Khalifa's authority. In 1887, the Mahdists were at war with Abyssinia. The year ended in victory at the battle of Debra Sin and the subsequent sack of Gondar, thanks to the skill of the Mahdist general Hamdan Abu 'Anja. Following a lull, hostilities were renewed in 1889 and this time Zaki Tamal won the battle of Gallabat, at which the Abyssinian king was killed, his body captured and his head sent to Omdurman. The only blot on this record was the inexplicable death of Abu 'Anja in early 1889.[19]

Although both foreign and domestic enemies were overcome, the Khalifa's authority was challenged by something totally outside of his control. In 1888, famine hit the land after the rains failed. The impact of the famine was severe owing to manpower losses, little agricultural development, and the movement of the Baggara people to Omdurman, who required feeding. Two years later, a plague of locusts wiped out the crops upon which the surviving population depended. In Omdurman, Slatin, noted that 'The dead lay in the streets in their hundreds; and none could be found to bury them', while the Nile was filled with 'hundreds of bodies of the wretched peasantry who had died along the banks – a terrible proof of the awful condition of the country'.[20] Nevertheless, the rains came and by 1896 cultivation had increased and the famine became a horrible, if recent, memory.

Omdurman, the site of the Mahdi's death, became the Mahdist capital in 1886 after the Khalifa had ordered the evacuation of Khartoum. As the Khalifa never ventured beyond its confines, Omdurman quickly grew in size. The city clung to the river and was longer in length than in width, some six miles to three miles respectively. The centrepiece of the city was the Mahdi's

Sir Rudolf Slatin. (Anne S K Brown Digital Archive)

---

18   A. B. Theobald, *Mahdīya. A History of the Anglo-Egyptian Sudan, 1881–1899* (London: Longmans, Green And Co Ltd, 1951), pp.145–149; Slatin, *Fire & Sword*, pp.249–253; Holt & Daly, *History of Sudan*, pp.100–102, 107–108.
19   Theobald, *Mahdīya*, pp.150–156.
20   Slatin, *Fire & Sword*, pp.272–276; Theobald, *Mahdīya*, pp.172–173; Holt & Daly, *History of Sudan*, pp.105–106.

tomb, with a dome some fifty feet high topped by a crescent and a large spearhead. The building was whitewashed to make it clearly visible for miles around. The tomb lay in a walled enclosure alongside the large mosque and the brick houses of the Khalifa, of his son Osman Shaykh al Din, of his brother Ya'qub, and those of the deputy khalifas, Muhammad al Sharif and Ali Wad Hilu. Within their own smaller enclosures to the north were the *Bait al mal* (treasury) and to the south the *Bait al amana* (arsenal). Evidently, the general population lived within its own tightly packed tribal areas, separated by only narrow lanes. 'In these', wrote Slatin, 'all the filth of the city is collected. Their wretched condition and the smells which emanate from these pestilential by-paths are beyond description.' The European prisoners lived in their own small part of the city near the market place. By 1896, they were under strict surveillance owing to some having escaped, including Slatin himself.[21]

Being the heart of the Mahdist empire, from Omdurman the Khalifa directed all its parts so as to preserve the dominion won by the Mahdi and to maintain the veneer of tribal unity. To do so, the Khalifa, as the fount of all authority, ensured that nothing could be done without his approval; he wanted to know everything and decide everything. For example, the legal system was now firmly based in Islamic Law, with the chief judge termed the *qadi al Islam*, a title taken from Islam's earliest times. However, the *qadi* was not an independent figure and would base his decisions on the Khalifa's wishes.[22] In the provinces, the Mahdi had established local governance based on the precepts of the Prophet, while everything else, including economic activity, came under the provisions of Islamic law. This system was also meant to sustain the army while it managed the local population and prepared to resume the *jihad*. Thus, each of these six provinces, or *'imalas*, were overseen by a local governor, or *amir*, who was also the *'amil*, the head of the administration: by 1896, all provincial heads were of the Ta'aisha tribe and they were answerable to Ya'qub. In imitation of the system at Omdurman, each *'imala* had within it a judge (*qadi*) and a treasury (*bait al-mal*) within which contained a granary, arms and ammunition and transport animals.

Most clerks and officials had worked for the previous regime and they continued to oversee the collection of taxes and these too were made to conform to early Islamic practice. The principal tax, the *zaka*, was incumbent on all Muslims to pay as a form of alms-giving and was the third pillar of Islam. It was paid in both coin and kind, particularly grain, and then stored in the treasury. The riverain tribes were the main providers of this tax and to add insult to injury it was collected by the hated Baggara. Indeed, British intelligence referred to it as 'the holy tax which covers wholesale plundering'. Although book-keeping and record keeping were of a high quality, something the Khalifa insisted upon, officials were poorly paid and bribery and corruption flourished. Merchants additionally paid a second tax, the *ushr*, charged on one tenth of their imported goods and often they had to pay it more than once. The third tax, the *ghanima* was essentially the plundering of

---

21 Slatin, *Fire & Sword* pp. 347-357; TNA: Kitchener Papers, PRO 30/57/12/K1, 'Intelligence Report on the Sudan 1890', pp.58–66.
22 TNA: Kitchener Papers, PRO 30/57/12/K1, 'Intelligence Report on the Sudan 1890', pp.45–46.

Islam's enemies, and in the Sudan this could mean anyone who angered the Khalifa. This became more prevalent as the list of the Khalifa's enemies, real and imagined, grew longer.[23]

The revenue collected from these taxes by the local officials was then sent to Omdurman's central *bait al-mal*, 'which was an immense treasury, store and auction market combined'.[24] Until 1890, this treasury was well administered by Ibrahim 'Adlan, but he fell out of favour with Ya'qub and then with the Khalifa, possibly because he had accrued too much wealth or possibly because he had shown hostility to the Khalifa's pro-Baggara policies, especially during the famine. Unfortunately for 'Adlan, administrative skills were not enough to save his life and he was hanged in early 1890. The administration of the *bait al-mal* at Omdurman was never the same again. For instance, 'Adlan had issued a new coinage, the value of which was readily accepted and used for trade with Egypt. After 'Adlan's execution, the Khalifa had the silver content reduced until the coins were simply pure copper thus undermining the rate of exchange and confidence.[25]

Nevertheless, the one trade that continued to flourish was the slave trade. This was certainly helped by the recent war against Abyssinia, where the Mahdists had captured men, women, and children, but also aided by operations in the south against the non-Arab black tribes living along the White Nile. As we shall see this trade was vital for filling the ranks of the army.

The Mahdist army was at the heart of the state and the administration was geared towards its support. Although by 1896 active operations had largely ceased, the army remained the bedrock of the Khalifa's authority and the instrument by which the late Mahdi's message could still be carried to neighbouring territories. The movement of the tribes of western Sudan to Omdurman meant that the army was now largely concentrated in the capital, although garrisons were kept at important positions such as Dongola and El Fasher. The army was known as the *ansar*, or helpers, a term used by the Prophet for his early supporters. All wore the same uniform of a long white cotton shirt or smock, the *jibbah* (or *jibba*, or *jubba*) and patched with coloured material, with white calf-length trousers (or drawers). Some soldiers wore sandals, although many did not, and some wore a skull cap or turban. The army by this time was a well-organised and well-supplied force, with weapons, including rifles and artillery pieces, although these were of low quality. Weaponry, in fact, was the basis of the army's organization, the division being between those who had rifles and those who did not and who were then obliged to carry swords and spears. The riflemen, many

---

23   For an account of tax collecting in the Gezira region see Bakri, *Memoirs*, pp.144–149. TNA: Kitchener Papers, PRO 30/57/12/K1, 'Intelligence Report on the Sudan, 1890' p.39; 'Ismat Hasan Zulfo, *Karari. The Sudanese Account of the Battle of Omdurman*, (London: Frederick Warne (Publishers) Ltd, 1980), pp.33, 41, 44. Peter Clark, 'The Battle of Omdurman in the Context of Sudanese History', in Edward M. Spiers, (ed.), *Sudan. The Reconquest Reappraised* (London: Frank Cass Publishers, 1998), pp.207, 209–211; Slatin, *Fire & Sword*, pp.336–337.

24   Theobald, *Mahdīya*, pp. 177, 181–182.

25   Slatin, *Fire & Sword*, pp.276–277, 334–343. Theobald, *Mahdīya*, p.181–183; Bakri, *Memoirs*, pp.202–203.

of whom were former slaves and captured while serving in the Egyptian army , were brought together and known collectively as the *jihadiya*. The continual taking of slaves from the south was thus an important means of keeping this rifle unit supplied with manpower. Their weapon was the Remington, a breech-loading, single-shot rifle, taken from the Egyptians during the Mahdi's campaigns. By 1896, it was obsolete but in the hands of a skilled rifleman it could still do damage. Hamdan Abu 'Anja had formed the *jihadiya* for the Mahdi and under his command the riflemen had become the crucial formation of the army, proving their worth not only against the Egyptians but also against the Abyssinians. At Shaykan, the riflemen had softened up Hicks' army for a day before the final Mahdist assault; against the Abyssinians at Debra Sin, the riflemen had stopped repeated charges until the exhausted enemy could be dealt with by troops carrying swords and spears. Discipline declined after Abu 'Anja's death in 1889 and his successors never quite appreciated the value of massed rifle fire.[26] By 1896, the rifles had rusted and their barrels had fouled. They had also been shortened to lighten them for long-distance travel but this damaged their accuracy and range, something that was not appreciated until it was too late. The *jihadiya* were regular soldiers in that they received rations and training. From them, the Khalifa recruited his guard unit, the *mulazimin* and from this came a special, picked force of 2,000 men for his bodyguard. These more elite troops were well paid from their own treasury, as well as being well trained and well fed. To emphasize their closeness to the Khalifa, the *mulazimin* commander was his son, Osman, Shaykh al Din. The bodyguard were not all riflemen, some, the *mushammaratiya*, carried long spears and were chosen for their physical appearance as well as their proficiency in arms and wore 'a two-horned skull cap'. While another group, the *khashkhashan*, were armed with elephant guns that were fired using a tripod rest and looked more like ancient matchlock muskets; they wore red waistcoats and red turbans.[27]

The bulk of the army comprised spearmen who carried one long, broad-bladed spear and four short spears, as well as a crossed handle sword. Few carried shields and it was usually the Beja that did. These foot soldiers were irregulars and indifferently trained, but made up for this by their religious fanaticism and their desire for martyrdom. Ideally, this group would deliver the final assault after the enemy had been shattered by rifle fire. On the other hand, the cavalry arm was mostly provided by the Baggara, who were superb horsemen and fearsome warriors. They provided their own mounts and weapons, a spear and a sword, except when given rifles for special duties. Because of this they had no particular organization and tended to wear red turbans.[28]

Most of the regular army gathered in Omdurman and would be joined by the townsmen and other reserve soldiers coming from the countryside. Every man was considered a warrior and was expected to serve when the call

---

26 Zulfo, *Karari*, p.14 & Note 2, p.23, p.34 & Note 6, p.46.
27 Zulfo, *Karari*, pp.35–36, 99–100. Donald Featherstone, *Omdurman 1898. Kitchener's Victory in the Sudan* (Westport, CT and London: Praeger, 2005), pp.22–25, 39.
28 Zulfo, *Karari*, p.34, 94; Slatin, *Fire & Sword*, p.329.

came. The Mahdist army was not simply a mass of men armed with a variety of weapons. Under the Khalifa, the army had been reorganized and various formations were established consisting of a mix of weapons. The primary unit was the *rub'*, meaning a quarter, because armies under the Mahdi were always divided into four whatever their size. A *rub'* comprised spearmen, riflemen (*jihadiya*) and cavalry, as well as a small staff group. The commanding officer, or *amir*, and his *rub'* always comprised 800 men, sometimes much more and this depended on the ability of the junior *amirs*, young men of high tribal standing, to recruit spearmen from their own tribes. Officers (*amirs*), were always mounted and identified by their own mounted flag-carrier, while more senior officers also had a drum. Everyone though knew the chain of command. A *rub'* was thus bedecked with large flags that would catch the eye of their opponents and provide reference points for movements and rallying points during a battle. Both the spearmen and the *jihadiya* were then divided into 'hundreds', which were then quartered, each quarter was commanded by a *muqaddam* and was known as a *muqaddamiya*. A *rub'* of the regular forces, such as the *mulazimin*, was fixed at between 800 and 1200 men.

There were eighteen *rub's* concentrated in Omdurman and these were organized into larger formations known as standards, the chief being the Black Standard because 'All the irregular elements came under its command, regardless of tribal origin. The Black Standard became the recruiting centre',[29] and was essentially a mass concentration of spearmen and numerous mounted *amirs*. It was organized by tribe, then by their *amirs*, and then sub-divided like any ordinary *rub'*. The Black Standard's importance was enhanced by the fact that its commanding officer was Ya'qub, the Khalifa's brother. When assembled for battle it would act in conjunction with the *mulazimin*, who would provide the necessary firepower for the Black Standard's attack.

There was also a Green Standard at Omdurman comprising mostly spearmen and under the nominal command of the deputy khalifa Ali Wad Hilu. It comprised fewer tribes than the Black Standard and was recruited mainly from those based along the White Nile and organized accordingly. Three tribes made up the Green Standard, the Dighaim, who also provided the cavalry, the Kanana and the Lahiwiyin.

The Red Standard had been abolished following the revolt of the *Ashraf* because it had been under the command of the deputy khalifa Muhammad al Sharif. But on the eve of the battle of Omdurman it was revived and Muhammad al Sharif gave the command of it to Ahmad `Abd al Karim. As the Red Standard was associated with the *Ashraf*, it would become the rallying point for northern Ja'alin and Dongolawi riverain tribes.[30]

The training of the Omdurman garrison was basic but often performed and ensured the men obeyed the junior *amirs* as they manoeuvred their units, allowing them to move together like some form of human murmuration. Consequently, the men were very fit indeed: 'Their slender frames, their supple muscles, their acclimatization to the rigours of life, an absence of

---

29   Zulfo, *Karari*, p.37.
30   Zulfo, *Karari*, pp.112, 136.

luxuries and also their light equipment all contributed towards their physical fitness.'[31]

Nevertheless, there were grave deficiencies within the Khalifa's army, especially the quality of marksmanship. The prevailing tactical doctrine was for the riflemen to shoot from the hip, sending an undirected hail of lead at the enemy, while the spearmen readied themselves for the massed assault: 'Misuse of rifle fire resulted from the prevailing idea of rushing forward to seek martyrdom without considering any other factor.' This was not how Abu 'Anja had used the *jihadiya*; he had appreciated how directed rifle fire could hurt the enemy. This decline in tactical thinking was to have grave consequences.[32]

The Mahdist army was not bereft of other forms of firepower because it also possessed artillery pieces and obsolete hand cranked-machine guns taken from the Egyptians. All were stored, along with rifles and ammunition, in the *bait al-amana*, the arsenal based in Omdurman. There were thirty-five field pieces, twenty-seven of which were obsolete smooth-bore muzzle loaders. The other eight were modern German Krupp guns, which were breech-loaders and rifled. Most of the crews comprised men who had served with the Egyptians and they maintained their guns to a high standard. However, both the artillery pieces and machine guns lacked ammunition. The Khalifa maintained several workshops for the manufacture of gunpowder and ammunition at Omdurman and elsewhere. These produced about 14,400 bullets a month and if local garrisons wanted more their requests had to go to Omdurman for the Khalifa's agreement. The provision of ammunition was strictly supervised and once agreed was despatched by camel and river transport. For the artillery, projectiles were only produced for the ancient muzzle loaders because the Krupp shells were just too complicated for the Khalifa's limited workshop resources and abilities. But since the gunpowder quality was poor the projectiles lacked sufficient power to inflict significant casualties on the enemy. Virtually all the artillery pieces and machine guns were kept in Omdurman, with most eventually positioned on the river front to face Kitchener's gunboats when the time came. The Mahdists were not great tacticians when it came to artillery deployment as they felt that the guns were better used against fortifications, rather than against enemy soldiers on a battlefield.[33]

By 1896, Mahdist Sudan had experienced several years of peace and stability, the Khalifa's position was secure and his authority could not be gainsaid. He had held the country together and defeated his enemies. He had reorganized the army which in spite of its weaknesses remained formidable. The fighting qualities of the men who comprised it had not diminished and they were still imbued with the zeal that had driven out the Egyptians and their British allies in 1885. The Mahdist army was still a force to be reckoned with and it retained a ferocity that was not to be underestimated.

---

31   Zulfo, *Karari*, p.96.
32   Zulfo, *Karari*, pp.100–101.
33   Zulfo, *Karari*, pp. 40–41, 44–45 101–102; William Wright, *Omdurman 1898*, (Stroud: Spellmount, 2012), pp.56–57.

Chapter 3

The Egyptian Army

The 1896 campaign to recover the Sudan for Egypt, and by extension assert British control over the Nile valley, was carried out by the Egyptian Army [EA], a force that had been reconstructed by the British after defeating the original army under Arabi Pasha in 1882. Commanded and led by its British senior officers, the EA, derided by the military authorities in Britain, was now given the opportunity to prove its detractors wrong. Initially, the campaign was to be of short duration, a limited advance south to divert the Mahdists from attacking the Italians following their defeat by the Abyssinians, and to help preserve the balance of power in Europe. But such was the EA's victorious momentum that it would advance all the way to the Mahdist capital Omdurman for the climactic battle with the Khalifa's forces.

Following the 1882 defeat of Arabi Pasha, the British decided that the EA required a root and branch reformation if it was loyally to support the Khedival government and protect Egypt's extensive territories because, according to one British officer, 'The old Egyptian army was almost unequalled for cowardice and incapacity.'[1] These traits had been ably demonstrated in the defeats suffered against the Abyssinians in the 1860s and against the British in 1882, while its remnants had collapsed fighting the Mahdists in the Sudan during 1883 and 1884. This 'incapacity' of the army, as its new British officers discovered, had everything to do with the fact that it was at war with itself and totally lacked any *esprit de corps*.

This can be seen in the way ordinary soldiers were recruited. All men aged between 19 and 23 were liable for conscription and the only way to avoid this was to be literate and rich, which most were not. Consequently, most recruits were peasants (*fellahin*) and most stayed in the army for life. The men were discharged when too old to be of any use and had to make their own way home to their villages, if they survived the journey. Once home, they became barely surviving, broken down examples, of the nature of military service, which 'did not seem to be a very desirable profession in

---

1   Colonel F. I. Maxse, *Seymour Vandeleur* (London: The *National Review* Office, 1906. Reprinted: London: Forgotten Books, 2015), p.132.

the eyes of the people'.[2] Once in the army, the conscript would be subjected to ferocious discipline and harshly punished for the slightest offence. Pay was desultory, food was unwholesome, and barracks were filthy. There was little in the way of medical care, while leave was never granted. All feared being sent to the Sudan as they knew it was unlikely they would ever return: 'Indeed, so degraded was the profession of arms that it would be difficult to devise a more certain system of destroying the spirit of any man, or knocking the manliness out of any soldier.'[3] The Egyptian officer class lay at the heart of the problem. Apart from robbing their men of their pay and taking no interest in their welfare, the officers also took no professional interest in soldiering generally. For many, their jobs were nothing more than stepping-stones for hasty promotion and social climbing. The further they were from the ordinary soldier the better.[4] Thus the task awaiting the British in late 1882 was indeed formidable.

The officer chosen to reform the EA as its *Sirdar* (commander-in-chief) was Major General Sir H. Evelyn Wood. He was paid a handsome £5,000 a year (about £600,000 in today's figures) and was expected to train and organize a force of 6,000 men with a budget of £200,000. Assisting Wood would be carefully selected British officers who would be expected to set an unimpeachable example to their men. The chosen officers also arrived with the cultural baggage of the times. They saw themselves as Olympian figures, above and beyond the Egyptians, who were regarded as degraded examples of men and naturally inferior to the British.[5] Nevertheless, one should not discount the officers' professional pride in accepting a challenge that would reflect their abilities as officers and trainers of men. Their reputations would be enhanced by ensuring the EA could fight. Thus, because the EA used several languages, owing to Egypt being a province of the Ottoman empire and having long economic and cultural connections with France, those officers chosen for the task were expected to know French and to become familiar with colloquial Arabic. To give orders, they would also need to know Turkish. Conscription would continue but be properly set at four years, with eight years in the Reserve. Egyptian officers found to be inadequate were removed over the next year, along with one British officer. Thus, by 1896, the EA had been transformed; its soldiers had regular pay, clean barracks and clothing, regular food, careful discipline, promotion by merit and yearly furloughs. 'They went home to their squalid villages smart in appearance and with plenty of money in their pockets. They were no longer ashamed of themselves and their calling.'[6]

The dedication of the British officers to their men had been displayed when cholera broke out in July 1883. All the Egyptian officers and medical

2   Lieutenant Colonel Andrew Haggard, *Under Crescent and Star* (Edinburgh and London: William Blackwood and Sons, 1895), pp.108–109.

3   Maxse, *Seymour Vandeleur*, p.134; Archie Hunter, *Kitchener's Sword-arm. The Life and Campaigns of General Sir Archibald Hunter* (Staplehurst: Spellmount, 1996), p.11.

4   Maxse, *Seymour Vandeleur*, pp.134–135.

5   Adam Dighton, 'Race, Masculinity and Imperialism: The British Officer and the Egyptian Army (1882–1899)', *War & Society*, 35:1 (2016), pp.4–7.

6   Maxse, *Seymour Vandeleur*, p.135.

An Egyptian Army battalion on parade. (*Illustrated London News*)

staff fled and it was left to the British officers to remain behind and nurse the infected men and even wash the bodies of the dead.[7] Nevertheless, these officers were well rewarded for their efforts. Initially, twenty-five were recruited for two years' service, unless they were dismissed after six months by the Egyptian government. Later, officers would sign up to the EA for five years before returning to their British regiments. Once selected, officers were immediately promoted while serving in the EA: for example, Captain H. H. Kitchener, second-in-command of the cavalry, rose to the rank of major and his pay increased accordingly.[8] In Britain a major was paid about £326 a year with allowances, although there were numerous expenses and the officer was expected to have a private income. Guards officers would have been paid about £488. In Egypt, Kitchener was paid in the region of £550, but he had to provide his own horse. With regard to the EA's infantry, four battalions were commanded by British officers, and these comprised the 1st Brigade under Lieutenant Colonel F. Grenfell, who was promoted to Brigadier General and earned £1,200 a year. His four regimental officers were made colonels and

7   Stephen Manning, *Evelyn Wood VC. Pillar of Empire* (Barnsley: Pen & Sword, 2007), pp. 168–172.
8   Henry S. L. Alford & W. Dennistoun Sword, *The Egyptian Soudan. Its Loss and Recovery* (London: Macmillan and Co., Limited, 1898. Reprinted: Dallington: The Naval & Military Press, 1992), p.39; Hunter, *Kitchener's Sword-arm*, p.12.

paid £750. In the British Army, they would have been paid, with allowances, about £550 annually. There were some nine officers, all promoted to major, who were known as supplementary officers because they had no active commands and helped with training and sundry duties; they were paid £450 a year.[9] Of the original twenty-five officers only two would still be in the EA as it prepared for the invasion of the Sudan – Kitchener, who was the Sirdar, and Colonel Leslie Rundle, who would act as his chief-of-staff for the coming campaign. By 1896, however, the EA comprised 120 officers and had grown to about 12,500 men. By the end of the campaign in 1898, the EA would number about 18,000.[10]

One element of the EA that was considered vital to its effectiveness was the use of former enslaved soldiers from southern Sudan. These men had been recruited since the time of Muhammad Ali, indeed his invasion of the Sudan in the 1820s had been motivated by his desire to acquire black slaves for his army. Huge numbers were captured, enslaved, and turned into soldiers, even then known as *jihaddiya*, whose primary task was to hold down the Sudan itself. Even the Mahdists prized these former slave-soldiers and absorbed many of them during and after the Mahdist rebellion. A large number of these slave-soldiers, though, preferred to stay loyal to the khedive and fled to Egypt or the port of Suakin. Once the British began the reform of the EA these soldiers were kept on and formed a hard core of men with valuable military experience. On 1 May 1884, the first Sudanese battalion, designated the 9th, was established. (In the EA, by the end of the campaign in 1898, battalions 1–8 and 15–18 were Egyptian, 9–14 were Sudanese).[11] Like the Egyptians, the British regarded the Sudanese as a so-called 'martial race', peculiarly fitted to a life of soldiering and, in consequence, only wanted men from certain areas of the Sudan, or whose parents came from those areas. These regions were southern Kordofan and Darfur, the southern White Nile regions of Equatoria and Bahr al Ghazal and even the Blue Nile valley. These soldiers were held in such high esteem by the British that their pay and service conditions were much better than those of the Egyptian conscript. Indeed, to maintain their morale and loyalty, the men were allowed to take wives and have families, some of whom would accompany their men on the forthcoming campaign. They were also paid 'family allowances' too, although these would be reduced over the years.[12] Having ordinarily been regarded as nothing more than slaves, these now highly valued men, and coming as they did from disparate areas, were also bound together by the shared experience of EA service. Life in the army gained these formerly enslaved

9   Ian F. W. Beckett, *A British Profession of Arms. The Politics of Command in the Late Victorian Army* (Norman: University of Oklahoma Press, 2018), pp.19–20; Haggard, *Under Crescent and Star*, pp.29–40; Corinne Mahaffey, The Fighting Profession. The Professionalisation of the British Line Officer Corps, 1870–1902, (Unpublished PhD thesis, University of Glasgow, 2004), p.200; Trevor Royle, *The Kitchener Enigma* (London: Michael Joseph, 1985), pp.52–54.

10   Alford & Sword, *Egyptian Soudan*, pp.294–305; Haggard, *Under Crescent and Star*, p.32; Hunter, *Kitchener's Sword-arm*, p.13.

11   Ronald M. Lamothe, *Slaves of Fortune. Sudanese Soldiers & the River War 1896–1898* (Woodbridge: James Currey, 2011), pp.12–26. Alford & Sword, *Egyptian Soudan*, p.38, 303–304.

12   Lamothe, *Slaves of Fortune*, pp.49, 73–76, 78–89.

Egyptian Army Camel Corps advancing on Dongola. (*Illustrated London News*)

men status and respect within the army generally, and 'by any objective measure Sudanese soldiers *were* "crack soldiers"'.[13] Nevertheless, these men never gained total respect by their new British masters because of cultural prejudices and preconceptions: Lord Cromer, for example, described these Sudanese recruits as 'little better than savages. They are difficult to control, and are as thoughtless, capricious, and wanting in foresight as children. They are not quick at drill, nor are they fond of it. The blacks are very excitable. On the other hand, their initiative, dash, and instincts of self-defence make them invaluable as fighting troops.'[14]

The British, in fact, perpetuated the slave soldier aspect of service because the men signed up for life and would only be discharged once they were too old or if they had been badly wounded. Furthermore, the British seemingly carried on the practice of branding each soldier for identification purposes and also used flogging to maintain discipline, although the latter was general punishment within the EA. As was then general practice in many armies, they could be, and were, shot for desertion. But even so, they were once again 'cut greater slack' and were not subjected to the full force of disciplinary military law, owing to 'the relative seniority and martial reputation of Sudanese soldiers'. In the same vein, the Sudanese soldiers were not forced to do manual labour, the preserve of the troops of the Egyptian peasant class. Such leniency towards the Sudanese was concerned with preserving the men's loyalty; they were considered a vital element in the war against the Mahdists as they would be given most of the hard fighting.[15] Against this leniency, however, was the fact that the Egyptian soldiers had better prospects for promotion. Four of the seven Egyptian battalions were officered solely by Egyptians, but all Sudanese battalions had British commanding officers as well as four more junior British officers within each battalion. Sudanese soldiers could rise to the rank of captain (*yuzbashi*) but never beyond that. This did have something to do with British prejudices, but also happened because most Sudanese were illiterate. One British officer later wrote that half of the Sudanese officers were 'men risen from the ranks … They can neither read nor write and their only home is the battalion'. Nevertheless, they were excellent soldiers being 'reliable, stout-hearted … hard as nails and commanding their men most efficiently'.[16] Thus, within the EA there were two forces – one made up of conscripted Egyptians whose ability as soldiers were questioned by the British; while the other force comprised Sudanese former slave-soldiers who made up a martial caste owing to the British perception of them as natural fighters, a belief that was both racist and correct. 'The truth is' opined Alfred Milner, who worked for the British administration in Egypt and who would become famous for provoking the war in South Africa against the Boers in 1899, 'that the two sets of men, with their widely different qualities, form a very

---

13   Lamothe, *Slaves of Fortune*, p.122, pp.121–134.

14   The Earl of Cromer, *Modern Egypt*, (London: Macmillan & Co., 1908), vol. 2, pp.476–477.

15   Lamothe, *Slaves of Fortune* pp. 31–34, 99–102.

16   Lamothe, *Slaves of Fortune*, pp. 93–99; West Sussex Record Office (WSRO): Maxse Mss 367: Frederick Ivor Maxse Papers, Maxse to his father, 9 April 1897, pp.7–8.

Sudanese troops of the Egyptian Army advancing towards Dongola. (*Illustrated London News*)

strong combination for fighting purposes'.[17] The proof of this assertion was about to be tested.

The campaign uniform of the Egyptian infantry comprised a khaki tunic or wool jersey and breeches, with blue puttees, although some might have reverted to their white kit during the summer months. The Sudanese troops tended to wear a blue wool jersey, khaki trousers and blue puttees. Both wore a red *tarbush* (fez), but this was covered by a khaki cloth on campaign and it often had a protective khaki neck cloth. British officers wore the British field service dress of tropical sun helmet, khaki tunic and blue puttees.[18] The EA's rifle was the Martini-Henry .450 with an 18½ inch sword bayonet, which when attached made the combined weapon some 5 feet 8 inches long. It was a single shot rifle, the bullet being loaded by pulling a lever which dropped the breech-block and ejected the old cartridge, thus allowing a new cartridge to be inserted into the chamber. The lead bullet sat within a brass cartridge that was propelled by black powder, and it had formidable hitting power: 'The soft lead slug was a man-stopper that smashed bone and cartilage and

17   Alfred Milner, *England in Egypt* (London: Edward Arnold), p.183.
18   G. Tylden, 'Egyptian Army Uniforms, 1882–1898' *Journal of the Society for Army Historical Research*, 20:77, (Spring, 1941), pp.56–57; Chris Flaherty, '1883 Till 1914 Army of Egypt Infantry', <http://www.ottoman-uniforms-.com/1883-till-1914-army-of-egypt-infantry/>, accessed 29 June 2020; Donald Featherstone, *Omdurman 1898. Kitchener's Victory in the Sudan* (Westport, CT & London: Praeger, 2005), p.19; Lamothe, *Slaves of Fortune*, pp.75–76.

left wicked wounds.'[19] Two bandoliers carried 100 rounds, one worn over the left shoulder the other around the waist. The Martini-Henry had three major drawbacks however: when fired it had a nasty kick that bruised shoulders; it produced too much smoke; and the barrel became quickly fouled with powder. [20] Nevertheless, the EA, and its Sudanese troops in particular, had become adept with this rifle and were excellent marksmen. [21] The Egyptian cavalry and camel corps tended to be dressed in a similar fashion to the infantry and carried the Martini-Henry carbine, a shortened version of the main rifle, and also a sword. The gunners of the EA artillery, who wore white jacket and trousers with blue puttees, started with a 65mm Krupp breech-loading field piece that could be broken down and carried by mule or camel, or could be fitted with wheels to be drawn along by mules. This equipment was gradually being replaced and by the time it reached Omdurman, the EA's artillery was equipped with 75mm Maxim-Nordenfelt guns. The horse batteries, however, continued to use the obsolete 75mm Krupp gun which was of a poorer quality in terms of rate of fire and shells. The EA also started the campaign with four Maxim machine guns under the command of Captain C.E. Lawrie. These were placed on carriages, with shields, and were drawn by horses much like artillery pieces. The Maxim was a formidable weapon, capable of firing 650 rounds a minute and would add greatly to the EA's firepower.[22]

As mentioned in Chapter One, the Sirdar of the Egyptian Army tasked with invading the Sudan was Major General Sir H. Herbert Kitchener. He was the third British sirdar and had succeeded Major General Sir Francis Grenfell on 13 April 1892. Grenfell later claimed that he had recommended Kitchener because he knew French and Arabic and had experience of both Egypt and the Sudan. This assertion is slightly contradicted by Sir John Maxwell, who served under Kitchener during the Sudan campaign and who told Kitchener's biographer, Sir George Arthur that Grenfell 'was doubtful if K. was the right man to succeed him … I believe it (the Egyptian command) was actually offered to others'.[23] Indeed, at the time Kitchener was very unpopular with his fellow officers and Grenfell was well aware of his lack of tact and good manners. Lord Edward Cecil, who would become one of Kitchener's *aides-de-camp* (ADC) in 1896 and was the son of the prime minister, Lord Salisbury, later wrote that Kitchener was 'uncouth and uncivilised', was 'inclined to bully his own entourage' and 'preferred to be misunderstood rather than be suspected of human feeling'.[24] Even Cromer, in his memoirs, hinted at Kitchener's failings by saying that his subordinates

---

19   Donald Featherstone, *Weapons & Equipment of the Victorian Soldier* (London: Arms and Armour Press, 1978; 1996), pp.24–25.

20   Featherstone, *Weapons & Equipment*, p.25.

21   Lamothe, *Slaves of Fortune*, pp.76–77.

22   Featherstone, *Omdurman 1898*, pp.13–16; Featherstone, *Weapons & Equipment*, p.65.

23   Field Marshal Lord Grenfell, *Memoirs* (London: Hodder & Stoughton, 1925), p.112; TNA: Kitchener Papers, PRO 30/57/93/GA3/30/ p.3, 'Reminiscences of Lord Kitchener' by General Sir John Maxwell.

24   Lord Edward Cecil, *The Leisure of An Egyptian Official* (London: Hodder & Stoughton, 1921), pp. 184–186.

only respected his 'strong and masterful spirit' and that this respect was not 'the affectionate obedience yielded to the behests of a genial chief'.[25]

Kitchener was disliked because he was aloof and was adept at cultivating political contacts. There were various paths for an ambitious officer to follow if he wanted to obtain promotion. One way was to gain successful battlefield experience and Kitchener certainly had plenty of that having served on the Gordon Relief Expedition in 1884–1885, having fought Osman Digna outside Suakin in 1888, being wounded in the process, having commanded a brigade at the battle of Gemeizah that same year, and then having commanded the Egyptian cavalry at the battle of Toski in 1889. All this fighting ensured Kitchener was noticed, and even Queen Victoria took an interest in his career following his wounding. Kitchener was lucky that there was plenty of active service between 1885 and 1892 and as his old comrade Andrew Haggard noted: 'to have once belonged to the Egyptian army was a distinct step in most instances on the road to fortune'.[26] Another road to advancement was patronage, from both senior army officers and politicians.[27] Kitchener had few army contacts at a time when having a senior benefactor was almost paramount for a junior officer. Instead, Kitchener cultivated the political elite and none more so than Lord Salisbury, prime minister between 1886 and 1892 and 1895 to 1902. Salisbury was impressed by Kitchener when they met at Hatfield in 1888 and ensured that on his return to Egypt he was promoted to Adjutant-General, effectively the EA's second in command. This just made him more unpopular among British officers within both the British and Egyptian armies.

In early 1890, Cromer demanded Kitchener take on the job of reforming the Egyptian police and appointed him its inspector general. There is some suggestion that Cromer sweetened the pill by promising to make him Sirdar once Grenfell left. As Maxwell asserts, when Grenfell resigned, 'Lord Cromer stepped in and fulfilled his promise'. The prime minister, Lord Salisbury also helped, because Egypt was the preserve of the Foreign Office, not the Colonial Office, and Salisbury was also foreign secretary.[28] For Cromer, Kitchener was by far the best choice for sirdar because his 'main merit was that he left as little as possible to chance' and, moreover, 'he did not think that extravagance was the necessary handmaid of efficiency'.[29] Kitchener had to operate on a tight budget because of the Caisse de la Dette's oversight of the Egyptian economy and because of Cromer's public works programmes. He thus used many expedients to save money and prepare the army for its war in the Sudan. Army uniforms and clothing were repaired and anything new was made from the cheapest materials. Old, worn leather was repaired too and not abandoned. Stores of clothing and equipment were quietly built up. To increase the army's reserve manpower, men were put into the reserve

---

25 Cromer, *Modern Egypt*, vol. 2, pp. 86–88.

26 Haggard, *Under Crescent and Star*, pp.30–31.

27 Beckett, *A British Profession of Arms*, chapters 2, 3 and 4.

28 TNA: Kitchener Papers, PRO 30/57/93/GA3/30/p. 3, 'Reminiscences of Lord Kitchener' by General Sir John Maxwell; Cecil, *Leisure*, p.183; Royle, *Kitchener Enigma*, pp.78–90.

29 Cromer, *Modern Egypt*, vol.2, p.87.

Colonel, later Major General,
Sir Archibald Hunter.
(*Illustrated London News*)

despite only having served two or three years. When the army was mobilised in 1896, this led to the formation of three new battalions.[30] As sirdar, Kitchener's aim now was to prepare the army for immediate combat, to be ready when the call came to avenge Gordon for it was for this that he had been planning ever since becoming sirdar. As Rundle later wrote, Kitchener 'kept his mind to one object and one object only – the recovery of Sudan and the avenging of the desertion of Gordon by England'.[31]

In the campaign ahead, Kitchener would rely particularly on two men, Colonel Archibald Hunter, who would end the campaign as a Major General, and Brevet Lieutenant Colonel F. Reginald Wingate. Hunter would be, in effect, the battlefield commander of the EA. He had served in it since 1884, his first command being the 9th Sudanese Battalion. Hunter had served in the Gordon Relief Expedition but did not see substantial action beyond skirmishing, although on the frontier afterwards the fighting became protracted and fierce. At the battle of Ginnis in 1885, Hunter was conspicuous with his Winchester rifle and was badly wounded, which event forced him to leave the EA for some three years. In 1889, he was back on the frontier serving under Colonel Joscelin Wodehouse and would take part in the battles of Argin (2 July) and Toski (3 August). At the latter, Hunter served with Kitchener for the first time and commanded a brigade with some aplomb. Having been noticed in 1892, Hunter, like Kitchener before him, became governor of the Red Sea Littoral. But two years later he was posted back to the frontier at Wadi Halfa, a more congenial posting to this man of action, who was given the lofty titles of 'Governor of the Nile Frontier and Officer Commanding of the Frontier Field Force'.[32] Hunter was highly regarded for his command and fighting skills. Both Wodehouse and Grenfell thought him a very competent officer and later accounts of the campaign written by journalists were favourable. Frank Scudamore, for instance, praised Hunter's capabilities, pointing out that throughout he laboured under the pain from the wound he received at Ginnis. It was G.W. Steevens who referred to Hunter as Kitchener's 'sword-arm' and that his role 'has become a holy mission, pursued with a burning zeal akin to fanaticism'.[33] Lord Edward Cecil, however, was not so complimentary and thought him, among other things, 'brutal and cruel'. Moreover, Cecil believed Hunter headed a group of British officers who disliked Kitchener's

30   Sir George Arthur, *Life of Lord Kitchener* (London: Macmillan & Co., 1920), vol. 1, pp.170–172.

31   Sudan Archive, University of Durham (SAD): SAD 231: Sir Reginald Wingate Papers, 231/2/31, Rundle typescript on Kitchener, p.2.

32   Hunter, *Kitchener's Sword-arm*, pp.10–36.

33   Scudamore, *A Sheaf of Memories*, (New York: E. P. Dutton & Company, 1925), pp.115–116; G. W. Steevens, *With Kitchener to Khartum* (Edinburgh and London: William Blackwood and Sons, 1898), pp.54–57; Hunter, *Kitchener's Sword-arm*, p.34.

administration of the army. The fact that Hunter was friendly with Rundle suggests a shared disdain for the Sirdar. Hunter and Kitchener were very different personalities. Hunter was admired for his more personable command style and liked to enjoy himself in Cairo fleshpots, complaining often of getting doses of the 'clap'. Kitchener was unlike Hunter on both accounts.[34] However, Hunter was vital to the success of the EA as a fighting force and ultimately to Kitchener's ambition. In consequence, Kitchener remained circumspect in dealing with Hunter and this allowed the latter a degree of latitude in his dealings with Kitchener, something afforded to no other officer. As Hunter's biographer states 'At this stage in his career Hunter … had less need of Kitchener than his chief had of him'. Yet Hunter was well aware that for such a campaign there was no better man than Kitchener.[35]

Colonel Sir Francis Reginald Wingate. (*Illustrated London News*)

If Hunter was of great importance to Kitchener for his battlefield skills, the man deemed most vital to the success of the campaign as a whole was Reginald Wingate. Frank Scudamore later asserted that, 'undoubtedly without Wingate's aid Kitchener could never have carried to success his enterprise of the reconquest of the Sudan'. Scudamore's memoir praises Wingate highly referring to his wide knowledge of the Sudan and Africa, to his linguistic abilities and to his sensitive handling, as press censor, of the journalists who accompanied the expedition. Steevens described him as 'the intellectual, as the Sirdar is the practical, compendium of British dealings with the Sudan'.[36] Wingate joined the EA in 1883 working under Wood and then Grenfell. But it was in the field of intelligence that Wingate excelled, especially when he was appointed the EA's Director of Military Intelligence when Kitchener became sirdar in 1892. Wingate built up an intelligence network based on highly paid Sudanese agents, that gave him an extensive knowledge of the Khalifa's armies and of conditions in Omdurman itself. This knowledge enabled Wingate to act as a cheerleader for the reconquest of the Sudan. To get his message across, and to get noticed and make some money, Wingate first wrote *Mahdism and the Egyptian Sudan*, published in 1891. This book set out all the facts and figures relating to life under the Khalifa, but although it was considered worthy, it was also rather dull, and did not sell well. Two other books soon followed, *Ten Years' Captivity in the Mahdi's Camp* (1892) and *Fire and Sword in the Sudan* (1896). Wingate was the official editor of these works being respectively the accounts of the escapes from captivity of the priest Father Ohrwalder and the former governor of Darfur, Rudolf Slatin. In these works, Wingate was not strictly the author

---

34   Cecil, *Leisure*, p.189; Hunter, *Kitchener's Sword-arm*, pp.35–36, 38.
35   Hunter, *Kitchener's Sword-arm*, pp.107–108.
36   Scudamore, *A Sheaf of Memories*, pp.106–108; Steevens, *With Kitchener*, p.64.

as he edited and re-wrote translations from the original German. The books were bestsellers and Wingate ensured that the Khalifa's regime was seen in the worst light possible. The books also propelled Wingate to the position as the foremost authority on Mahdist Sudan: he had now been noticed. In 1895, it was Wingate who had debriefed Slatin, meeting him for the first time, and then wrote a lengthy report based on Slatin's testimony. In it, Wingate altered aspects he did not agree with and changed them to back up his own views. This was the case over the Bahr al Ghazal territory to the south. Slatin thought this territory unimportant, whereas Wingate on the other hand knew that the French and Belgians were lurking around this part of the White Nile valley. Consequently, Wingate doctored the report by stating that Slatin considered the area of vital importance to the Sudan and Egypt.[37] Wingate and Slatin became firm friends, hence Wingate's editing of Slatin's memoir. Slatin was quickly appointed assistant director of military intelligence, as his knowledge of local Arabic and Omdurman became vital once the campaign began, indeed, 'His earthy Arabic was well attuned to questioning deserters and spies; it was the language that they themselves spoke; they felt at ease when they talked with him.'[38] Alongside Slatin, Wingate had an impressive staff who had been carefully selected, especially for their linguistic skills. Coptic (Christian) Egyptians and Ottoman Syrians were recruited, the most prominent being Na'um Shuqaqqir. With highly paid agents criss-crossing the Sudan, Wingate and his staff were soon assessing intelligence coming from Omdurman as well as the frontier districts, and began building up a thorough appreciation of life under the Khalifa. As Steevens later remarked, 'it is due to the system of native intelligence he (Wingate) has organised, that operations in the Sudan are now certain and unsurprised instead of vague, as they once were.'[39] Wingate was a superb intelligence chief and he was well aware of his own importance. He believed his skills were unrecognised by Kitchener, and like Slatin had 'a morbid sensitiveness to fancied slights'.[40] Even before his appointment as director of military intelligence in 1892, Wingate wrote that he was not on good terms with either Kitchener or Rundle, despite the latter being his brother-in-law, and whom he knew later was corresponding with the War Office behind Kitchener's back. 'Service under chiefs in whom I have neither much confidence nor very much respect is likely to become difficult', he wrote. Indeed, once in post he was soon arguing with Rundle.[41] Wingate often argued with Kitchener over his marriage and his desire to see his wife, something Kitchener found irksome because Wingate would be away from

37   M. W. Daly, 'The Soldier as Historian: F. R. Wingate and the Sudanese Mahdia', *Journal of Imperial and Commonwealth* History, 17:1 (1988), pp.100–105; Sir Ronald Wingate, *Wingate of the Sudan. The Life and Times of Sir Reginald Wingate* (London: John Murray, 1955), pp.88–92; William Beaver, *Under Every Leaf* (London: Biteback Publishing, 2012), pp.234–235.

38   Richard Hill, *Slatin Pasha* (London: Oxford University Press, 1965), pp.46–51.

39   Steevens, *With Kitchener*, p.64.

40   Hill, *Slatin*, p.46.

41   M. W. Daly, *The Sirdar. Sir Reginald Wingate and the British Empire in the Middle East* (Philadelphia: American Philosophical Society, 1997), pp.44, 50; Beckett, *Profession of Arms*, p.107.

his work. Near the end of the campaign, for example, Wingate was reluctant to ask for leave because, as he told his wife, it would 'always bring out a sneer in which he aims his views on the mistake of officers marrying. I am not going to subject you or myself to his boorish insults'. Grenfell, however, had noted that Wingate lacked tact and 'the power of commanding respect'.[42] As will be seen, in spite of their disparate personalities, Kitchener, Hunter, and Wingate would work well together, recognising the strengths as well as the follies of each other. Now the task they had waited for with growing impatience was upon them and it would be up to them to make it a success not just for the benefit of their own careers, but also for the promotion of British interests generally in north-east Africa.

---

42   SAD: SAD 233: Wingate Papers, 233/5/17, Wingate to his wife, 13 May 1898; Daly, *The Sirdar*, p.50.

Chapter 4

To Dongola 1896

Sir Garnet Wolseley had been in a hurry during the Gordon Relief Expedition and had sent troops forward in the forlorn hope of saving Gordon. The 1,500 strong Desert Column had been Wolseley's final gambit; revealing that he had 'lost control of his campaign … he ceased to be the director of operations and became a spectator instead.'[1] Kitchener had witnessed this calamity and, in contrast, would make sure that his own campaign would be managed differently and in a way that complemented his own temperament. Kitchener would exercise a tight grip on every aspect of the advance, keeping his plans firmly within his own head and avoid delegation as much as possible. The reconquest of the Sudan was Kitchener's task and he was going to do it his way. His brother Walter was appointed to command the camel transport for the duration of the campaign, and later wrote that Kitchener was 'a real autocrat – he does just as he pleases.'[2] But Kitchener was not actually free to do as he pleased because, as already discussed, he would be constrained by the Nile and the desert and it would be these natural elements that would dictate the pace of the campaign and its requirements.

By 6 June 1896, the EA, having been strung out along the Nile, was concentrated at Akasha, just 16 miles north of the Mahdist position at Firket. During the ten weeks or so since Akasha's occupation, it had steadily prepared for its first major engagement, having amassed reinforcements, supplies and ammunition. Two battalions, the 9th and 10th Sudanese had come from Suakin. The 9th Battalion arrived first, having been relieved at Suakin by the 16th Egyptian Battalion, which comprised reservists. To get to the front, the 9th had been shipped to Kosseir from where it had marched across the desert to Kena, covering some 120 miles in four days, with temperatures at times reaching 115° F (45°C) in the shade. From Kena, the troops were then brought forward to Akasha. The second unit, the 10th Sudanese had been delayed owing to Osman Digna causing trouble around Suakin and had finally been released in late May, once a contingent from India arrived to replace it. The 10th reached Akasha about 4 June. While all

---

1   Colonel Mike Snook, *Beyond the Reach of Empire. Wolseley's Failed Campaign to Save Gordon and Khartoum*, (London: Frontline Books, 2013), p.xviii

2   Philip Magnus, *Kitchener. Portrait of an Imperialist* (London: John Murray, 1958), p.95.

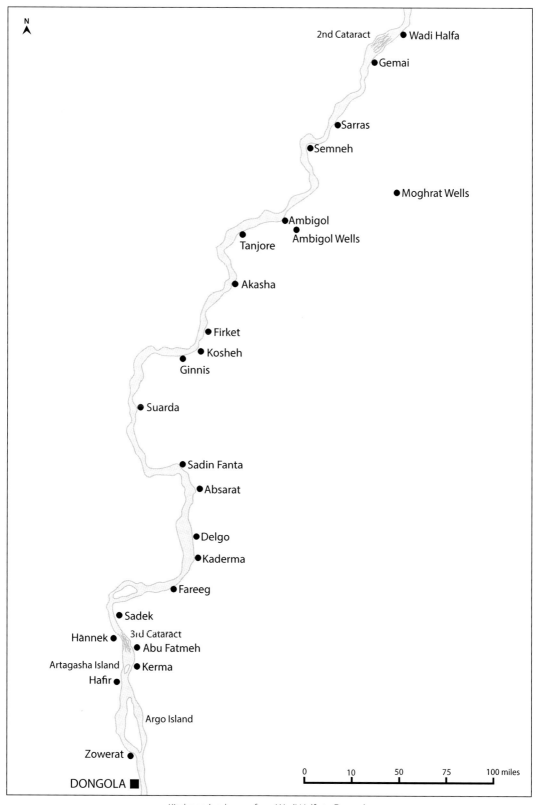

N

2nd Cataract ● Wadi Halfa
● Gemai

●Sarras
●Semneh

● Moghrat Wells

●Ambigol
● Ambigol Wells
● Tanjore

● Akasha

● Firket
● Kosheh
Ginnis

● Suarda

● Sadin Fanta
●Absarat

●Delgo
●Kaderma

● Fareeg
● Sadek
3rd Cataract
Hannek ● ● Abu Fatmeh
Artagasha Island ●Kerma
Hafir ●

Argo Island

Zowerat ●
DONGOLA ■

0   10   50   75   100 miles

Kitchener's advance from Wadi Halfa to Dongola.

this was happening, the Mahdists in Firket, under their ineffectual leader, the Emir Hammuda, had been joined by Osman Azrak, 'the contriver of the most daring and most brutal raids', according to Churchill. He was sent to galvanize Hammuda or even supersede him, but his appointment was too late: as Kitchener's army gathered, the Mahdists 'watched in senseless apathy the deliberate machine-like preparations for their destruction'.[3]

The ability to concentrate virtually the whole of the EA with speed and efficiency owed a great deal to Kitchener's foresight and restless energy. The Nile was unreliable at that time of the year and camel transport could not bring up enough supplies: the only solution therefore had been to build a railway. This would enable troops, food, water, and ammunition to be brought forward with despatch. Once Akasha had been occupied on 20 March, the railway was immediately begun from Wadi Halfa, or as the British soldiers would call it 'Wadi Hell-Fire'.[4] Although 33 miles of track existed between there and Sarras, the original line running to Akasha had been destroyed by the Mahdists, but not thoroughly. The old embankment still existed, as did the rails, for they had been thrown down towards the river. Even so, there was precious little material to be had and so Kitchener and his five chosen Royal Engineer subalterns, one of whom, Lieutenant Percy Girouard, was put in command of the whole enterprise, had to make do and mend and use their initiative. Kitchener certainly did; he had the barracks at Wadi Halfa demolished because some old rails had been used in their construction.[5] The availability of engines and rolling stock was limited, thus old rusting, abandoned engines were patched up, and old trucks were purloined. Labourers were found by resorting to conscription, while later, Mahdist prisoners would also be used for the project. Egyptian plate layers were, however, labelled 'useless scoundrels', while engine drivers were actually stokers with no experience. The work was done in searing heat, usually 116° F (47°C) in the shade, with 129° F (54°C) being recorded at one point. Speed, though, was the order of the day and the railway was built as far as Ambigol Wells. Although the quality of the construction was poor, it sufficed, however, to get men and material forward without a major incident.[6]

Meanwhile, Major Walter Kitchener had managed to get the camel transport well organised and manned, although again using conscript labour. It was noted that the Egyptians lacked knowledge of how to handle camels and each conscript had to be trained thoroughly, after which he made 'the most excellent transport man'.[7] Thus, the EA was now well prepared for its first major battle of the campaign.

---

3   Winston Spencer Churchill, *River War. An Historical Account of the Reconquest of the Soudan* (London: Longmans, Green, And Co.) vol. 1, pp.185–222; An Officer (Lieutenant H. L. Pritchard), *The Sudan Campaign 1896-1899* (London: Chapman & Hall Ltd., 1899), pp.24–25, 30.

4   Henry S. L. Alford & W. Dennistoun Sword, *The Egyptian Soudan. Its Loss and Recovery* (London: Macmillan and Co., Limited, 1898. Reprinted: Dallington: The Naval & Military Press, 1992), p.81.

5   TNA: Kitchener Papers, PRO 30/57/93/GA3/12, p.1: 'Memories of Kitchener in Egypt and the Sudan' by Major General N M Smyth.

6   An Officer, *Sudan Campaign*, pp.16–19, 27.

7   An Officer, *Sudan Campaign*, pp.19–22.

Intelligence on the Mahdist position at Firket was very good. Wingate knew every aspect of the place and provided briefings for the officers. In addition, the commander of the EA cavalry, Major J. F. Burn-Murdoch, along with one of the squadron commanders, Captain R.G. Broadwood, and even Hunter, had carried out thorough surveys of Firket themselves, getting close to the village to observe the Mahdists at their leisure. The village itself was a mile long and 300 yards wide, a straggling aggregate of mud houses that hugged the bank of the Nile, but was overlooked by high ground to the north and east. The Mahdists, numbering some 2-3,000 infantry and 300 Baggara cavalry, had three main positions. To the north of the village lay the camp of the Ja'alin tribe; to its south lay that of the Baggara cavalry; to the east, occupying some of the high ground were the *jihadiya* riflemen. Some of the houses behind the Ja'alin had been prepared for defence.[8] Kitchener accepted Hunter's plan for the EA to approach Firket by night in two columns: one, the River Column, would hug the road by the river bank, while the Desert Column marched around the high ground to the east, outflanking the Mahdists and cutting off Firket from the south. The latter would be under the command of Burn-Murdoch and would comprise the Camel Corps, the cavalry, the Horse Artillery battery, the camel mounted 12th Sudanese battalion, and two Maxim machine guns. Forming the River Column, Kitchener and Hunter led the infantry, comprising three brigades of three battalions each. Major D.F. Lewis commanded the 1st Brigade; Major H. MacDonald, an officer who had risen through the ranks, the 2nd; while Brevet Major J. Maxwell commanded the 3rd Brigade. All these officers were long-serving members of the EA. They would be supported by two field artillery batteries and two Maxim machine guns.[9] Timing would be all-important and it is said that Broadwood set the times for each column to appear owing to his knowledge of the ground through scouting.[10] The time set for the arrival of the two columns was 4:30 a.m.

At 5:00 p.m. on 6 June 1896, Kitchener led out the River Column for the 18-mile march, its orders written out by Rundle who had stayed behind. The column was forbidden to smoke and use bugle calls, and any Mahdists encountered were to be dealt with by bayonet. The column was headed by the 1st Brigade, then the Maxims, the artillery, Kitchener and his staff, the 2nd Brigade, the 3rd Brigade, the Field Hospital, and finally a half battalion from the 3rd Brigade making up the rearguard. The march orders for the Desert Column were more limited; Burn-Murdoch was directed to occupy the eastern hills opposite Firket and then to face west, 'taking care you do not come under fire of the Infantry Brigade advancing along the river bank'. He was, however, told how to deploy his force: the Egyptian Cavalry were to be placed on the left, the Camel Corps in the centre, and the dismounted

---

8   Edward M. Spiers, 'Intelligence and Command in Britain's Small Colonial Wars of the 1890s', *Intelligence and National Security*, 22:5, (2007), p.665; An Officer, *Sudan Campaign*, pp.25–26; Archie Hunter, *Kitchener's Sword-Arm. The Life and Campaigns of General Sir Archibald Hunter* (Staplehurst: Spellmount, 1996), p.45; Churchill, *River War*, vol. 1, p.228.

9   Alford & Sword, *Egyptian Soudan*, pp.86–87.

10   An Officer, *Sudan Campaign*, p.30.

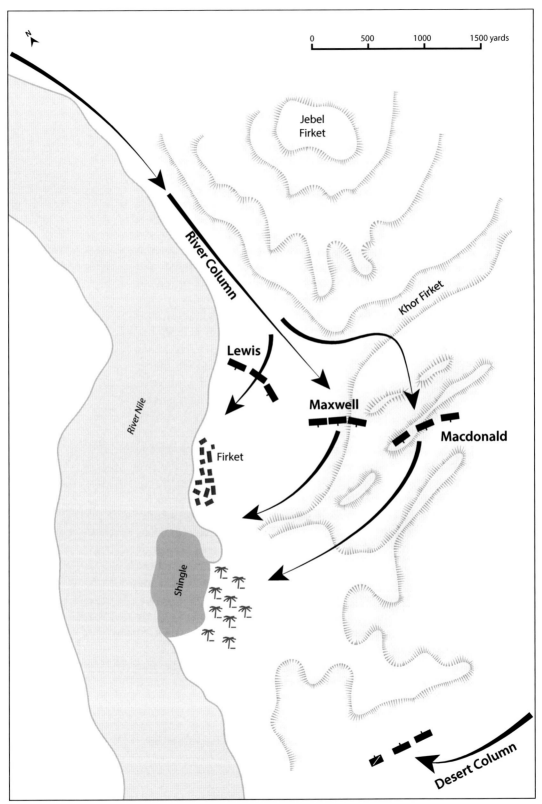

Battle of Firket, 7 June 1896.

12th Sudanese on the right. The deployment of the artillery and the Maxim guns was left to Burn-Murodoch's discretion. After the enemy was defeated the cavalry and Camel Corps were expected to move south as far as Suarda, which they were ordered to occupy and fortify.[11]

Taken at face value, Kitchener's adumbrated despatch following the battle suggests that the night march was rather straightforward.[12] Accounts by those who took part tell a different story. The night was only starlit and very dark and the River Column had to negotiate a landscape of steep hills divided by numerous dried river beds known as *khors*. The ground was so broken that at one point the column had to march in single-file along a ledge overlooking the river. The march discipline, however, remained excellent. By 4:30 a.m., the River Column was in position and a little after 5:00 a.m., it was spotted by a Mahdist outpost and the battle began. Immediately, the sound of artillery was heard towards the south, which meant the Desert Column was engaged as well. The plan had worked perfectly.

MacDonald's brigade on the left soon cleared the crest of high ground that led off from the mountain known as Jebel Firket, and headed for the *jihadiya* defences on the slopes to the brigade's front. Using a combination of volley fire and movement over the undulating ground, MacDonald's men soon drove the *jihadiya* from their positions, in spite of their spirited resistance, forcing them to retreat towards Firket. Lewis's brigade on the right advanced towards the village, driving the Ja'alin before it, while Maxwell's brigade was brought forward to fill the gap between the two other brigades and form the centre. Soon, all three brigades were engaged in and around Firket, clearing the enemy from their camps and any houses they occupied. In the house-to-house fighting, 'no quarter was given and none asked'.[13] Within two hours the battle was over: the firepower of the EA had proved decisive, its fire discipline had been exemplary, while the Maxims and artillery had proved their worth. The Emir Hammuda had been killed, while Osman Azrak had escaped. Despite being heavily outnumbered, the Mahdists in general had fought with tenacity and discipline, although their shooting had been poor, mostly going high. Their conduct, however, elicited the comment that: 'It is sad to think that men with such innate pluck should be such brutes'.[14] Mahdist casualties were horrendous: some 800 were killed, with about 500 wounded and 600 taken prisoner, many of whom, especially those of the *jihadiya*, were then recruited into the EA. However, although the fighting in Firket had been bitter and no mercy shown by either side, the journalist A.H. Atteridge pointed out that elsewhere 'There had been no massacre. Quarter had been

---

11 TNA: WO 32/6142: Operations. 'Report by Major General H. Kitchener relating to Dongola Expedition and capture of Firket, Sudan': 'Orders for the River Column', from Rundle, Chief-of-Staff, 5 June 1896; 'Orders for the Desert Column', Rundle to Burn-Murdoch, 6 June 1896.

12 TNA: WO/32/6142: Operations. 'Report by Major General H. Kitchener relating to Dongola Expedition and capture of Firket, Sudan': 'Sir H. Kitchener's despatches on the advance on Dongola', Brigadier General Sir H. H. Kitchener to The General Officer Commanding The Force in Egypt, 9 June 1896.

13 A. Hilliard Atteridge, *Towards Khartoum. The Story of the Soudan War of 1896* (London: A. D. Innes & Co., 1897), pp.182–194; 212; Alford & Sword, *Egyptian Soudan*, pp.88, 90.

14 Alford & Sword, *Egyptian Soudan*, pp.90–91.

Battle of Firket, 7 June 1896. 1st Brigade advances. (*Illustrated London News*)

given to all who accepted it. The wounded were not only spared but taken care of.'[15] Some Mahdist wounded did try to fight on and were then killed; the journalist E.F. Knight was attacked by one who he thought was dead. 'Many of the wounded Dervishes acted, as is their wont, in such a manner as to forfeit all right to clemency'. This refrain would be heard throughout the coming campaign, especially following the battle at Omdurman.[16]

---

15 Alford & Sword, *Egyptian Soudan*, p.213; Colonel F.I. Maxse, *Seymour Vandeleur*, (London: The *National Review* Office, 1906. Reprinted: London: Forgotten Books, 2015), p.162; Churchill, *River War*, vol. 1, pp.232–233.

16 E. F. Knight, *Letters from the Soudan* (London: Macmillan & Co., 1897), pp.121–122.

Battle of Firket, 7 June 1896,
1st Brigade advancing against
enemy positions. (*Illustrated
London News*)

The EA had, according to all who had been there, fought well: the action had been 'A red-letter day in the history of the Egyptian army'. Knight felt that the troops had experienced 'an increase of soldierly pride and spirit'.[17] Hunter, though, was more circumspect pointing out that the EA had outnumbered the enemy, as they had in earlier engagements, and 'We have never asked them to do anything that was not within the easy compass of attainment.' He was still not sure whether an Egyptian soldier 'could stand a charge of Baggara horse'.[18] As planned, Suarda was soon occupied. It was now crucial for the railway to be brought forward and the Nile utilised and its control taken from the Mahdists. But now, the campaign started to go awry.

Kitchener was never going to do things in a rush but the campaign had to be concluded before the Nile flood began to fall. Preparations for the next stage, therefore, had to be done quickly and without hindrance. Unfortunately for Kitchener's already considerable anxiety this was not to be the case. There occurred three almost calamitous events, all beyond human control, and which would test the strength, ingenuity and adaptability of the whole EA and its commander-in-chief.

Firstly, the army was struck by cholera, compounding problems already caused by an outbreak of typhoid. The cholera epidemic had reached Wadi Halfa by 30 June and had there infected the North Staffordshire Regiment. To

---

17   Knight, *Letters*, p.123; Alford & Sword, *Egyptian Soudan*, p.92.
18   King's College London: Liddell Hart Centre for Military Archives (LHCMA): Major General Sir J. Frederick Maurice Papers, General Sir Archibald Hunter Letters: 2/1/2/, Hunter to Maurice, 12 July 1896, pp.1–3.

outrun it, the North Staffordshires had been moved to Gemai, but to no avail. 'One after another of our men was carried off by it; and for the greater part of July our existence might be summed up in the question "Whose turn next?"'[19] The EA succumbed too, although the battalions at Kosheh were moved into the desert, and the army was not free of the disease until August. By the end of the epidemic, it had suffered 1,218 cases, of whom 919 had died, with most of those, numbering 640, being 'Followers', those Egyptians working on the logistical side. In terms of fighting troops, the army had lost 260 men, from 406 infected cases. The British Army, including North Staffordshires and Royal Engineer officers working on the railway, lost 19 men, from 24 infections. In 1896, more soldiers died from the cholera than were killed by the Mahdists. These bare figures, fairly low as they were, cannot however provide much of an idea, as one historian has remarked 'of the disgusting manifestations of this disease, a hellish picture of men suffering and dying uncomforted in crushing heat and overpowering stench'.[20] Unsurprisingly, morale among all the troops – be they Egyptian, Sudanese, or British – plummeted.

Secondly, soon after the battle of Firket, Hunter was tasked with bringing the steamers and sail boats over the Second Cataract, so that they could assist the advance upriver. This Hunter would achieve, but his men had to expend considerable energy in doing so, owing to the vagaries of nature. By then, the Nile flood ought to have been well underway but it had arrived late and it was not until mid-August that Hunter could start the process, which eventually took three weeks. About 1,000 Egyptian soldiers would be used to haul the boats over the rocks, supplemented by 400 men from the North Staffordshires. The gunboats, their armaments removed and unable to use their engines, were pulled over the cataract by the troops using two great steel hawsers on each side, with one at the bow to steady the boat, plus a system of blocks and tackles. In searing heat, the men heaved each boat over huge, black granite slabs, against a current made fierce by the onset of the flood. At a narrow gorge, known as 'the Big Gate', where 'An enormous churned-up mass of water rushes through', it took the men, working in relays, an hour and a half to pull one gunboat through.[21] Four gunboats and three steamers were pulled through in about a week, leaving the sailing boats, known as gyassas to come next. The flat-bottomed barges (nuggars) could not take the rough water and had been left behind. Three soldiers were killed during this operation.[22]

The four gunboats were all stern-wheelers, 89 feet long with 18 feet beams. Known as the *Tamai*-class, they comprised the *Tamai*, the *Metemma*, the *Abu Klea*, and the *El Teb*, and although built in 1885 they had not yet seen any action. British designed and built, the boats were formidably armed: each had a Mark I, 12-pdr, quick–firing gun, that could fire either

---

19   Alford & Sword, *Egyptian Soudan*, p.97.

20   Churchill, *River War*, vol. 1, pp.242–245; An Officer, *Egyptian Soudan*, pp.43–44; Henry Keown-Boyd, *A Good Dusting. A Centenary Review of the Sudan Campaigns 1883–1899* (London: Book Club Associates, 1986), pp.168–170.

21   Alford & Sword, *Egyptian Soudan*, pp.104–106; An Officer, *Sudan Campaign*, pp.45–46; Churchill, *River War*, vol. 1, pp.245–249.

22   Hunter, *Kitchener's Sword-arm*, pp.50–51.

Hauling a gunboat over the second cataract. (*Illustrated London News*)

high-explosive or shrapnel shells at ranges of up to 11,750 yards. They were supported by a rapid-firing Maxim-Nordenfelt 1-pdr, known as a 'pom-pom' because of the noise it made, and four Maxim machine guns. They were ideal river craft, having shallow-draughts of two feet, six inches even when full of men and ammunition. They would soon be joined by the first of a bigger type of gunboat, the *Zafir*, which was 128 feet long, with a beam of 23 feet. Again, of British design and build, the *Zafir* and its sisters, the *El Nasir* and the *El Fateh*, would have a fully laden draught of two feet, nine inches. Armed with the same weapons as the *Tamai* class, they also carried two quick-firing six-pdr guns. For protection, both classes were covered in steel plates but the gun positions were vulnerable, with only the guns' shields and sandbags offering any cover. Later, for the final part of the campaign in 1898, the gunboat flotilla would be joined by three new, more powerful, *Sultan*-class boats, the *Sultan*, the *Sheikh* and the *Melik*. These were 145 feet in length, with a beam of 24 feet, six inches. They were armed with two 12-pdr guns and six Maxim machine guns. In addition, they could carry two five-inch field howitzers, suitably adapted. The main difference between this class of boats and the two others was that they were driven by underwater screw propellers, thus making their propulsion safer from enemy fire. All the gunboats' boilers were designed to burn coal, but could use wood if necessary, although this was not ideal. Thus, the supply of coal was a necessity and this 'among other things, was a deciding factor' in the building of the future Sudan Military Railway. Although, the *Sultan* class gunboats might have made excellent river boats, they were nevertheless flawed when faced with the demands of the campaign since all gunboats were expected to tow other boats laden with troops and supplies. The *Sultan* class's shallow draught of two feet, six inches was a handicap because it meant the boat lacked 'a sufficient grip of the water' and could tow only at very low speeds against the current, unlike the stern-wheelers. However, when in action the gunboats would not be towing barges and when almost stationary at Omdurman, they would prove their worth.[23]

In 1896, then, for the second stage of the Dongola campaign, Kitchener could now rely on added firepower from his gunboats as well as a river fleet to bring up supplies and troops to supplement the work done by the railway. The EA now controlled both sides of the Nile river bank, making Mahdist positions insecure and any movement extremely hazardous. The gunboats forced the Mahdists further into the desert, denying them their main supply route and line of communication. However, technology is only good when it works and on 11 September, soon after the *Zafir* was launched, having been brought in pieces from Britain and carried on the railway all the way from Egypt, and with Kitchener on board, one of its boilers blew up and could only be replaced by a new one. Kitchener was distraught and locked himself away on another boat to work through the disappointment. It seems that with his nerves stretched, this was one blow too many for the sirdar to take.

---

23   Angus Konstam, *Nile River Gunboats 1882–1918*, (Oxford: Osprey Publishing, 2016), pp.9–10, 12, 14, 16–17, 20–21, 23–24, 34–35; Alford & Sword, *Egyptian Soudan*, pp.107, 237–238; Bennet Burleigh, *Khartoum Campaign 1898. Or the Re-conquest of the Soudan* (London: Chapman & Hall Limited, 1899. Reprinted Cambridge: Ken Trotman Ltd, 1989), pp.73–74.

The *Metemma* reaches calmer waters at the second cataract. (*Illustrated London News*)

According to Maxwell, Kitchener 'was so upset and distressed at this, that he completely broke down, and cried like a child'.[24]

Kitchener's mood is understandable when it is appreciated that in addition to the cholera outbreak and the delay getting the boats over the Second Cataract, there was another major, natural disaster waiting in the wings. By late August, the railway had been brought forward to Kosheh and preparations were nearly ready for the final advance. But between 25 and 27 August, three unseasonal storms broke over the desert. The wind had changed direction and was now coming from the south, bringing first searing heat, and then, as it increased, sandstorms, drenching rain, thunder and lightning. Such an event was practically unprecedented. The storms were powerful enough to wash away altogether about twenty miles of railway track, the camp of the railway battalion and most of the telegraph wires.[25] Kitchener acted immediately, taking charge himself by rounding up 5,000 men to rebuild and repair the broken line. Speed was of the essence to ensure the EA could still take advantage of the high Nile water. Kitchener patrolled the railway line, making sure sufficient men were made available. The job was completed after 12 days, although as one officer remarked, the repair was 'just sufficiently well to enable the line to work'.[26]

The storms also inflicted casualties upon the men, especially those of the 1st Brigade. On 23 August, Kitchener sent MacDonald's 2nd Brigade from Suarda to occupy Absarat. It was quicker to march across the desert because of a small bend in the river and it was not far, being some 21 miles. However, because of the southerly wind bringing extreme heat, the troops found the march arduous, a number collapsed with heat stroke and two died. In response, Kitchener had water tanks and water bags dropped at two points, ready for Lewis's brigade that would march the 37 miles from Kosheh to Absarat. After a delay, the brigade, including Hunter, marched out late on the 27 August and was hit by the third storm, before it reached the first watering point. The storm, combined with the ferocious heat, fairly wrecked the brigade, with large numbers falling back to Kosheh and then more men falling along the wayside. The brigade came into Absarat in dribs and drabs on the afternoon of 28 August, totally exhausted by the experience. Although later deemed the 'Death March', only eight men died, while the stragglers were helped by Kitchener's order to send every camel and horse available to help bring them in. Hunter, though, never forgave Kitchener and wrote him a stinging letter of protest, along with a follow-up missive a month later. His anger might also have been fuelled by what he considered to be Kitchener's ingratitude following his efforts to get the boats over the Second Cataract. Whether Kitchener received the first letter, or even read it, is a moot point, because he did not react to Hunter's insubordination,

---

24   TNA: Kitchener Papers, PRO 30/57/93, GA3/30, p. 4: 'Recollections of Kitchener' by General Sir John Maxwell.

25   Alford & Sword, *Egyptian Soudan*, p. 108; Atteridge, *Towards Khartoum*, pp.318–321; Knight, *Letters*, pp.243–246.

26   An Officer, *Sudan Campaign*, pp.49–54; TNA: Kitchener Papers, PRO 30/57/93, GA3/12/p. 2: 'Memories of Kitchener in Egypt and the Sudan' by Major General N M Smyth.

perhaps being unwilling to alienate Hunter further. Hunter himself shared some culpability for not calling off the march and was angry that the men blamed him. Churchill though defended Kitchener for the lack of transport animals that might have helped, owing to the 'pitiless economy' marking the campaign.[27]

Kitchener was not one to give praise lightly, if at all. He expected officers to get their jobs done, whatever the circumstances. One account we have of Kitchener by a junior officer sheds some light on the sirdar at this anxious time. Kitchener, 'has tremendous energy and has the knack of getting an extraordinary lot of work out of the people under him. He is supposed to have shown want of feeling about the numbers who have died or got sick … but I think that is purely a private matter. Soldiering under him is hard too as he considers nothing as regards one's comfort etc., when he wants anything carried out but I think we ought to expect that on active service.'[28] Since March, Kitchener had worked his army hard, to deal with the Mahdists, to facilitate the advance and to overcome the vagaries of the desert and the Nile. Come September, the army was given some rest but the timetable was dictated by the Nile and its flood state and this could not go to waste, especially as it would enable the river flotilla to cross over the Third Cataract as it moved on Dongola.

On 5 September, the final part of the Dongola campaign began as the EA began to move south. By 18 September, the EA, reinforced by the 4th Brigade under Brevet Major E. F. David, as well as the North Staffordshire Regiment, had concentrated at Sardek, ready to move the short distance towards Kerma, where the Mahdists had concentrated. On the river, the gunboats, minus the *Zafir*, patrolled ahead, ready to lend their considerable firepower to the coming battle. The Mahdist commander, whose force of about 5,600 was heavily outnumbered, was the Emir Wad Bishara, the governor of Dongola, and he was conscious of his army's inferiority. On the 19 September, the EA advanced to find Kerma empty but soon afterwards realised that Bishara and his army were on the other side of the river, dug in along the river bank at Hafir, a village covered on its northern and southern sides by boggy ground caused by flood water. Altogether, it was a formidable position and Kitchener, to use Wellington's phrase, had been 'humbugged'. This was surprising considering that intelligence received in July had already suggested that Wad Bishara would fight at Hafir.[29] Thus, the only action to occur on the 19th was the attempt by three gunboats, the *Tamai*, the *Metemma* and the *Abu Klea*, (the fourth boat, the *El Teb* being stuck on a rock in a smaller cataract), supported by the Horse Battery, to dislodge the Mahdists from their riverside trenches, buildings and palm–trees. In the

---

27   Hunter, *Kitchener's sword-arm*, pp. 51-54; John Pollock, *Kitchener* (Combined paperback edition, London: Robinson, 2002), vol. 1, pp.100–101; Churchill, *River War*, vol. 1, pp.249–252.

28   National Army Museum (NAM): 1984-12-50: Fredrick Gore Anley Papers, to his mother, 24 August 1896.

29   SAD: Sudan Intelligence Reports (SIR): Main Sequence, Intelligence Report, Egypt, No. 49, 22 June – 18 August 1896, supplementary to 27 August 1895(6), p. 5, F.R. Wingate, 18 August 1896; Appendix A (8), 15 July, 1896, Letter from Mohammed El Haj, pp.12–13. <https://www.dur.ac.uk/library/asc/sudan/sirs; http://palimpsest.dur.ac.uk/slp/sirs1.html>, accessed 1 Sept. 2020.

Egyptian gunboats attacking Dongola. (*Illustrated London News*)

early morning light, the gunboats fired for all they were worth and were answered in kind by the Mahdists rifles and their eight old brass cannons. The whole area was covered with smoke, while the bullets and shells made the river boil. The gunboats eventually withdrew, unable to dislodge the enemy. Kitchener then decided to change his tactics. He deployed all the army's artillery, Maxim guns and even a rocket battery on an island near Hafir and began a massive bombardment of the Mahdist defences. Enemy snipers in the palm trees were a particular target, as they had caused problems for the men servicing the gunboats' guns. Under cover of this fire, the gunboats, still blazing away, surged past Hafir and on to Dongola. Wad Bishara, badly wounded, as was Osman Azrak, deciding the threat to his base was too great, ordered a retreat, and left behind up to 200 dead and many more wounded. The Mahdists might have repelled the gunboats, but their bullets and shells had proved inadequate to sink or disable any of them, an indication of the poor quality of the Mahdist gunpowder. Although one shell penetrated the *Abu Klea*'s magazine, it did not explode, while three shells hit the *Metemma*. Once the Mahdists had decamped, Kitchener ordered the EA to be ferried over to Hafir and by 22 September, it was camped six miles from Dongola. That night the EA marched on the town and in the morning stood in battle array awaiting Wad Bishara and his army, which soon appeared. However, without firing a shot, the Mahdists turned in precipitate retreat, bypassing Dongola and not stopping until they reached Abu Hamed, although Wad Bishara, Osman Azrak and the Baggara horse headed for Metemma, across the Bayuda desert. Evidently, years later, it was discovered that Wad Bishara had wanted a death or glory charge against the EA, but his emirs had decided that it was a futile action and had arrested him, bound him and carried him away. The EA marched into Dongola and pursued the retreating Mahdists, capturing some 900 in the process. Many of the *jihadiya* were recruited into the EA and sent north for training. The gunboats advanced 200 miles further up river and soon EA units were placed in Korti, Debba, and then Merawi, within striking distance of Abu Hamed. The 1896 campaign was over. The EA, exhausted though it was, had achieved all that had been asked of it and it had proved to be a formidable force in its own right. Admittedly, the EA had not come up against the whole might of the Khalifa's army, which was still located around Omdurman, but it had achieved the task it had been given. Overall, Kitchener's campaign had been a huge success.[30]

---

30 Churchill, *River War*, vol. 1, pp. 254–274; Alford & Sword, *Egyptian Soudan*, chapters 8–11. An Officer, *Sudan Campaign*, pp.56–71; 'Ismat Hasan Zulfo, *Karari. The Sudanese Account of the Battle of Omdurman*, (London: Frederick Warne (Publishers) Ltd, 1980), pp.64–67.

Chapter 5

To Berber, 1897

In his despatch following the capture of Dongola, Kitchener outlined the campaign's achievements. About 450 miles of the Nile valley, which included 300 miles of fertile country, had been liberated, all this 'to the intense delight of the large and suffering population', who were now delivered 'from the barbarous and tyrannical rule of the savage and tyrannous Baggaras'. By so doing, the EA had 'demonstrated … high qualities of endurance and bravery', while 'the high spirit and eagerness which the troops have displayed under very trying circumstances is beyond praise'. Kitchener could look back with satisfaction and relief to a very successful campaign that had lost few lives, most from cholera, and had cost only £[Egyptian]715,000: 'A figure which bore testimony to the Sirdar's economical administration', according to Cromer's measured praise. The sulky Hunter received the acknowledgement he felt his due, being promoted to major general and appointed governor of Dongola province. Everyone on the British and Egyptian side could consider the campaign a job well done.[1] Lord Salisbury asked of Lord Lansdowne, 'I hope you are going to do something for Kitchener in the way of reward', to which Lansdowne replied that Queen Victoria had already agreed his promotion and that an 'advancement in the order of the Bath' was in the offing. Although Lansdowne felt that Mahdist resistance had 'not been serious', he acknowledged that Kitchener 'has overcome the other obstacles brilliantly'. Thus, Kitchener was promoted to major general in the British Army and was awarded the honour of KCB. Lansdowne signed off by writing, 'I shall be surprised if we are not pressed hard to let him go ahead.'[2]

To 'go ahead' was very much on Kitchener's mind when he returned to Cairo to discuss the next stage with Cromer. Kitchener explained that in 1897 he wanted to advance to Berber, and implied that if permission was not forthcoming then the strategic situation might change for the worse because

---

1   TNA: WO 32/6142: Operations: 'Sudan Campaign. Dongola Expeditionary Force', Kitchener to Knowles, 30 September 1896; Knowles to Brodrick, 14 October 1896. The Earl of Cromer, *Modern Egypt*, (London: Macmillan, 1908), vol. 2, p.91; Archie Hunter, *Kitchener's Sword-Arm. The Life and Campaigns of General Sir Archibald Hunter* (Staplehurst: Spellmount, 1996), p.57.

2   BL: Lansdowne Papers, 88906/19/6, Salisbury to Lansdowne; Lansdowne to Salisbury, 25 & 29 September 1896.

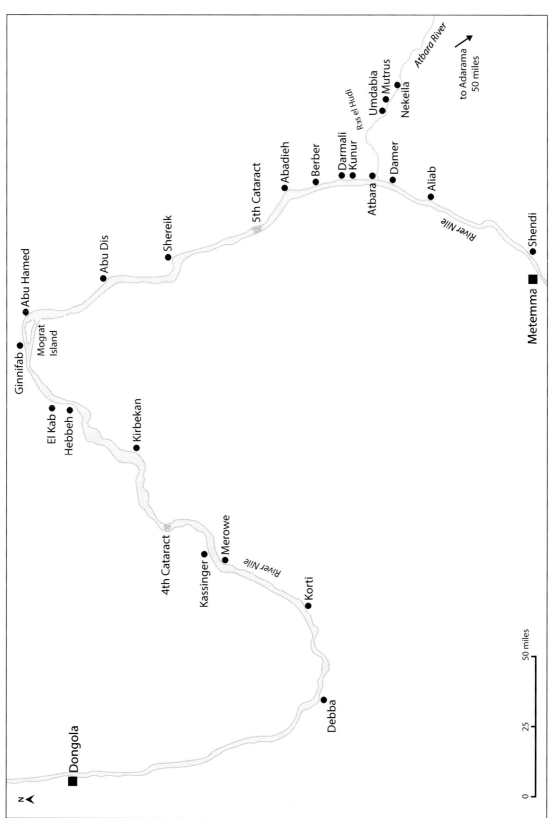

Atbara River

to Adarama
50 miles

Umdabia
Mutrus
Ras el Hudi
Nekeila

Abadieh
Berber
Darmali
Kunur
Damer
Atbara
Aliab

5th Cataract

Shereik

Abu Dis

Abu Hamed

Mograt
Island

Ginnifab

River Nile

Shendi

Metemma

El Kab
Hebbeh

Kirbekan

Merowe
River Nile

4th Cataract

Kassinger

Korti

Debba

Dongola

N

Kitchener's advance from Dongola to Metemma.

50 miles

0   25   50 miles

67

Wingate had information that the French were intriguing with Abyssinia in order to gain influence over the equatorial areas of the Nile. Thanks to the work of the army's Intelligence Division, the government knew that the French were on the move towards Fashoda, situated on the upper Nile in the Bahr al Ghazal region of the Sudan. The outcome of this concern would be a British mission to the Abyssinian emperor, Menelik, in early 1897, which would include Wingate and the prime minister's son, Lord Edward Cecil.[3] Meanwhile, Cromer was now convinced something should be done in 1897 even though 'I had thought … to stop two or three years at Dongola'.[4] Cromer thought he might get the money from the Caisse de la Dette and indeed he did, despite French and Russian objections. However, they appealed to the Court of Appeal (the Mixed Tribunals) and won their case and on 6 December 1896, Egypt was forced to give back the £500,000 initially granted, a decision Cromer had anticipated.[5] Kitchener, however, had already gone to London to put his case in the hope and expectation that London would outflank the French and the Russians.

Salisbury had told Queen Victoria that a further advance was unlikely because it is 'purely a question of money. There is no Egyptian money available. If it is done, it must be done with English money … my impression is that the House of Commons would *not* be disposed to authorise the expenditure'.[6] Moreover, a formidable hurdle awaiting Kitchener was the Chancellor of the Exchequer, Sir Michael Hicks Beach. Kitchener arrived in London on 9 November and one week later was writing to Cromer that he had won his case. To do so, he employed not only his political friends but even royalty in the shape of the Queen and her cousin, the Duke of Cambridge, the former commander-in-chief of the British Army. Nevertheless, Kitchener had explained his plans very well, including that for building a new railway to support the advance on Abu Hamed and Berber. With the latter place captured, he ventured, the Suakin garrison could be reduced. Kitchener had done his sums and provided an estimate of £500,000, which included money for the railway (£240,000) and three new gunboats (£75,000). As Hicks Beach's biographer wrote: 'The business-like terseness of the proposition and the care shown for economy of means commended themselves at once to the Chancellor of the Exchequer'. In the end the loan was nearer £800,000 and Cromer negotiated an interest rate of 2.5 percent.[7]

Once back at the front following his 'victory' over the Chancellor, Kitchener began his pet project without further delay. On 1 January 1897,

---

3   Philip Magnus, *Kitchener. Portrait of an Imperialist* (London: John Murray, 1958), pp.101–102; William Beaver, *Under Every Leaf* (London: Biteback Publishing Ltd, 2012), pp.250–256.

4   Quoted in Magnus, *Kitchener*, p.102.

5   Cromer, *Modern Egypt*, vol. 2, p.92; Roger Owen, *Lord Cromer* (Oxford: Oxford University Press), p.290.

6   Quoted in R. Robinson & J. Gallagher with Alice Denny, *Africa and the Victorians* (London: Macmillan, 1981), p.358.

7   TNA: Kitchener Papers, PRO 30/57/11/J/11, Kitchener to Cromer, (tel), 16 November 1896; Lady Victoria Hicks Beach, *Life of Sir Michael Hicks Beach (Earl St. Aldwyn)* (London: Macmillan & Co. Ltd., 1932), vol. 2, pp.41–45; Magnus, *Kitchener*, pp.102–103; Owen, *Cromer*, p.290.

Laying the telegraph wire and building the railway. The railway was built mostly by conscripts and prisoners of war and they were often not treated kindly. (*Illustrated London News*)

digging commenced for the new railway that would cross the Nubian desert. Evidently, Kitchener had had this project in mind since April 1896 and to him, it was the only viable route towards Abu Hamed, a town, whose strategic importance, like all the towns southwards from that point, could not be gainsaid.[8] From there, the route was directly south towards Omdurman with the Sixth Cataract at Shabluka being the only natural obstacle to overcome. Even so, the Nubian desert route was not without its pitfalls: it was not suitably mapped, information about it was scanty and it was considered to be waterless. Hunter, was against the idea because of these issues and with only the 'beastly water' at Murat Wells available 'half-way'. His idea was for the railway to follow the Nile. Hunter's letter was shown to Wolseley, who then passed it on to Lansdowne, 'Of course', he wrote, 'you know how fully I agree with him [Hunter] as regards this railway from either Korosko or [Wadi] Halfa to Abu Hamed'.[9]

Nothing daunted, Kitchener chose Wadi Halfa as the starting point because of the abundant materials gathered there, its concentration of workshops ablaze with activity and noise, full of British, European, and Arab workers, speaking seven languages and where 'The malodorous incense of civilisation was offered to the startled gods of Egypt', in Churchill's florid phrase. This 'brown and squalid' town, according to G.W. Steevens, that was all length – three miles along the river – and little width, some 400 yards, was now 'the decisive point of the campaign' because 'being forged [was] the deadliest weapon that Britain has ever used against Mahdism – the Sudan Military Railway'.[10] The building of this railway changed the strategic outlook of the campaign, for it would ensure that Kitchener's expanding army could be supplied without relying on the vagaries of the Nile. Both the river and the Mahdists would be decisively outflanked. Yet, when the project began, the EA lacked almost everything to run on it and so keep the construction moving. Two men were ordered to bring forth the desert railway: the newly promoted Lieutenant Colonel J. Maxwell, formally commander of the 3rd Brigade and now governor of Nubia, and Lieutenant P. Girouard, who had done so much to build the unfinished Nile railway. Maxwell was tasked with finding the manpower, and Girouard the material and the machines. Kitchener had chosen both men well, Maxwell, more a staff officer than battlefield commander, 'was eminently qualified for the job', while Girouard, now Director of Railways, was described as 'the personification of cheerfulness ... revelling in the mastery of every difficulty'.[11] Girouard was sent to buy the necessary equipment throughout the year, eventually buying 15 locomotives and 200 trucks. Five engines had been earmarked for Cecil

8   Lieutenant Colonel E. W. C. Sandes, *The Royal Engineers in Egypt and the Sudan*, (Chatham: Institution of Royal Engineers, 1937), p.192.

9   BL: Lansdowne Papers, 88906/19/28, Wolseley to Lansdowne, 3 January 1897, enclosing Hunter to Maurice, 12 December 1896.

10   Winston Spencer Churchill, *River War. An Historical Account of the Reconquest of the Soudan* (London: Longmans, Green, And Co.) vol. 1, p.208, 290; G. W. Steevens, *With Kitchener to Khartum* (Edinburgh and London: William Blackwood and Sons, 1898), p.22.

11   Sir George Arthur, *General Sir John Maxwell*, (London: John Murray, 1932), p.45; Sandes, *Royal Engineers*, pp.173, 225.

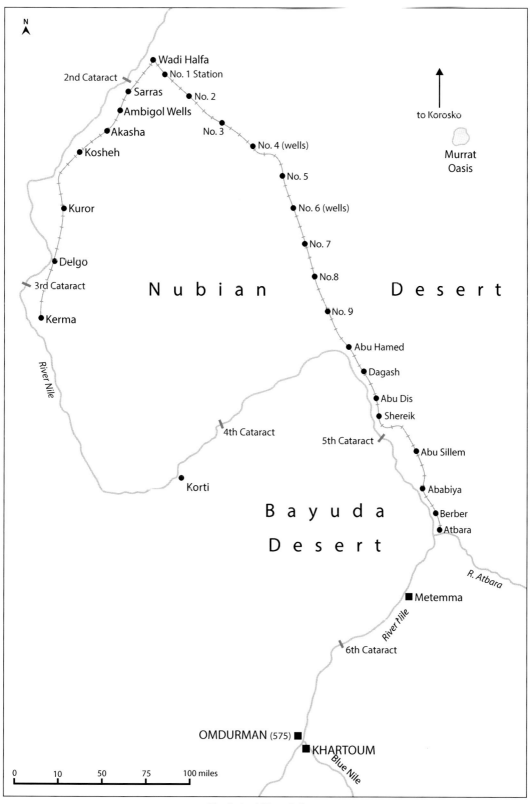

The Sudan Military Railway.

Rhodes's Cape Railway, while three engines had to be purchased from the United States owing to an engineering strike in Britain. Churchill scathingly pointed out that these American engines were more reliable, better made and a lot cheaper than if they had been built in Britain.[12] At first, progress was slow with only 40 miles of track laid by May. Then, on 4 May 1897, the Nile line reached Kerma and was deemed to be finished, thus releasing men and material for work on the desert railway. Thereafter, progress was rapid and by July, 130 miles had been built, with small stations about every 23 miles. These stations often comprised a tent, a wooden hut, and a water tank. Station No. 6 was described as the 'Swindon of the desert' for 'Every train stops there half-an-hour or more to fill up with water, for there is a great trifoliate well there.' It was also where drivers were changed for 'here is a little colony of British engine-drivers … There they swelter and smoke and spit and look out at winking rails and the red-hot sand, and wait till their turn comes to take the train'.[13] The crucial phrase of the above quote is that relating to the water supply because Kitchener had a hunch and an enormous stroke of luck, 'quite Kitcheneraic', according to Maxwell. It should be noted, however, that throughout the building of the railway the supply of water was never a desperate issue. There were times when it had to be rationed and the water-train arrived just in time. Indeed, the minimum water requirement for the workers at Railhead (the furthest point of construction) was 9,000 gallons daily. Thus, the further the advance, the greater the need for water because 'the material trains would have one-third of their carrying power absorbed in transporting the water for their own consumption'. To ease this problem some one hundred 1,500 gallon tanks were bought and the engines could be seen pulling 'enormous boxes on wheels, on which the motive power of the engine and the lives of the passengers depended'.[14] Nevertheless, finding a supplementary water source was crucial, especially for the engines that would bring up the troops and supplies. Kitchener had some basic information provided by officers in 1895 and in early 1897 he sent out a Royal Engineer officer, Lieutenant E. H. S. Cator to survey the ground upon which the railway was to run. Cator, who unfortunately died of typhoid not long afterwards, found the desert ground good, if gently uphill, and the possibility of water at points marked by Kitchener on his map. Indeed, at Station No. 4, 77 miles from Wadi Halfa, work started in early July and after five weeks digging water was found at a depth of 90 feet. Not until October, however, was the second well dug, at Station No. 6, which yielded a bountiful supply. 'They [the wells] substantially increased the carrying capacity of the line and reduced the danger to which the construction gangs were exposed.'[15] By July, the railway was well advanced, but the workers and troops at Railhead were still exposed to danger because they were now much nearer to Abu Hamed,

12 Sandes, *Royal Engineers*, pp.173, 226–227; Churchill, *River War*, vol. 1, p.298.

13 John Pollock, *Kitchener* (Combined paperback edition, London: Robinson, 2002), vol. 1, p.108; Steevens, *With Kitchener*, p.29.

14 An Officer (Lieutenant H. L. Pritchard), *The Sudan Campaign 1896-1899* (London: Chapman & Hall Ltd., 1899), pp.78, 102–103; Churchill, *River War*, vol. 1, p.289.

15 Churchill, *River War*, vol. 1, p.295; Pollock, *Kitchener*, vol. 1, p.107

Packed into gunboats, troops sail up the Nile. (*Illustrated London News*)

about 100 miles away, and at the risk of a Mahdist raid. It was now imperative that the town be captured, not only for the sake of the railway, but because the Nile was rising.

Meanwhile, it seemed the Mahdists in Abu Hamed were unaware of the desert Railway and their attention was fixed on the EA's positions along the Nile to the south west. This was exemplified in June, when an EA detachment was sent to look for Mahdist raiders and was ambushed by a Mahdist force as it returned. A sharp skirmish ensued and the EA patrol beat off the Mahdist attack. Precautions were then taken by the EA to keep the Mahdists away from the railway, particularly by using friendly Ababdeh tribesmen, under Abd el Azim, who patrolled about 40 miles ahead and managed to observe Abu Hamed, bringing back vital intelligence about the garrison and its defences.[16] Abu Hamed itself appeared to be beyond the Khalifa's horizon, existing in a form of splendid isolation from the main army farther south. The garrison commander, Emir Muhammad al Zayn, had about 800 men, with less than half armed with rifles. He was eventually ordered to stand and fight, an order supported by his wife who did not want him to become another Wad Bishara at Dongola.[17] While Abu Hamed awaited its fate, the Khalifa was concentrating his forces at Omdurman, a process which had begun in late 1896. The most significant arrival was that of the Emir Mahmud Ahmed, his cousin, from Kordofan with some 10,000 warriors and a host of women and children.

---

16   An Officer, *Sudan Campaign*, pp.98–99, 102–104.
17   'Ismat Hasan Zulfo, *Karari. The Sudanese Account of the Battle of Omdurman* (London: Frederick Warne (Publishers) Ltd, 1980), p.69, fn., 1, p.80.

Prefabricated parts of a gunboat arrive at Kosheh to be re-assembled. (*Illustrated London News*)

War artist, R. Caton Woodville's depiction of a Dervish, or Mahdist, chief, probably a Baggara horseman. He wears his patched jibba and is well-armed. (Anne S. K. Brown Military Collection)

Kitchener's entry into Berber during the final days of the campaign. (Anne S. K. Brown Military Collection)

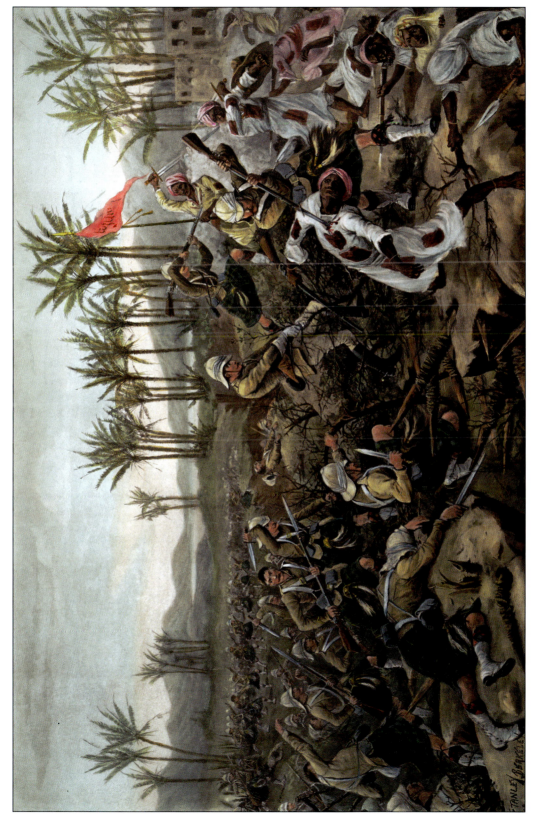

Battle of the Atbara, 8 April 1898. Highlanders attacking the Mahdist *zariba*. (Andre S. K. Brown Military Collection)

Following the end of the Battle of the Atbara, the captured Mahdist commander, the Emir Mahmud, was briefly interviewed by Kitchener. (Anne S. K. Brown Military Collection)

The British 1st Brigade, under Brigadier General Andrew Wauchope, begins its final advance towards Omdurman. (Anne S. K. Brown Military Collection)

'The way cleared for civilization.' A. Sutherland's contemporary view of the first phase of the Battle of Omdurman. Sutherland deliberately coloured the khaki uniforms of the British red so that the regiments could be easily identified. (Anne S. K. Brown Military Collection)

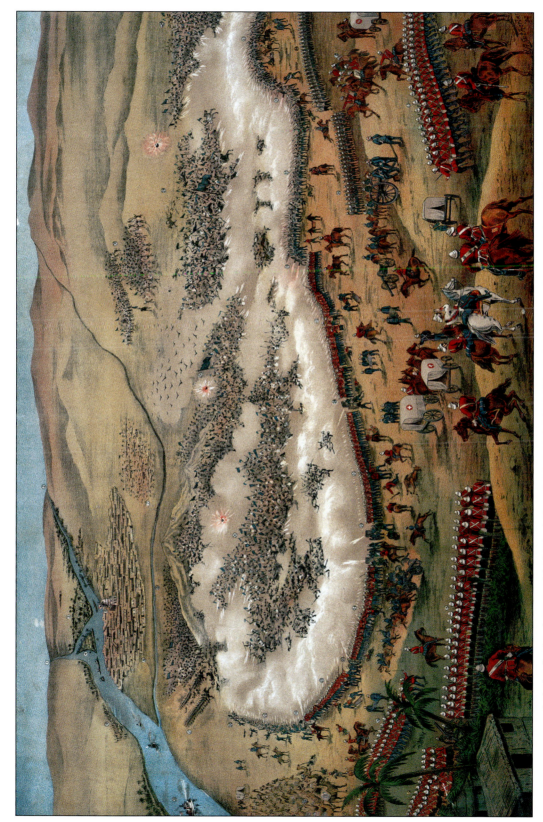

Sutherland's other depiction of the battle which even includes the charge of the 21st Lancers, top left. (Anne S. K. Brown Military Collection)

British troops repelling the Mahdist attack. (Peter Dennis © Helion & Company)

MacDonald's brigade fights off the last desperate assault of the Mahdists. (Peter Dennis © Helion & Company)

Egyptian Army Lancer circa 1896. From a sketch by Richard Caton Woodville. (Anne S. K. Brown Military Collection)

The hero of Omdurman: Major General Hector MacDonald. (Anne S. K. Brown Military Collection)

The charge of the 21st Lancers depicted just before they crashed into the main Mahdist line hidden in a *khor* or dried river bed. (Anne S. K. Brown Military Collection)

A trooper of the 21st Lancers. (Anne S. K. Brown Military Collection)

Kitchener and his staff amidst the ruins of Khartoum on 4th September 1898. (Anne S. K. Brown Military Collection)

Mahmud, 'daring and ambitious, as he was conceited and incapable',[18] had taken command of the Khalifa's western forces following the death of the efficient Osman Wad Adam. By May 1897, Mahmud's army had arrived, meaning more Baggara mouths to feed. Very quickly, Mahmud and his host were sent north to Metemma, a strategic position that guarded the Nile from incursions from Korti across the Bayuda desert, the route that Wolseley's ill-fated Desert Column had used in the campaign of 1884-1885. Mahmud's advance north had been the first major stirring of the Mahdist forces, which until now had been content to sit and await attack. Metemma was the capital of the Ja'alin, whose disdain for Baggara governance was combined with dislike of those tribes from the west. The Ja'alin chief, Abdallah Wad Saad was summoned to Omdurman and told by the Khalifa that the Ja'alin would host Mahmud's rapacious army, but would at the same time evacuate Metemma to keep out of their way because of his fear of violence. Abdallah objected but was sent away having been verbally abused by the Khalifa. Wingate's subsequent report suggests that the Khalifa suspected the loyalty of the Ja'alin, 'and decided to force it into rebellion on the first opportunity'. Furthermore, all Wingate's sources agreed that if the Ja'alin had acquiesced, they would have been plundered of their goods and women. Unsurprisingly, the Ja'alin decided to revolt and on 24 June, letters arrived at Kitchener's HQ asking for help. There was little Kitchener could do in a hurry and 1,000 Remington rifles were sent off with the Camel Corps from Korti to Jakdul Wells in the Bayuda desert. There they came across Ja'alin refugees who were given the rifles and who joined the friendly tribesmen already based there. The EA learnt that Mahmud had moved quickly against Metemma and on 1 July his army had stormed the town massacring over 2,000 inhabitants, including Abdallah Wad Saad. His orders successfully carried out, Mahmud camped outside Metemma awaiting both the EA and further instructions. Ironically, the massacre at Metemma would be the largest action fought by the Mahdists in 1897. Afterwards, Kitchener remarked with satisfaction that 'Things are looking well in the interior. The dervishes are divided amongst themselves … I am in communication with a good many in the interior who desire to upset his [the Khalifa's] rule'.[19]

Things were soon looking even better for Kitchener because the EA was now poised to take Abu Hamed. The town needed to be secured so that work on the railway could proceed. To that end, Hunter was tasked with Abu Hamed's speedy capture because enemy reinforcements were supposedly on their way. Hunter was given a 'flying column' for the job, a force of about 3,000 mostly infantry able to move quickly. These comprised MacDonald's brigade of four battalions, three Sudanese and one Egyptian. They were supported by a battery of field artillery, two Maxim machine guns, one Gardner and one Nordenfelt, both hand-cranked and obsolete machine guns. A troop of

---

18   Churchill, *River War*, vol. 1, p.313.

19   NAM: 1968-07-234: Kitchener-Wood Letters, Kitchener to Wood, 3 July 1897; SAD: Main Sequence: SIR: Intelligence Report, Egypt, No. 54, 1st June – 17 July, 1897, p. 2, F.R. Wingate, 8 August 1897, <https://www.dur.ac.uk/library/asc/sudan/sirs; http://palimpsest.dur.ac.uk/slp/sirs1.html>, accessed 5 Sept. 2020.

cavalry also accompanied the infantry. Additionally, there was a column of camels laden with supplies bringing up the rear. Hunter set out on 29 July, following the bank of the Nile, and in very hot weather that would kill at least three men and incapacitate many others. The ground over which the column marched was described by a veteran as having the 'appearance of a stormy ocean suddenly petrified into solid, red trap-rock and left to bake for centuries in the sun – a wilderness of volcanic hillocks rising in ragged ridges hundreds of feet above the water'.[20] Surprisingly, the wheeled artillery and Maxims managed to navigate the chaos of rocks and sand, although at one time the latter had to be sent on a detour over the hard desert because the main 'road' was too difficult for them to traverse. Wingate's subsequent report gave the distance covered as 133 miles, which was accomplished in 205 hours: 73½ marching and 131½ resting in camp. Much of the march was conducted at night because of the heat, adding to the difficulties caused by the terrain. For the troops, night marching 'has a drawback of depriving men of their sleep, as no one can sleep well in the hot day'. After a prodigious feat of marching, averaging 15 miles a day, the column reached a point just two miles from Abu Hamed on 7 August.[21]

Having prepared a *zariba*, a stockade made from thorn bushes, for the baggage camels and half the 3rd Egyptian Battalion, the column set off again at 5:30 a.m. and within an hour were positioned on the eastern side of Abu Hamed. The town itself ran north to south, as the river there still ran from the south northwards, before it turned towards the west. As it clung to the river, it was like most Sudanese Nile towns, all length and little width, this time being 500-600 yards long to 100-150 yards wide. On its eastern side, the land rose gently, 20-30 feet, to a plateau, upon which were three watch towers. Just outside the town, the Mahdist commander, Muhammad al Zayn, had dug some shelter trenches that were barely visible. Hunter's force, in line of battle, advanced to the top of the plateau and then down the slope towards the town. The artillery opened fire at 6:30 a.m., but the Mahdists showed excellent fire discipline and waited until MacDonald's brigade was 100 yards away before they delivered a great, loud, smoky volley that caused virtually all the EA's casualties that day, including two British officers. Thankfully for the EA, much of the fire was high. Having fired, the Mahdists ran for the town, hotly pursued by MacDonald's men. The fighting became one of bayonets and bullets against mostly spears and swords within the narrow streets and alleys, as well as within the houses themselves. Indeed, one house had to be demolished by artillery fire to subdue the defenders. In spite of the Mahdists' valour, they were quickly overwhelmed. The Sudanese soldiers, evidently, had quickly worked out a method of house-to-house fighting. They would fire volleys into a house from outside because the mud brick

---

20   Colonel F. I. Maxse, *Seymour Vandeleur* (London: The *National Review* Office, 1906. Reprinted: London: Forgotten Books, 2015), p.176.

21   SAD: Main Sequence: SIR: Intelligence Report, Egypt, No. 55, 18 July – 30 September 1897, p.3, F.R. Wingate, 30 September 1897, <https://www.dur.ac.uk/library/asc/sudan/sirs; http:// palimpsest.dur.ac.uk/slp/sirs1.html>, accessed 5 Sept. 2020; An Officer, *Sudan Campaign*, p.105.

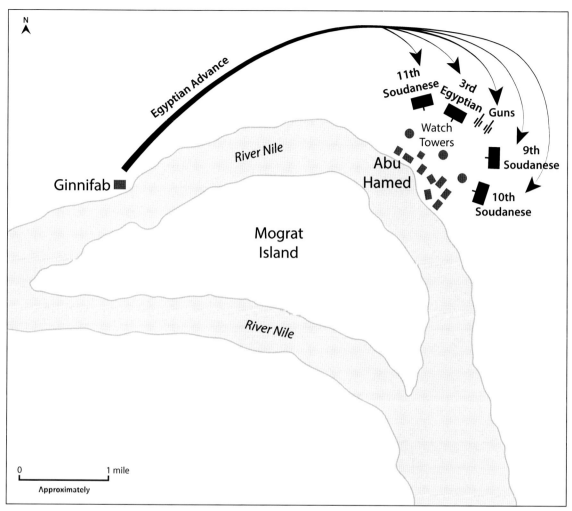

The Battle of Abu Hamed,
7 August 1897.

was soft, shooting anyone or anything inside, and then bayonet survivors who emerged. They also fired blindly around corners in case of any lurking Mahdists, making the streets doubly dangerous for any unwitting comrades. 'Nevertheless', as one officer remarked, 'they are A1 at clearing an enemy out of a village'.[22] Mahdist losses were high: Hunter recorded 450 killed, 180 prisoners, including the Mahdist commander, Muhammad al Zayn, and 50 having fled. Over 100 Baggara women and children were also captured.[23] The EA lost just 23 killed and 61 wounded, although some of the latter died soon afterwards. This was to be the EA's biggest fight of 1897 and the capture of Abu Hamed secured the success of the Desert Railway and thus Kitchener's faith in the whole project.

It was now imperative to move the gunboats up to Abu Hamed, especially as the Nile was rising, but the fourth cataract proved trickier than expected. On 5 August, the *El Teb* was wrecked when it spun round against the current

---

22   An Officer, *Sudan Campaign*, p.110.
23   Hunter, *Kitchener's sword-arm*, p.67.

The 11th Sudanese charging Mahdist positions at Abu Hamed. (*Illustrated London News*)

and was swept downriver onto the rocks. Only on 13 August was the Nile high enough for the *Metemma* to pass over the cataract, the other gunboats soon following. By 29 August, they were all located at Abu Hamed, including the three new stern-wheelers of the *El Zafir* class. These could now project the EA's power farther up the Nile towards Berber and beyond. Berber was a strategic town because it met the road from the port of Suakin. Its governor, Emir Zaki Osman, had been promised help from Mahmud but none had been forthcoming. On 24 August, the mutinous condition of his troops and the fear of being trapped had forced Zaki Osman to flee Berber for Shendi, where he arrived on 31 August. Hunter, aware of something amiss, sent a scouting party of Ababdeh tribesmen, under Ahmed Bey Khalifa, towards Berber. Eventually, on 3 September they reported back that the town was unguarded. Three days later, having passed over the fifth cataract with the gunboats, Hunter and 350 men landed in Berber and the town, 10 miles long, with rudimentary sanitation, and with a population of 12,000, was Egyptian once more. Soon afterwards, a fort and gunboat base were built where the river Atbara joins the Nile, just a few miles south of Berber. Success, however, often breeds extra complications and the serendipitous occupation of Berber was no exception. The EA was now terribly overstretched, with only five battalions available to garrison Berber by October. Indeed, the railway would reach Abu Hamed only on 31 October, thus adding to Kitchener's and Hunter's anxieties. Berber, so easily won, remained vulnerable as it was now in striking distance of Mahmud's substantial force, which had been reinforced by Osman Digna's small army. If the Khalifa himself stirred, then Berber

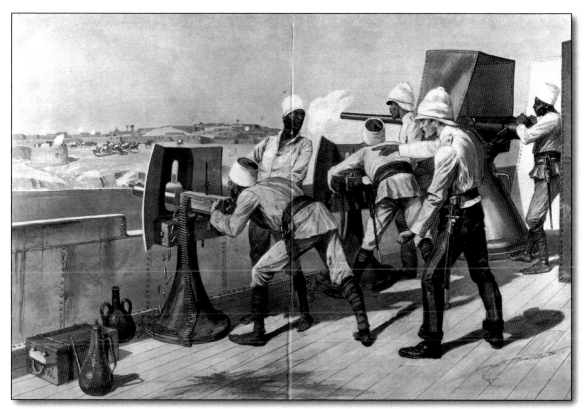

The gunboats made it extremely difficult for Mahdist forces to move along the banks of the Nile. Here, Baggara horsemen are fired on by artillery and maxim machine guns. (*Illustrated London News*)

might be attacked by the whole Mahdist host before adequate reinforcements arrived. Thus, there would be no more fighting in 1897, beyond the gunboats patrolling the river and shelling any Mahdist forces they saw. For Kitchener, and for the whole command of the EA, the next few months would be full of stress and worry.

On 18 October 1897, Kitchener sent his resignation to Cromer, writing that 'I feel the position in which I am placed leaves me no alternative.' The immediate reason, as he explained, was his disagreement with Sir Elwin Palmer, Director General of Accounts, in Cairo, who was demanding economies and not paying out enough money for the railway. 'If Palmer will point out how the thing can be done I shall be glad to meet him, but I must protest against the manner in which I am being asked to make financial impossibilities possible and called responsible for estimates that cannot be more than approximate'. In addition, Kitchener pointed out the precarious military situation, with Mahmud's force nearby, one with 'better fighting qualities and far greater numerical strength than we have ever met before'.[24] Cromer did not accept the resignation and recognised that Kitchener was under severe strain and that other issues, not just financial, weighed heavily on his mind. In the first place, Grenfell, Kitchener's predecessor as Sirdar, had just been appointed to the command of the British Army of Occupation in Egypt. His appointment in July made Lord Salisbury complain that the decision 'has so much that is

---

24   TNA: Kitchener Papers, PRO 30/57/11/J13, Kitchener to Cromer, 18 October 1897.

political in its character that his opinion [Cromer's] should have been heard'. He thought 'the news will be very unwelcome. It is imagined that Grenfell would not be sorry to oust Kitchener from effective command.'[25] Indeed, the next stage of the campaign would have to be carried out with the aid of British troops and Kitchener feared that he would be superseded by another officer. The probable deployment of British troops was of concern to Cromer too; he feared War Office interference and the imposition of a general he could not control. Cromer was concerned about the costs involved and also whether British troops could take the climate. Lansdowne, now in favour of British troops being sent, responded to Cromer's concerns by quoting a letter Kitchener had sent Wolseley in which he cast aspersions on the fighting abilities of his Egyptian troops, and who stated that with a completed railway and river steamers he could easily get British troops to the front, who could then be used 'in a healthy time of year without having to undergo the long march to get to the front'. The EA, he wrote, was like St John the Baptist, 'preparing the way'.[26] Kitchener found himself now caught in a cleft stick: he needed British troops to ensure the defeat of the Mahdists, yet he risked being superseded by a British Army general of superior rank.

The other anxiety Kitchener faced was the fate of Kassala, to the east of Omdurman near the Abyssinian frontier, then garrisoned by the Italians. They had announced they would be evacuating the town and for Kitchener this was an important post needed to cover his left flank. It was then imperative that the EA should occupy it instead, 'but I do not see where I am to get the troops'. If he had the funds, he could send some of the Suakin garrison there. Kitchener also complained to Grenfell about this issue, about Palmer's recalcitrance over the cost and the lack of troops should the EA be attacked by large Mahdist forces.[27] Cromer, having by then received Kitchener's resignation letter, was willing to pay the costs, although it would strain Egypt's resources to the limit. But the EA could advance no farther, not for a long time, 'it may be some years', and this meant that British troops would not be called upon. In a further memorandum, Cromer reiterated his views and batted away a suggestion by Wolseley to 'advance this winter'. Cromer was not for turning.[28]

Kitchener paid a visit to Cairo on 11 November 1897 and discussed matters with Cromer and Grenfell. The Kassala issue was settled, with Cromer finding the funds for its occupation and he managed to persuade Kitchener to visit Massawa, the Italian port on the Red Sea to sort out the arrangements and have a break, which he did. The 16th Egyptian Battalion under Colonel Parsons would now march as the new garrison to Kassala from

25   BL: Lansdowne Papers, 88906/16/21, Salisbury to Lansdowne; Lansdowne to Salisbury refuting his view, 7 July 1897.

26   BL: Lansdowne Papers, 88906/16/21, Memorandum by Lansdowne, 30 June 1897; Lansdowne to Cromer, 27 June, 1897.

27   NAM: 1968-07-234, Kitchener-Wood Letters, Kitchener to Wood, 22 & 30 September 1897. TNA: Kitchener Papers, PRO 30/57/10/14, Kitchener to Grenfell, 14 October 1897.

28   TNA: Cabinet Papers, CAB 37/45/46/Nos. 1 & 3, Cromer to Salisbury, 22 October 1897; 5 November 1897; BL: Lansdowne Papers, 88906/16/21, Wolseley to Lansdowne, 26 October 1897; Lansdowne to Salisbury, 28 October 1897; Lansdowne to Cromer, 29 October 1897.

Suakin, arriving there in December. 'I have had to fight for money', Kitchener wrote, 'but I have got enough to keep the Army in a state of efficiency in its present positions & take Kassala. I do the latter for £40,000 less than it cost the Italians.'[29]

Nevertheless, the feeling of insecurity continued to pervade the officers of both the EA and the British Army in Cairo. Rundle, Wingate, and the Deputy Assistant Adjutant General in Cairo, Major Charles á Court all lamented the advance to Berber and that there would be no continuation of the campaign.[30] Á Court's letter of 10 December was sent to Wolseley, who passed it on to Lansdowne and who then sent it to Lord Salisbury. Salisbury did not care for its tone and wondered who would pay for a British brigade that á Court and Wolseley wanted. He stated, following Cromer, that Kitchener would give them 'timely warning' should the need arise for British reinforcements.[31] But as the arguments between soldiers and civilians raged, intelligence began to emerge that the Khalifa was gathering his forces and preparing to march north. According to á Court, Hunter had heard this from a 'reliable native', while at the same time, two men arrived at Korti bearing news and were swiftly questioned by Slatin, who confirmed Hunter's information. Slatin, evidently, 'credits their report, the Sirdar, who at first doubted, is also of opinion that an advance is intended'. Consequently, Kitchener had the Dongola garrisons stripped of troops and sent from Kerma to Abu Hamed, via Wadi Halfa, in four days, a remarkable journey that justified the whole railway project.[32] On 31 December 1897, Cromer received a telegram from Kitchener stating that the Khalifa's army was ready to move north to join Mahmud by 25 January. 'This is the confirmatory information I have had of the intentions of the Khalifa … to seriously attack us,' he wrote, 'I think British troops ought to be ready to move up the Nile.' The decision to send for British troops was made after a long discussion with Wingate, and once this had been made Kitchener acted as if the weight of the world had been lifted from his shoulders. Cromer promised to ensure Kitchener remained in command, which was confirmed by the British cabinet on 4 January, a point that even Wolseley had endorsed. Very soon four British battalions would be on their way to Abu Hamed.[33] The campaign of 1898 would now start sooner rather than later.

29   TNA: Cabinet Papers, CAB 37/45/46/No.2, Cromer to Salisbury, 11 November 1897; TNA: Kitchener Papers, PRO 30/57/10/I14, Grenfell diary extracts, p. 4; NAM: 1968-07-234, Kitchener-Wood Letters, Kitchener to Wood, 19 November 1897.

30   SAD: SAD 267: Wingate Papers, 267/1/147, Rundle to Wingate, 16 December 1897; 267/1/201, Wood to Wingate, 28 December 1897; BL: Lansdowne Papers, 88906/19/6, á Court to Colonel (?), 10 December 1897.

31   BL: Lansdowne Papers, 88906/19/28, Wolseley to Lansdowne, 20 December 1897; 88906/19/6, Lansdowne to Salisbury, 21 December 1897; Salisbury to Lansdowne, 25 December 1897.

32   TNA: WO 32/6380: Sudan Campaign. Á Court to Fairholme, 24 December 1897.

33   Pollock, *Kitchener*, vol. 1, pp.112–113; Magnus, *Kitchener*, p.116; BL: Lansdowne Papers, 88906/19/16, Lansdowne to Salisbury, 29 December 1897.

Chapter 6

To the Atbara, 1898

Following Kitchener's request for British troops, the War Office, in consultation with Grenfell, decided to send a brigade to the Sudan while another was kept in readiness for future use. Kitchener soon confirmed that one brigade of four battalions was 'sufficient for defence' but wanted another brigade, with cavalry, artillery and Maxim guns to be ready for 'offensive operations'.[1] By 10 January, however, it was becoming clear that the Khalifa's army was not marching north. According to Wingate's sources, a dispute between the Khalifa's brother, Ya'qub, and the Khalifa's son, Osman Shaykh al Din, over the loyalty of the Ja'alin and whether all their chief men should be killed, had led to the Khalifa's hesitation. Moreover, the Khalifa had been unable to concentrate sufficient of his forces and, although Wingate felt the Khalifa had 'intended to wipe us out', he also thought that as time was 'fast slipping by, [this] may induce him to adopt a less offensive policy'. Wingate now considered the situation from the viewpoint of the Anglo–Egyptian Army as 'a distinctly satisfactory one: it allows for all possible emergencies & admits also of an offensive-defensive policy'.[2] Thus the news emanating from Omdurman, that the Khalifa was not on the move after all, eased the apprehension of the British authorities; they could now plan for the next phase of the campaign.

By mid-February, three battalions of the British brigade were concentrated at Abu Dis, just north of Berber. These were the 1st Battalion, Lincolnshire Regiment, the 1st Battalion, Royal Warwickshire Regiment and the 1st Battalion, Queen's Own Cameron Highlanders. The 1st Battalion, Seaforth Highlanders was on its way from Malta and would not reach the front until 16 March. These battalions were the first to use the new Sudan Military Railway and although it was better than marching, there were many complaints about the accommodation: a Seaforth NCO thought the 'rough wagons' were

---

1   TNA: WO32/6380: Sudan Campaign, Wolseley to Lansdowne, 2 January 1898; Wolseley Memorandum, 5 January 1898; Intelligence Division Report, 5 January 1898; BL: Lansdowne Papers, 88906/20/7, Grenfell to Lansdowne, (copy), 4 January 1898, BL: Lansdowne Papers, 88906/16/21 Lansdowne to Salisbury, 4 January 1898; TNA: WO32/6380: Sudan Campaign, Lansdowne to Grenfell, (GOC, Egypt), (tel.), 5 January 1898; Wolseley to Grenfell, (GOC, Egypt), nd, (5 January 1898); Grenfell (GOC Egypt) to Lansdowne, (tel.), 5 January 1898.

2   SAD: SAD 266: Wingate Papers, 266/1/8, Wingate to á Court, 10 January 1898, (copy).

'like the iron ore ones at home, only rougher & dirtier'. Private Teigh of the Lincolns thought that they were 'similar to coal trucks in England, 30 men in each truck and we were very much crushed up'. The men had little sleep because 'there was not room to turn oneself round.'[3] At least they were not travelling in the heat of summer.

The British soldiers, however, were much better equipped than their Egyptian counterparts. Their rifles were the recent five-bullet-magazine .303 Lee-Metford that had a higher rate of fire than the Martini-Henry. These bullets contained the smokeless cordite propellent which meant they flew at a higher velocity and had a greater range, but they lacked the explosive power to bring down a man instantaneously. To remedy this 'defect', the troops were ordered to file down the bullet tips to make them more explosive when they entered a man's body. While in camp waiting to move forward, the men had to use upturned rails to file down three million rounds, at 80,000 per day, a task that displeased both officers and men. Lieutenant Cox of the Lincolns found that the magazines would not work with the filed bullets and complained on 2 February that 'all available men and officers [were working] 6 hours daily for 30 days to file off the tops'. These bullets were eventually used up by May and a new bullet was introduced: the journalist, Bennet Burleigh, relating that 'The latest pattern "man-stopper" was a bullet fashioned with a hollow or crater at the point, the nickel casing being perforated'. Later, having seen its effects, Burleigh noted that 'it generally spread on hitting, and made a deadly wound, tearing away bone and flesh at the point of exit'.[4] The longer Lee-Metford rifle was accompanied by a bayonet shorter than that used by the EA. It was a 12-inch sword-bayonet of pattern 1888 made by the Wilkinson Sword Company.[5]

The British wore a full khaki uniform, the only colour being provided by the flashes on their helmets, which differentiated each battalion, and their white ammunition pouches – soon discoloured by the desert dust – that carried 100 rounds. The Scottish battalions wore kilts which broke up the monotony of khaki, with tartan socks instead of puttees, although khaki spats hid most of their colour. The British uniforms also contained quilted spine pads as protection against the sun and their helmets were the foreign-service helmet made of cork and which had a quilted neck cover attachment for added sun protection. The worst part of the soldiers' kit was a pair of sub-standard boots. One soldier complained that when the brigade marched to Berber in February, 'the soles had left the uppers and were flapping up and down all the way until they got too far then they had to come off at the

---

3   NAM 1979-06-139: Fraser Letters, to his Father, 14 April 1898; John Meredith (ed.), *Omdurman Diaries 1898. Eyewitness Accounts of the Legendary Campaign* (Barnsley: Leo Cooper, 1998), p.16.

4   Meredith, (ed.), *Omdurman Diaries*, pp.33–38; Bennet Burleigh, *Khartoum Campaign 1898 or the Re–Conquest of the Soudan* (London: Chapman & Hall, Limited, 1899. Reprinted: Cambridge: Ken Trotman Ltd, 1989), p.17, 36–37, 72–73; Beatrice Gatacre, *General Gatacre. The Story of the Life and Services of Sir William Forbes Gatacre 1843–1906* (London: John Murray, 1910), pp.190–191.

5   Donald Featherstone, *Weapons & Equipment of the Victorian Soldier* (London: Arms and Armour Press, 1978, 1996), p.38.

Major General W. F. Gatacre, commander first of the British Brigade and then of the British Division. (*Illustrated London News*)

waist leaving only the insole. I'll leave you to guess how comfortable these were marching on stones and rock'. In the end the British were given sturdier boots from the EA's stores.[6]

One major problem suffered by the British troops throughout the 1898 campaign, and much more than the EA, was the incidence of typhoid or enteric. British water discipline was poor: once at the front soldiers often ignored advice and suffered accordingly. In fact, most campaign deaths during 1898 would be caused by typhoid, with many men dying in Egypt on their return. The death rate from typhoid amounted to 64 per cent of all deaths and Dr W. Taylor, who wrote the campaign medical report, opined: 'There is no' doubt that if boiling were strictly carried out it would prevent water being a source of enteric fever and dysentery.' When the army began to march in August the heat was severe and Bennet Burleigh noted that at one stop, 'We were ourselves too parched to care about the impurities of the Nile, and soldiers and officers swallowed great draughts of the soupy stuff'. Filters were available but easily blocked by sediment, as one officer wrote: 'My filter gone "fut."' With little fuel available there was a general disinclination to boil water when marching. The incidence of typhoid was not reported by the press correspondents as it appeared to be just one of those things that happened on campaign, a view, it seems, that was shared by the brigade's commander, Major General William Gatacre,[7]

A fitness fanatic, Gatacre was restless and full of energy, and he put his brigade through excruciating route marches in blazing heat to ensure the troops were conditioned to the climate. On 11 February, for example, the brigade marched between 15 and 20 miles, with two rounds given to each man and 'we attacked several rocks', according to one soldier. Even when miles from the front, the men had to be ready to repel a night attack. One soldier complained that 'We slept dressed in all clothing, boots and puttees, accoutrements on and rifle slung on right shoulder, very pleasant with 127 rounds of .303 in the puches [*sic*], 3 coils of strap sticking in the back and a bayonet and scabbard on left side …' He also grumbled that once awake the brigade was put through 'evolutions never known to any "drill book" or the best tacticians'. [8] Unsurprisingly, Gatacre's nickname among the troops was 'Backacher'. On 25 February, Gatacre took the men on a morning route

6   Donald Featherstone, *Omdurman 1898. Kitchener's Victory in the Sudan* (Westport, CT & London: Praeger, 2005), p.79; NAM: 1998-06-144/3–4: Letter by Senior NCO of the Royal Warwickshire Regiment, to Fred, 16 October 1898; Edward M. Spiers, 'Campaigning Under Kitchener', in Edward M. Spiers (ed.), *Sudan. The Reconquest Reappraised* (London: Frank Cass, 1998), p.57.

7   Philip D. Curtin, *Disease and Empire. The Health of European Troops in the Conquest of Africa* (Cambridge: Cambridge University Press, 1998), pp.194–201; Meredith (ed.), *Omdurman Diaries*, p.33.

8   NAM: 1998-06-144/2, Senior NCO to Fred, 16 October; Meredith(ed.), *Omdurman Diaries*, pp.38–39.

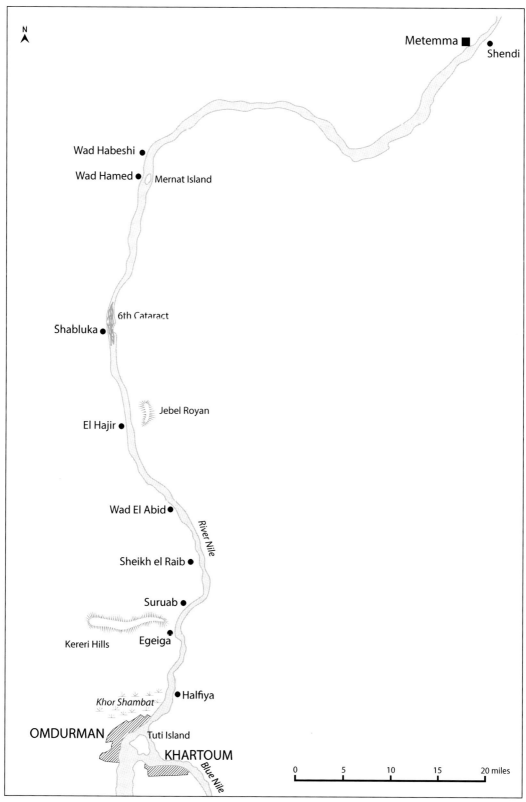

N

Metemma ■
● Shendi

Wad Habeshi ●
Wad Hamed ● ◯ Mernat Island

6th Cataract
Shabluka ●

Jebel Royan
El Hajir ●

Wad El Abid ●

River Nile

Sheikh el Raib ●

Suruab ●

Kereri Hills
Egeiga ●

Khor Shambat
● Halfiya

OMDURMAN
Tuti Island
KHARTOUM
Blue Nile

0   5   10   15   20 miles

The Final Advance from Metemma to Omdurman.

march, covering 16 miles through intense heat. Then, on returning, news was received that the brigade was needed at the front. Gatacre told the men they would need to march there in four days to save the lives of many women and children. The brigade, without the Seaforths who were still awaited, eventually reached Darmali, 15 miles south of Berber in five days, with one day's rest. They had covered about 122 miles, an impressive feat of marching.[9] Nevertheless, hundreds of men fell out and were put on camels, officers' horses or picked up by gunboats. On reaching Berber, the brigade was met by Kitchener and several EA battalions whose bands played the British in, giving them a timely morale boost. However, as one officer noted critically, 'all the talk of saving Berber was mainly Gatacre's imagination. We were not expected to arrive for another week at least, and our confidence in him was shaken'.[10] In Gatacre's defence he had told Kitchener that he would arrive at 'Atbara camp' on Wednesday, 2 March. It is not known whether Kitchener acknowledged this message, although the EA was ready to receive the British when they arrived. Kitchener, it seems, was content to let Gatacre get on with his job and, surprisingly perhaps, despite their ordeal the British brigade was ready for its first major action about a month later.[11]

Gatacre's haste was the result of the forward movement of Emir Mahmud's army of Mahdists. The latter's fateful decision to advance was based on the erroneous assumption that the EA had insignificant numbers both at the Atbara fort as well as at Berber, and that there was a chance to inflict a crushing defeat on the enemy. Thus, on 15 February the gunboats patrolling the Nile found that Mahmud had crossed the river over to the east bank and was now concentrated at Shendi, news that was confirmed by refugees and secret agents. Finally, by 17 March, Mahmud's army had reached Aliab, 30 miles farther north. Wingate's agents brought news that the Khalifa had adjudicated a dispute between Mahmud and Osman Digna over strategy. The latter wanted to move in a north-east direction towards the Atbara, cross the river, and then outflank Atbara fort to threaten both it and Berber. If Mahdist assumptions had been correct about the EA's numbers this would have been a good way of cutting its lines of communication, to use manoeuvre rather than a head-on assault on Atbara fort favoured by Mahmud. On 18 March, letters arrived from the Khalifa backing Osman Digna and that day, at 3:00 p.m., Mahmud's army began to march north-east across 40 miles of waterless desert. The army, encumbered by hundreds of women and children, in spite of having left many behind at Shendi, reached the Atbara river two days later. Osman Digna had argued that the army could be supplied by raiding local tribes. He knew the country as the nearby settlement of Adarama had been a recent base. However, on 21 March a Mahdist patrol clashed with one from the EA, a nasty surprise for Mahmud and Osman Digna who had not appreciated the nearness of the EA. In consequence, Mahmud chose to fortify his camp or *dem* by constructing entrenchments and also a *zariba*. This was the easier decision of three possible choices, the other two being either to

---

9   Meredith (ed.), *Omdurman Diaries*, pp.49–55.

10   Meredith, (ed.), *Omdurman Diaries*, p.55.

11   Gatacre, *General Gatacre*, p.192.

Commander Keppel's gunboat, *Zafir*, engages Osman Digna's position at Shendi. (*Illustrated London News*)

retreat to Shendi, which would have destroyed his badly provisioned army and wrecked his reputation, or to launch an attack against the EA, which he now appreciated was larger than first imagined. Having made his choice, Mahmud's camp was now well hidden within dense bush and scrub that lined the river banks, but the food supply was critical.[12]

In response, the British troops had been brought forward. Once the Seaforths arrived on 16 March the new brigade had been concentrated at Kunar alongside the EA, which had been reinforced by the 4th Egyptian Battalion, having marched the 270 miles from Suakin to Berber in 13 days. On 20 March, the Anglo–Egyptian Army (AEA) moved south-east along the Atbara river to Hudi, thus denying a fording point for Mahmud's army and in effect hustling it farther away from Atbara fort, as did another march the next day to Ras el Hudi. Here the AEA stopped and encamped behind its own *zariba*, broiling in the 115 F daytime heat and rejoicing in the cool of the night. For the British troops, many awaiting their first actions, this was a time of high tension made worse by Gatacre's frequent blood-chilling exhortations about an impending attack. On the night of 20/21 March, following one of Gatacre's speeches, a sentry shot at a stray donkey and caused uproar in the camp which thought it was under attack. In the commotion, jittery Seaforths bayoneted Lincolns, with one man dying of his wounds. Lieutenant Meiklejohn wrote indignantly in his diary that Gatacre was 'very angry. Yet the whole affair was entirely due to his continual talk of being attacked at any moment, and the unnecessary strain he puts on all of us.'[13]

12   Henry S. L. Alford & W. Dennistoun Sword, *The Egyptian Soudan. Its Loss and Recovery* (London: Macmillan and Co., Limited, 1898. Reprinted: Dallington: The Naval & Military Press, 1992), pp.174, 208–209; SAD: Main Sequence: SIR: Intelligence Report, Egypt, No. 59, 13 February – 23 May 1898, pp.2–5, <https://www.dur.ac.uk/library/asc/sudan/sirs; http://palimpsest.dur.ac.uk/slp/sirs1.html>, accessed 15 Sept. 2020.

13   Winston Spencer Churchill, *River War. An Historical Account of the Reconquest of the Soudan* (London: Longmans, Green, And Co.) vol. 1, pp.375–377; Alford & Sword, *Egyptian Soudan,*

In spite of Gatacre's warnings, Mahmud refused to venture out of his *dem* and as Kitchener could not afford to ignore his presence – for Mahmud commanded about 14,0000 warriors – he was now obliged to find his lair. On 30 March, Hunter was sent out with a sizeable force, consisting of all the Egyptian cavalry under their new commander, Brevet Lieutenant Colonel Broadwood, Burn-Murdoch having left at the end of 1896, and the Horse artillery, plus two Maxim guns. Hunter was only able to observe the part that protruded from the scrub and with impeccable fire discipline the Mahdists kept quiet and hidden. The newly arrived Captain Douglas Haig, the cavalry's chief-of-staff, told his sister: 'Tho' [*sic*] our guns fired 29 shells at it [the camp] at 1,000 yds range and the maxims over 2,000 rounds, the Dervishes stayed in their trenches and took not the slightest notice'.[14] Nevertheless, Hunter and others had ridden perilously close to the *zariba* and managed to have a good look, noting lines of trenches and stockades, but such was the density of the scrub that they could not discern the *dem's* depth and what lay within.[15] Hunter's report to Kitchener and Gatacre led to one of the more bizarre episodes of the campaign. Gatacre was all for attacking, while Hunter, normally a fire-eater, urged caution, leaving Kitchener caught between the two viewpoints. For Kitchener, who was not an experienced battlefield commander, having left Hunter to manage the battles in 1896 and 1897, the responsibility of having to decide whether to attack a well-entrenched and numerous enemy, coupled with the fear that a repulse might mean being replaced by Grenfell or another British general, engendered a loss of nerve. On 1 April, Kitchener asked Cromer for advice: 'I have little doubt of the success of our attack on his present entrenched position', he wrote, 'although it would probably entail considerable loss … I should be glad to learn your views on the subject'. Cromer, not competent to judge, sought the advice of Grenfell and Lord Salisbury, with the latter referring the matter to the War Office. Grenfell, meanwhile, supported Hunter; while the British government said Kitchener should do what he thought best. Cromer, on receiving these views urged caution, but by then Hunter had decided on attack and on hearing of this from Kitchener, Cromer then changed tack himself. Fortified now by the unanimity of Gatacre, Hunter, and Cromer, Kitchener decided to attack the *dem* but not before Hunter had carried out another reconnaissance.[16]

According to Hunter afterwards the whole enterprise, carried out on 5 April, was a waste of time: 'It was a certainty I would learn no more than I had already.' Hunter's irritation might have had something to do with the fact that this time the Mahdists decided to make a fight of it, with Baggara horsemen attempting a pincer movement against Broadwood's cavalry, backed up by a substantial number of *jihadiyya*. In spite of the support of the Horse Artillery

---

pp.203–204; Meredith, *Omdurman Diaries*, pp.65–66.

14   Douglas Scott (ed.), *Douglas Haig. The Preparatory Prologue 1861–1914. Diaries and Letters* (Barnsley: Pen & Sword Military, 2006), p.82.

15   Archie Hunter, *Kitchener's sword-arm. The Life and Campaigns of General Sir Archibald Hunter* (Staplehurst: Spellmount, 1996), pp.80–81.

16   Philip Magnus, *Kitchener. Portrait of an Imperialist* (London: John Murray, 1958), pp.119–120; Hunter, *Kitchener's sword-arm*, p.81; Gatacre, *General Gatacre*, pp.200–201.

and the Maxims, there was hand-to-hand fighting and Hunter's force extricated itself with difficulty. Haig later noted that the artillery had fired 57 assorted shells, while the Maxims had expended some 5,500 rounds. Haig had shown bravery during the fight by rescuing a wounded Egyptian NCO and bringing him back safely to the artillery line.[17]

Kitchener, his resolve restored, accepted Hunter's demand to attack on Good Friday, 8 April. In the meantime, the AEA had moved closer to the *dem* and on 6 April stopped at Umdabia, within eight miles of the enemy. On the evening of 7 April, the AEA began its final advance, halting at 9:00 p.m. at the abandoned village of Mutros for some rest before starting again at 1:00 a.m. in bright moonlight, moving into the desert to avoid the scrub and adding two miles to the march. By 4:30 a.m., the AEA was in position about 600 yards from the silent, watchful *dem*. The Mahdist camp was well prepared to resist an assault. It was 'a large irregular enclosure strongly entrenched all round, palisaded in parts, with innumerable cross trenches, casemates, and straw huts, besides ten palisaded gun emplacements, the whole surrounded by a strong *zariba*'. It was almost impossible to gauge the *dem*'s full extent because all that could be seen was a 'dense jungle of sunt trees, dom palms, and undergrowth'.[18] This thick scrub grew similarly on the other side of the river, making an attack from that side impossible, hence the approach over familiar terrain.

Lieutenant Colonel G. R. Broadwood, here pictured in later life. In 1898 he commanded the Egyptian cavalry and the Camel Corps. (*Illustrated London News*)

The rising sun soon revealed the AEA in full panoply of battle, a steady line some 1,500 yards long. The British brigade was on the left and the EA on the right. The Egyptian cavalry, supported by its two Maxim machine guns, was on the extreme left. Once the AEA had advanced to within 600 yards of the *zariba*, the artillery, with its 24 guns, supported by Maxims and a rocket battery under Lieutenant Beatty of the Royal Navy, all commanded by Colonel Long, opened fire at 6:15 a.m. The visual effect was quite stunning: the thirteen 24 lb Hales rockets 'hissed and screamed as they left the troughs and jerked eventually towards the *zeriba*' [sic].[19] The artillery fired over 1,300 shells, mostly shrapnel that exploded in the air, although others tore the ground. The whole encampment was blanketed by shells and rockets that wreathed the area in smoke and caused the straw huts, *tukls*, to burn. For about 90 minutes the bombardment continued, the noise of explosions adding to the choking smoke. The cacophony was not ended when the guns stopped, for immediately the loud noise of martial music swept the area as

17 Hunter, *Kitchener's sword-arm*, pp.81–82; Churchill, *River War*, vol. 1, pp.399–412; *Scott, Haig*, p.84.

18 SAD: Main Sequence: SIR: Intelligence Report, Egypt, No. 59, 13 February – 23 May 1898, p.6. <https://www.dur.ac.uk/library/asc/sudan/sirs; http://palimpsest.dur.ac.uk/slp/sirs1.html>, accessed 15 Sept. 2020.

19 Churchill, *River War*, vol. 1, p.423.

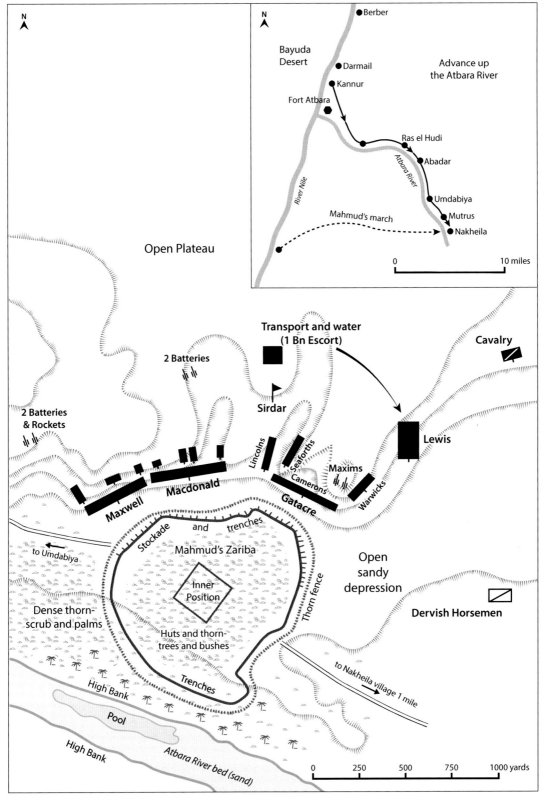

The Battle of the Atbara, 8 April 1898.

the AEA began its advance, the whole accompanied by fifes, drums, bagpipes and the bands of the Sudanese battalions. The EA, some 10,000 strong, had two brigades in the front line, MacDonald's on the left and Maxwell's on the right.[20] Lewis's 3rd Egyptian Brigade was held back in support. At first, the EA brigades, like the British, advanced slowly firing volleys that covered the entrenchments with hails of lead; then at 300 yards, the Mahdists opened fire with a crashing volley but with most bullets going high. The EA then changed tactics and began to fire and move forward at a rush. Captain Hugh Fitton, the EA's DAAG, told his sister: 'We advance with bands playing and the men cheering'. In response to the Mahdist volley, 'Our men opened a perfectly tremendous & very rapid fire … & so we went on in 4 or 5 rushes'. Hunter, the only mounted senior officer in the AEA, waved his helmet urging his men on; Fitton was duly impressed: 'Townshend … had been foremost in the rushes, but this surpassed anything I have seen or expected to see'.[21]

The EA was nearest to the *zariba* and it was Townshend's 12th Sudanese Battalion that was the first to cross it, although Lieutenant Vandeleur of the 9th Sudanese Battalion claimed his was the first through. Townshend had trained his men well in fire and rush tactics and they were soon into the first entrenchments. These had by now been abandoned, but the surviving *jihadiyya*, arranged in a second line, kept up a galling fire with their Remingtons. The Mahdists had also exploded some mines and according to Townshend, one man 'had the top of his head blown off'. The 12th Sudanese was soon into the trenches and it was now a matter of bayonet work: 'the scene in the trenches was awful: dead and dying Dervishes, all black riflemen, like our own men. No quarter was given, and they did not ask for it'.[22] Lieutenant Ready of the 2nd Egyptians was a bit more critical of the Sudanese battalions: 'Just for a second I was afraid our firing line was getting out of hand that they would never get through the bush.' The support of his battalion he claimed was crucial as it came 'along in excellent order & we pushed straight along. I quite see now why they never could put Sudanese troops in support or reserve because they shoot their rifles off up in the air & … they get quite mad and dance along holding their rifles over their heads'. Even so, Ready was critical of his own men despite their advance 'in column, under a heavy fire … without having been able to fire themselves [which] was a pretty severe test'. Ready 'hit one or two on the head with a big stick I had & made them hold their heads up instead of crouching on the ground like a frog & they saw me walk about tho' probably I was in a greater funk than any of them myself'.[23]

The British brigade approached their task in a different manner. Gatacre had his battalions in columns, the Warwicks on the left, the Seaforths in the centre and the Lincolns on the right. The Camerons, however, were posted in

---

20   Maxwell had been restored to command of the 1st Brigade following the completion of the railway to Abu Hamed.

21   NAM: 1994-10-42: Fitton Letters, to his sister, 13 April 1898.

22   N. S. Nash, *Chitral Charlie. The rise and fall of Major General Charles Townshend* (Barnsley: Pen & Sword Military, 2010), pp.102–104; Colonel F. I. Maxse, *Seymour Vandeleur* (London: The *National Review* Office, 1906. Reprinted: London: Forgotten Books, 2015), p.208.

23   NAM: 1966-09-142: Ready Diary, 14 & 18 April 1898.

Battle of the Atbara, 8 April 1898. Here the Seaforth Highlanders fight their way into the Mahdist *zariba*. (*Illustrated London News*)

front and deployed in line. Their task was to blast their way to the *zariba* and then take it down, allowing the other battalions to surge through while they then reformed and followed. But, as one Cameron officer, Neville Cameron, related, 'Well, these orders were carried out exactly with the exception of the last order', for no Cameron was going to let the Seaforths or English battalions have all the glory. The troops of the Camerons were told to advance slowly, firing volleys, then at about 200 yards they switched to independent fire. By then, the Mahdists had started to fire 'the bullets seemed to come in a perfect hail', as Neville Cameron explained.[24] In the Lincolns it was noted how the bullets went 'whizzing overhead' but started to hit bodies the closer they got. Lieutenant Cox had one bullet through his helmet: 'I then spoke to Sgt. Malone on my left who fell shot in the mouth'. A Mahdist gun was fired at the Warwicks as Lieutenant Meiklejohn recounted: 'a shell whined and screeched over our heads and burst nearly ½ mile in rear. The men all laughed'. Then, 'an angry buzz passed me rather like some huge infuriated bee'. It took him a moment to realise what it was 'and it was not too pleasant'. Meiklejohn saw a group of Mahdists who ventured out to attack wiped out by Maxim and rifle fire, 'but one or two survivors disdainfully turned round and strolled unconcernedly away. They are gallant fellows!' The Camerons easily pulled away the *zariba* and Meiklejohn wrote scathingly afterwards: 'The much vaunted *zariba*, which Gatacre had led us to esteem such a terrific obstacle, was a miserable affair. A few branches of tangled camel thorn only 4 ft high and a few feet thick'. Meiklejohn decided to vault it, was snagged by thorns and fell flat on his face, his men thinking he had been shot.[25] The Camerons, meanwhile, had suffered the most casualties, although a Seaforths' officer grudgingly remarked that they had 'had the excitement of firing'. The Seaforths, Warwicks and Lincolns, following up behind had been unable to fire and they had 'nothing to do, except watch their men dropping, and all the bleeding and doctoring and stretcher work'.[26] Soon, all the battalions were through, including the Camerons, with Gatacre on foot up among them and accompanied by a soldier carrying a large Union Jack, who was soon shot. The men threw themselves at any survivors in the trenches and then against those manning the stockade behind. Meiklejohn noted that 'There was some angry work with bayonets and rifles. Everyone went mad.' One Mahdist grabbed a soldier's bayonet but was then shot, 'blown away a foot or so'.[27] The Mahdists were fighting hard 'all firing point blank as fast as they can load'. Gatacre was nearly speared, but was saved by Private Cross of the Camerons, who bayoneted the spearman. The British troops were shocked to find that 'Many unfortunate blacks were chained by both hands and legs, in the trenches, with a gun in their hands and their faces to the foe': some survived and were rather pleased to do so.[28]

---

24   NAM: 1983-05-55/1: Cameron Letters, to his father, 13 April 1898.

25   Meredith (ed.), *Omdurman Diaries*, pp.90–93.

26   Quoted in Edward M. Spiers, *The Scottish Soldier and Empire, 1854–1902* (Edinburgh: Edinburgh University Press, 2006), p.140.

27   Meredith (ed.) *Omdurman Diaries*, p.93.

28   Alford & Sword, *Egyptian Soudan*, pp.220–225; Meredith (ed.), *Omdurman Diaries*, p.96.

The Senior NCO of the Warwicks was, like most men in the brigade, in action for the first time and on hearing the bugle sound the charge 'then's the time your hair rises with pride ... How our fellows cheered and charged up to that Zereba [sic]'. They went through it 'and over, full of thorns and splinters, one on top of another ... now began the glory of an Englishman's fight – the bayonet – and they did use it with a vengeance. In that little scrape I accounted for 3 in as many seconds, not bad for a novice is it[?]'[29] As the British and Sudanese battalions surged into the *dem*, they came across the worst effects of the artillery bombardment. All the Mahdist gun emplacements were wrecked, their crews dead or dying and where fires burned 'there was a horrible smell of roasting flesh'. Alongside dead and wounded donkeys and camels, could be found the bodies of women and children. One female survivor, described as an 'Amazon stripped to the waist', attacked Meiklejohn, but she was stopped by his men and 'fought and bit like a wild cat'. She had a baby nearby but later was seen being fed by the soldiers who dandled her child. Another woman shot a man of the Camerons and was killed with seven bayonets.[30] One problem that became apparent as the fighting moved through the *dem* was that of 'friendly fire'. British officers would complain about the wild shooting of the Sudanese battalions. Neville Cameron remarked that one officer was hit by a Martini-Henry bullet and only the Sudanese carried those. But by now, the British line had lost cohesion. Captain Egerton of the Seaforths wrote later that the assault 'now degenerated into groups of soldiers, who undoubtedly in this confused bush fighting got very much out of hand'. The Sudanese were close to the British and carried on firing inside the *dem* and this 'from our flank and rear really became much worse than the enemy's fire, and altogether it was very unpleasant indeed.[31] Little mercy was shown to the Mahdists; Cox wrote 'the Englishman ... spared nothing except the animals' and that one man who threw down his weapons and threw up his arms was quickly bayoneted. But, he explained, 'one must remember what perfect devils these dervishes are – their frightful cruel habits – Gordon's murder – and their treatment of the Jaalins [sic]'.[32] In spite of the smoke and the smell the Mahdists were driven through the *dem* towards the Atbara river. At an inner stockade a tough battle ensued with Mahmud's bodyguard, who numbered about 1,000 men. The 11th Sudanese took the brunt of the fighting, one company was practically wiped out. Piper Stewart of the Camerons fell dead shot by up to seven bullets. Joined by the 10th Sudanese, the stockade was rushed, the bodyguards killed and Mahmud was captured. He was taken off to see Kitchener for a cursory interview. The Mahdist commander showed no fear, 'his expression was cruel, but high'. After a brief exchange, Mahmud was photographed with his Sudanese captors and later autographed the

29   NAM: 1998-06-144/8, Senior NCO to Fred, 14 October 1898.
30   Meredith (ed.), *Omdurman Diaries*, pp. 89, 94.
31   NAM: 1983-05-55/1, Cameron Letters, to his father, 13 April 1898; Granville Egerton, *With the 72nd Highlanders in the Sudan Campaign* (London: Eden Fisher & Co. Ltd, 1909), p.16; Lieutenant Colonel Charles à Court Repington, *Vestigia* (London: Constable and Company Ltd., 1919), pp.160–161.
32   Meredith (ed.), *Omdurman Diaries*, pp.87–88.

The Battle of the Atbara, 8 April 1898. The British Brigade advancing into the Mahdist encampment. (*Illustrated London News*)

picture. On 14 April, Kitchener at the head of MacDonald's brigade held a triumphal march through Berber with Mahmud on display for all to see and take note. Most sources, like the journalist Bennet Burliegh, say he marched with his hands tied behind his back, 'but walked with head elate, as a central personage in the parade.' Later, Burleigh would interview Mahmud on the train north to Wadi Halfa and the latter told him that the Khalifa was waiting for them and 'has 60,000 soldiers [and] many guns'. 'My error', Mahmud said, 'was in listening to Osman Digna, and leaving Metemmeh and the Nile'.[33]

Meanwhile, the EA and the British soon reached the dried bed of the Atbara, where only stagnant pools survived. Many Mahdists were now killed as they fled towards the scrub on the other side, the survivors rushing on to uncertain fates at the hands of the Kassala garrison, unfriendly local tribes or the harshness of the desert. The battle had lasted between 30 and 45 minutes. Osman Digna, his followers and the Baggara horse had fled, having ridden out of the *dem* early in the battle and in all about 4,000 Mahdists escaped but few would return to Omdurman.

When the 'ceasefire' sounded, 'The Soudanese danced with delight, and went wildly around shaking hands with everyone they came across'. Many

---

33   Alford & Sword, *Egyptian Soudan*, pp.223, 228; 'Ismat Hasan Zulfo, *Karari. The Sudanese Account of the Battle of Omdurman* (London: Frederick Warne (Publishers) Ltd, 1980), p.79; Bennet Burliegh, *Sirdar and Khalifa or the Re-conquest of the Soudan* (London: Chapman & Hall, 1898), pp.269–278; Ronald Lamolle, *Slaves of Fortune. Sudanese Soldiers and the River War* (Woodbridge: James Currey, 2011), p.147.

soldiers, especially the British, drank from the pools, some of which contained bodies. The infantry now moved back out of the *dem*. As Meiklejohn related: 'I had lost most of my company in the general confusion, but men of different regiments followed me as we made our way back to the entrance of the *zariba* and formed up as a general crowd … We were not a pretty sight. Officers and men smoke begrimed, and covered with dust and blood.'[34]

The Mahdist camp was then systematically looted, mostly for weapons and flags and the occasional chain mail shirt. Kitchener and his staff came inside and were given three hearty cheers by all the troops. Losses were quickly computed amidst the stink and heat. According to the intelligence report, signed off by Kitchener on 16 April, the British suffered 28 killed and 89 wounded. The EA lost 57 killed and 391 wounded (although the numbers listed actually make it 56 killed and 384 wounded).[35] Mahdist numbers were imprecise with most accounts giving some 3,000 killed in and around the *dem* (it was probably more) and possibly several thousand more dying of wounds whilst fleeing. Some 1,000–2,000 were taken prisoner, with hundreds being sent north into Egypt to be trained for service in the EA. The dead of the AEA were quickly buried wrapped in blankets, just outside the *zariba*, and the bodies of the British troops were treated separately to those of the EA. The rest of the army moved to higher ground to rest and prepare for the march back in the evening cool. In so doing, they had to contend with a daytime temperature of 108° F with little cover beyond anything they could make to shield themselves from the sun. The Mahdist dead were buried in the trenches or left where they fell, to be picked apart by vultures, crocodiles and other animals. Some corpses would be found months later desiccated by the sun.

Contrary to Kitchener's official despatch, the medical arrangements for the British brigade proved wholly unsatisfactory. Captain Reginald Brooke, Gatacre's A.D.C., wrote later of the shortage of chloroform and a complete lack of operating tables, while Lieutenant Cox mentions that the hospital was 'very much under strength in doctors'. At the battlefield, there were only 19 men and five doctors. Indeed, the EA had to carry the British wounded back on stretchers in the evening, all of them having had to wait in the sun beforehand. Lieutenant Ready of the 2nd Egyptians thought this appalling not only because of the language problem but 'it rather gives the Egyptians a very poor idea of the Englishman'. Moreover, the EA had to pitch tents for the British, who just looked on and 'it is not what I call playing the game'. It took three nights of marching before the wounded reached the hospital at Dakheila. Kitchener, evidently, was enraged and reprimanded the chief medical officer, Lieutenant Colonel MacNamara, described by one officer as a 'weak, theoretical, silly old man'. Cromer brought this matter to the attention of the War Office, with Wood explaining that the EA had selected

34   Alford & Sword, *Egyptian Soudan*, pp.223–224. Meredith (ed.), *Omdurman Diaries*, p.94. Churchill, *River War*, vol. 1, pp.436–438.

35   SAD: Main Sequence: SIR: Intelligence Report, Egypt, No. 59, 13 February – 23 May 1898, pp.21–22. <https://www.dur.ac.uk/library/asc/sudan/sirs; http://palimpsest.dur.ac.uk/slp/sirs1.html>, accessed 15 Sept. 2020.

men, whereas doctors in the British Army 'are very much inclined to sit down and wait on Providence or some helpful man who would tell them what to do'. He wished that the four battalion commanders had 'a little of the superfluous energy of Gatacre'.[36]

Dealing with the wounded was not the only problem facing the British medical authorities. Soon after the battle, the brigade was hit by dysentery and typhoid because the troops had drunk from the polluted pools in the Atbara river bed and from the Nile. Over 500 cases occurred within three weeks and men volunteered to help the medical orderlies in the hospital because there was so much sickness. There would be a steady number of fatalities, including Private Cross who had saved Gatacre's life. Soon, however, the camp would have large Berkfeld filter pumps to help clean the Nile water, but cases of illness would linger on for weeks.[37]

Gatacre's battle tactics raised some questions afterwards. Hunter wrote that the British formation 'was as bad as bad could be. Ours was the correct one'. The advance 'was as slow as a funeral .., everybody got jumbled together'. The EA's formation, he argued, allowed for better control by the officers, it being 'elastic & gives ample fire development, units are supported by themselves & so there is no mixture of corps nor confusion of movement', and allowed for a competitive element between battalions.[38] Captain Egerton of the Seaforths felt the same and wrote later that the 'commanding officers' all objected to the plan and he thought that Gatacre 'was in error'. If the brigade had 'attacked on ordinary lines ... we should have suffered considerably less loss'.[39] Gatacre's widow later argued that the formation chosen was not 'peculiarly destructive' because the EA had a higher ratio of casualties.[40] Rough calculations show the EA having 5.5% losses relating to its three brigades, while those for the British brigade show 3.4%. The EA had concentrated more on getting inside the *dem*, which it had done quickly and so began hand-to-hand fighting sooner. The slower British advance had through its effective volley firing kept the Mahdists down, but once at the *dem* the formation had proved costly, for it was here that most of the losses were incurred as the Camerons awaited support. If the British brigade had advanced in line it is likely that casualties would have been less. The overall approach to the battle had been left to Hunter and Gatacre and it was not a sophisticated plan. But if they had tried to manoeuvre Mahmud out of the *dem* by going around it, using the scrub as cover, it is probable that Mahmud would have rushed out and in that sort of environment the Mahdists would

---

36 NAM: 1983-05-55/10, Cameron Letters, Brooke to Cameron's father, 29 May 1898; Meredith (ed.), *Omdurman Diaries*, p. 101; NAM: 1966-09-142, Ready Diary, 14 April 1898; BL: Lansdowne Papers, 88906/20/7, Cromer to Lansdowne; Wood to Lansdowne; Lansdowne to Cromer, 22 May, 1 June, 7 June 1898; Major General Sir Frederick Maurice (ed.), *The Life of General Lord Rawlinson of Trent. From His Journals and Letters* (London: Cassell & Co. Ltd, 1928), p.34; Henry Keown-Boyd, *A Good Dusting. A Centenary Review of the Sudan campaigns 1883–1899* (London: Guild Publishing, 1986), p.201.

37 NAM 1998-06-144/10, Senior NCO to Fred, 14 October 1898; Meredith (ed.), *Omdurman Diaries*, pp.104–106, 110–113.

38 NAM: 1983-05-55, Cameron Letters, Hunter to Cameron's father, 25 April 1898,

39 Egerton, *With the 72nd*, p.14.

40 Gatacre, *General Gatacre*, p.203.

The Emir Mahmud being paraded through Berber. In this depiction his hands are not tied in anyway. (*Illustrated London News*)

have had an advantage. As it was, the size of the AEA had obliged Mahmud to stay behind his defences.

Although Mahdists were killed indiscriminately, including the wounded who had shammed death in order to strike the unwary, there had been no official policy to kill the wounded or those surrendering. 'We got verbal orders to be careful of passing enemy wounded as their trick was to feign death and then stab from behind. Even the genuinely wounded might do this. If a man held up his hands he was to be spared', wrote Lieutenant Meiklejohn.[41] Churchill recorded that Kitchener had issued 'distinct orders that quarter was to be given to all who asked for it and that wounded Dervishes were not to be despatched unless they were dangerous'. The British troops were even told the Arabic word for mercy, "Aman". Moreover, wounded Mahdists were captured and were well treated. Some came into camps days later seeking medical aid. Private Teigh saw about 20 Mahdists working with the camel transport despite 'some with arms off and others with legs off, but they are very happy and say that "English very good"'.[42]

Kitchener's combined army had now been 'bloodied', with its British soldiers especially gaining valuable battle experience and knowledge of their enemy. The AEA had struck a significant blow to the hopes and expectations of the Khalifa. However, it was still not strong enough to bring the campaign to a finish and a second British brigade would soon be on its way as reinforcements. For the Khalifa, the defeat of Mahmud's army had been a severe blow, not only in the loss of soldiers but in damaging his prestige and authority. He now had to plan the final battle in the hope of keeping Mahdism alive in the Sudan.

---

41   Meredith (ed.), *Omdurman Diaries*, p.83.
42   Churchill, *River War*, vol. 1, pp.444–445; Meredith (ed.), *Omdurman Diaries*, p.114; Major General W. Gatacre, 'After the Atbara and Omdurman', *The Contemporary Review*, 75, (Feb. 1899), pp.300–301.

Chapter 7

To Kereri 1898

After the destruction of Mahmud's army the AEA settled down to await the rise of the Nile and the arrival of a second British brigade. Meanwhile, the Sudan Military Railway continued its inexorable journey south and on 14 July reached the Atbara, enabling the rapid build-up of a month's supplies for the British brigades and two months' supplies for the EA. Atbara fort became 'a busy port containing streets of tinned beef boxes, biscuits, blankets, barrels and bales, and more than 200 sailing craft'.[1] Three new gunboats were added to the river flotilla during this time, bringing welcome additional fire power. Owing to the bad luck it had suffered earlier in the campaign, the *El Teb* was renamed the *Hafir*, and in all, there were now ten gunboats patrolling the Nile.

The 2nd British brigade under Brigadier General Sir Neville Lyttelton began to arrive during the first two weeks of August and comprised four infantry battalions – the 1st Battalion, Grenadier Guards, the 1st Battalion, Northumberland Fusiliers, the 2nd Battalion, Lancashire Fusiliers, and the 2nd Battalion, The Rifle Brigade. The 1st British Brigade was placed under the command of Brigadier General Andrew Wauchope with Gatacre now in charge of what became known as the British division. This extra responsibility, however, did not deter Gatacre from behaving as before. He soon annoyed the new arrivals especially with his ideas regarding the formation of squares: 'everybody… thought they were rotten', complained Lieutenant Loch of the Grenadier Guards, 'and I hope it will never be practised in earnest'. He also noted that, 'It is an extraordinary thing how unpopular [Gatacre] is among all officers here. It is all from want of a little tact now and then'. Later, Loch revealed that Gatacre 'comes around with a lantern in the middle of the night and examines the men and officers to see they have their boots and kits on. He must be mad'. Lyttelton, though friendly with Gatacre, found him 'a very trying man to serve under … His great fault is that he cannot keep himself to his own work … I have never seen such a restless & often misdirected energy'.[2]

---

1   Colonel F. I. Maxse, *Seymour Vandeleur* (London: The *National Review* Office, 1906. Reprinted: London: Forgotten Books, 2015), p.212; John Meredith (ed.), *Omdurman Diaries 1898. Eyewitness Accounts of the Legendary Campaign* (Barnsley: Leo Cooper, 1998), p.123.

2   NAM: 1986-08-66: Diary of Lieutenant The Hon E. D. Loch, 30 July, 13 August and 24 August 1898, pp.4–5, 14, 21; Queen Mary, University of London [QM]: NL/2: Sir Neville Lyttelton

The only British cavalry regiment to take part in the campaign, the 21st Lancers, also arrived. In appearance its troopers looked like infantrymen except that they wore breeches with soft leather sewn on the inside as protection against wear from the saddle. Like the infantry they also wore quilted cotton neck covers and spine pads. Their main weapon was the lance which until 1885 had been made from bamboo, but thereafter was replaced by ones made from ash. It was nine feet long, weighing just over 4 lbs and carried a steel spearhead about one foot in length. They also carried the unpopular 1890 sword which like its predecessors often bent when striking an enemy. More useful was the Lee-Metford carbine, a shorter version of the main infantry weapon, the bullets for which were carried in a bandolier worn around the chest. Instead of their usual great chargers, the Lancers rode smaller Syrian horses as these were a better breed for service in the Sudan. These hardy mounts had to carry about 20 stones in weight (280lbs): the rider, his weapons, saddles, feed, and other pieces of equipment.[3] Also on their way were two British artillery batteries, the 32nd Field Battery comprising six 15-pdr breech-loading field guns that fired mostly shrapnel shells, and the 37th Field Battery comprising six new 5-inch howitzers that fired 50lb shells armed with the new lyddite high explosive. Attached to this latter battery were six Maxims. For the march on Omdurman, the artillery was placed under the command of Lieutenant Colonel C. J. Long. In total, for the final part of the campaign the combined AEA would have at its disposal 44 field guns and 20 Maxim machine guns.[4]

The summer months were very trying for the troops left behind at the camps near the Atbara. The ordinary soldiers were drilled, worked fatigues, played sports, fished, and put on and attended concerts. The heat became excessive, well over 100° F most days, although Lieutenant Loch thought the dry heat efficacious: 'The climate is lovely, one wakes up in the morning just as fit as possible'. Captain Douglas Churcher of the Royal Irish Fusiliers, who commanded a battery of Maxims was not so keen on the climate because of the dust which covered everything even when cooking; his sausages were inedible because 'they were black with dust before we could eat them'. The journalist Bennet Burleigh found the heat oppressive because it 'bore down like a load upon head and shoulders and enveloped us like a blast from a roaring furnace'.[5]

Relief for the troops was soon underway. From August the army began to move south: first, units of the EA were sent to the forward base between Wad

Papers, NL/2/9/NGL/KL/508, to his wife, 9 September 1898; Meredith (ed.), *Omdurman Diaries*, p.167.

3   William Wright, *Omdurman 1898* [Stroud: Spellmount, 2012], p.53. <http://www.uniformology.com/LANCERS-11,html>, accessed 30 October 2020. G. W. Steevens, *With Kitchener to Khartum* (Edinburgh and London: William Blackwood and Sons, 1898), p.219.

4   Donald Featherstone, *Omdurman 1898. Kitchener's Victory in the Sudan* (Wesport, CT and London: Preager, 2005), p.61. Donald Featherstone, *Weapons & Equipment of the Victorian Soldier* (London: Arms and Armour Press, 1978, 1996), pp.85–87.

5   NAM: 1986-08-66, Loch diary, 7 August, p.11; NAM: 1978-04-53: Diary of Captain Douglas Wilfred Churcher, 12, 15 and 18 August, pp. 4–6; Bennet Burleigh, *Khartoum Campaign 1898 or the Re–Conquest of the Soudan* (London: Chapman & Hall, Limited, 1899. Reprinted: Cambridge: Ken Trotman Ltd, 1989), p.55.

Habashi and Wad Hamed, some 15 miles north of the Sixth Cataract, known as Shabluka Gorge. MacDonald's and Maxwell's brigades went first, the men packed onto the gunboats and the new double-decker barges which were lashed to the steamers' sides. These also towed one or two *gyassas* carrying kit and equipment. 'Thus in this land of impossibilities' wrote Steevens, 'a craft not quite so big as a penny steamer started to take 1,100 men, cribbed so that they could not stretch arm or leg, 100 miles at rather under a mile an hour'. Although many would soon be joining their men and marching with them to Omdurman, 'The faithful women, babies on their hips, screamed one more farewell'. The Egyptian cavalry and the Camel Corps were ferried across the river and then marched south towards Wad Hamed. Other EA battalions were called upon, such as the 5th Egyptian Battalion, which was summoned from Suakin and reached Berber after marching 260 miles in 18 days. This was a feat, according to Steevens that 'was a record for marching troops, and it is not likely that anybody but Egyptians will ever lower it'.[6]

The 1st British Brigade began to leave soon afterwards and one thing the newly promoted Captain Cox noticed on his steamer were '4 field hospitals and 2 communication hospitals on board, they certainly are not going to run short this time – got X rays on board'.[7] Meanwhile, on 13 August, Kitchener and his staff left Atbara fort on gunboats to join their men. From 18 August, the 2nd British brigade began moving south. One feature of the voyage noticed by Lieutenant Loch were the stragglers from the 21st Lancers, who were escorting the massive transport column of mules and camels. 'Several stops to pick up sick men from Lancers', he wrote. Having no transport of

---

6   Steevens, *With Kitchener*, pp.192–193, 205–206; Ronald M. Lamothe, *Slaves of Fortune. Sudanese Soldiers & the River War 1896–1898* (Woodbridge: James Currey, 2011), pp.85–89; Burleigh, *Khartoum*, pp.42–43, 59–60.
7   Meredith (ed.), *Omdurman Diaries*, p.167.

their own, the Lancers had to leave behind those men and horses that fell out. The latter especially fell by the wayside because they had just come off the trains and were not acclimatised to the rigours of the Sudan. Loch thought the Lancers had lost some ten per cent of their horses because they were unfit and were worked too soon.[8] The cavalry and journalists had to pass through the abandoned town of Metemma, where Mahmud had massacred the Ja'alin the year before. 'It was truly an awful Golgotha', wrote Burleigh, 'the remains of thousands of dead animals scattered all over the town'. Steevens saw 'Bones, skulls, and hides of camels, oxen, horses, asses, sheep and goats. The stillness and the stench merge together … exuding from every foot of this melancholy graveyard – the cenotaph of a whole tribe'. From the river, Cox saw 'The whole place strewn with skeletons of human beings, and I also saw the gallows where some were hung...'[9] These sights simply added to the troops loathing of the Mahdists. By 24 August, as the 21st Lancers came wearily into camp, the concentration of the AEA was complete. Kitchener had four Egyptian brigades, the two brigades of the British Division, the nine squadrons of the Egyptian cavalry, eight companies of the Egyptian Camel Corps, and the four squadrons of the 21st Lancers. In addition, the AEA had its 44 field guns and 20 Maxim machine guns as noted above. On the river, there were ten gunboats, disposing 36 guns and 24 Maxims. Accompanying the army on its march south would be at least 15 journalists making this final stage of the campaign one of the best covered of the Victorian period.

The concentration at Wad Hamid and then the march south that started on 24 and 25 August had gone smoothly thanks to the inaction of the Khalifa. There had been concern that the Mahdists would fight at Shabluka Gorge, where the Nile forced its way through the rock of its Sixth Cataract, rather than finding a way through the softer desert. Although the Nile was high, the gunboats and sailing craft would still have to fight their way through against a strong current and would have been vulnerable to the fire from any Mahdist fortifications. The high ground on the western side, a broken jumble of rocks, would have provided strong defensive positions to any Mahdist warriors positioned there. Clearing this area would have been a formidable undertaking for the AEA. In Omdurman, the strategic advantage of the gorge had not been lost on the Khalifa and his generals and there had been some serious discussions. Again, as over the fate of the Ja'alin, Osman Shaykh al Din was pitted against his uncle, Ya'qub. The former, supported by Ibrahim al Khalil, wanted to fight at Shabluka, whereas Ya'qub preferred to fight outside Omdurman. In May, a major gathering, influenced by the views of Osman Digna, persuaded the Khalifa to fortify Shabluka and to fight a major battle there. Work on these fortifications began quickly and seven forts were built, although several of them were subsequently flooded by the high Nile. At the same time the Emir 'Abd al Baqi was despatched with 300 cavalry to watch and report on the movements of the enemy which he did to the very end. But at the beginning of July, the Khalifa ordered a halt to construction work

8   NAM: 1986-08-66, Loch Diary, 20 August 1898, pp.17–18; Steevens, *With Kitchener*, pp.223–225.
9   Burleigh, *Khartoum*, p.88; Steevens, *With Kitchener*, pp.228, 231–232; Meredith (ed.), *Omdurman Diaries*, p.169.

because he could no longer supply the small force doing the building work. Realisation dawned that to supply an army so far from Omdurman would be impossible. The area, anyway, was unknown to him and too far away for him to exert his authority; Shabluka was therefore abandoned to the enemy. Instead, the Khalifa ordered eleven forts to be built along Omdurman's river front, another two at Khartoum, two on the east bank and two on Tuti Island, thus covering the point where the White and Blue Niles met. The Khalifa had decided to await his Anglo–Egyptian enemy at Omdurman and deal with it on familiar ground at the heart of his domain.[10]

The AEA marched around Shabluka, a detour of eight miles, without incident but shadowed constantly by the scouts of 'Abd al Baqi. The only mishap, on 27 August, being the loss of the gunboat *Zafir*, whose basic repairs, carried out the previous year, finally collapsed near Shendi. All the crew were lucky to survive, including Commander Keppel, who transferred to the *Sultan*. The flotilla was now reduced to nine gunboats for the final voyage to Omdurman. On 28 August, the AEA reached Royan and on Royan Island nearby established a field hospital and a supply base. Then it began its approach march to Omdurman made harder by natural, but not Mahdist, obstacles. The Nile had flooded water courses that could not be crossed and instead the army had to march around them adding to the distance covered. Moreover, the ground was littered with sharp stones that damaged both boots and ankles. The weather made the marches almost unbearable. Men collapsed from the heat during the day and at night the troops had to suffer sandstorms and torrential rain. In spite of these trials on 1 September the AEA crested the Kereri hills overlooking the Kereri plain. The cavalry headed farther south towards the next ridge around the high point of Jebel Surgham, while the rest of the army occupied the deserted village of El Egeiga which became the base camp. The AEA would now await the Khalifa, many hoping they would not have to go and seek him out in the narrow streets and alleys of Omdurman itself.

Meanwhile, on the east bank of the Nile river, a column of some 2,000 friendly tribesmen, many of whom were Ja'alin, were led south by Major Stuart-Wortley, a veteran of the Gordon Relief Expedition, Lieutenant Charles Wood, a son of General Sir Evelyn Wood, acting as his chief-of-staff, and also Hassan Effendi Sherif and Tannus Shihadi, two Arab members of the Intelligence Department who were to act as interpreters and make reports. On 1 September, in conjunction with six gunboats under Keppel, the 'Friendlies' attacked Mahdist positions south of the village of Halfaya and cleared the two forts on that side of the river. Tuti Island was found to have been flooded, swampy and in range of the guns and rifles of the Omdurman forts, so the howitzer battery was landed on the east bank, some 3,000 yards

---

10   'Ismat Hasan Zulfo, *Karari. The Sudanese Account of the Battle of Omdurman* (London: Frederick Warne (Publishers) Ltd, 1980), pp.114–123; Winston Spencer Churchill, *River War. An Historical Account of the Reconquest of the Soudan* (London: Longmans, Green, And Co., 1899) vol. 2, pp.58–60; SAD: Main Sequence: SIR: Intelligence Report, Egypt, Report, No. 60, 25 May to 31 December 1898, p.2, <https://www.dur.ac.uk/library/asc/sudan/sirs; http://palimpsest.dur.ac.uk/slp/sirs1.html>, accessed 12 December 2020.

The gunboat, *Sultan*, engaging Mahdist positions by the Mahdi's tomb. Note the damage already done to the tomb's dome. (*Illustrated London News*)

from the Mahdi's tomb which it began to shell at 3:00 p.m. The dome was soon shattered, sending up clouds of dust. Buildings around the tomb were also hit and civilians killed. The Khalifa had been warned by Kitchener that this might happen because on 30 August he had sent a letter urging him to send civilians 'to a place of safety'. The letter also urged the Khalifa to surrender otherwise 'the responsibility for such bloodshed will be on your head'. While the Mahdi's tomb was being bombarded, the gunboats departed to fight the forts along the Omdurman river bank which they did very effectively. At daybreak the following day, the bombardment started again and great holes were blown into the walls along the river bank. Soon, a greater noise could be heard from the Kereri plain as the great battle of Omdurman commenced.[11]

By 1 September, the Khalifa had determined to fight Kitchener's army on the Kereri plain and not within the streets of Omdurman. His decision had been influenced by emirs who had been persuaded to support this course by Wingate's agents.[12] For the Khalifa, the battle was going to be a repeat of Shaykan in 1883, where Hicks Pasha had met disaster. The day before, when his army was mobilised, including much of the adult male population

11   SAD: Main Sequence: SIR: Intelligence Report, Egypt, No.60, Operations of Friendly Arabs on East Bank, 25 August 1898 to 5 September 1898; Appendix 7, Report of Major E. M. Stuart-Wortley, 5 September, pp.33–35; Report of Tannus Shihadi, 13 September 1898, pp.35–38; Appendix 6, Copy of Letter sent to the Khalifa before the battle of Omdurman, 30 August 1898, p.32. <https://www.dur.ac.uk/library/asc/sudan/sirs; http://palimpsest.dur.ac.uk/slp/sirs1.html>, accessed 12 December 2020.

12   Zulfo, *Kereri*, p.137.

of Omdurman, the Khalifa 'delivered a fiery oration urging his followers to sacrifice themselves in the [*jihad*] against the infidels'. Indeed, since May 'men were preparing their souls for death' as Babikr Badri, one of the warriors, noted.[13] On 1 September, the Mahdist army moved out of Omdurman as if to confront the enemy. Watching from high ground to the north, Winston Churchill, like many others who saw the Mahdist army arrayed for battle, was awe-struck: 'It was perhaps the impression of a lifetime; nor do I expect ever again to see such an awe-inspiring or formidable sight'.[14] Kitchener, too, had seen the Mahdist advance from the high point of Jebel Surgham. On his way back to camp he saw Hunter who related afterwards that Kitchener looked 'as if he'd seen a ghost'. He told Hunter that 'the enemy were only 5 miles beyond the hill, advancing 50,000 strong against us'.[15] They pushed back the Egyptian cavalry, the Camel Corps and the 21st Lancers who had advanced to some low hills south of the large water-course known as the Khor Shambat. There was some skirmishing but the British and Egyptians withdrew safely, the 21st Lancers remaining on the western ridge of Jebel Surgham until night fall. The Mahdist advance caused the AEA to form positions around El Egeiga in a half-circle facing westwards, ready to meet their assault, but in the end nothing happened. It was now 1:45 p.m. and the whole Mahdist army, as one, stopped, fired a volley in the air and camped in and round the Khor Shambat, which was damp and full of pools of water, the main flood having dissipated. Soon, as the Lancers moved back to the eastern ridge, noisy Mahdists went up Jebel Surgham, and could see the Mahdi's tomb being bombarded by British howitzers: according to Babikr Bedri, 'the people were dumbfounded, their shouting ceased, even the neighing of the horses was stilled'.[16]

As his army settled down, the Khalifa called his principal advisers to discuss the plan of attack. It was decided that this would take place after dark as this would give the Mahdists a better chance of getting close to the enemy. This was an operation that Kitchener and his staff feared, so Wingate and Slatin persuaded two villagers to go to the Khalifa and tell him that the enemy planned themselves to attack in the night. This they did and were then sent back to spy on the AEA but were arrested and held until after the battle. Fearful of being attacked, the Khalifa called another meeting as darkness fell, this time with his generals present. An argument broke out between Osman Shaykh al Din and Ibrahim al Khalil, the youngest commanders. The latter wanted to attack at night and was backed by Osman Digna. But Shaykh al Din wanted to attack in daylight and his view was now supported by the Khalifa. Three reasons for this change of mind suggest themselves: first, the need for clear visibility for the riflemen of the *mulazimin* and the *jihadiya*; second, the need to maintain control of the army, even now a difficult undertaking; and third, the desire for prestige. Shayhk al Din wanted his riflemen to receive

---

13   SAD: Main Sequence: SIR: Intelligence Report, Egypt, Report, No. 60, 25 May to 31 December 1898, p.4, <https://www.dur.ac.uk/library/asc/sudan/sirs; http://palimpsest.dur.ac.uk/slp/sirs1.html>, accessed 12 December 2020; Babikr Bedri, *The Memoirs of Babikr Bedri*, (London: Oxford University Press, 1969), p.226.

14   Churchill, *River War*, vol. 2, pp.85–87.

15   LHCMA: Maurice Papers, Hunter Letters, 2/1/5: Hunter to Maurice, 14 October 1898.

16   Bedri, *Memoirs*, pp.233–235.

much of the glory and to be seen acquiring it and it would also be good for the Khalifa to be seen to be in command. One historian also suggests that the Khalifa did not think his generals were competent enough, especially compared to those who had fought for the Mahdi. As darkness enveloped the area, the AEA's gunboats illuminated the plain with their searchlights making the success of a night attack even less likely.[17]

Once the decision had been made the battle plan was outlined. The army of Ibrahim al Khalil was placed on the right flank. Aged 24, he was the youngest general and described as one of the 'ablest military strategists in the field'. Tactically, though, he would be found wanting but this had much to do with the fact that he had never faced Kitchener's forces. He was a cousin of the Emir Mahmud and had been brought up in the Khalifa's household, alongside Osman Shaykh al Din, with whom he did not get on. At the age of 20, Ibrahim al Khalil had put down a rebellion in the Nuba hills and had commanded in the far west, hence the designation 'Kara army' for his troops. Earlier in the year, he and his men had been summoned to Omdurman. He commanded some 4,000 men and their task would be to ascend Jebel Surgham and then attack the enemy's left flank in conjunction with the Mahdist centre, commanded by Osman Azrak.[18]

In 1896, Osman Azrak had judiciously fled the field at Firket and had survived being wounded near Dongola. He was about 53 and close to the Khalifa, having made his name raiding the frontier with Egypt. He was essentially a cavalryman but was put in charge of a force comprised of infantry: riflemen taken from Osman Shaykh al Din's command as well as sword and spearmen that altogether numbered some 8,000 men. Osman Azrak was expected to soften up the AEA by breaking into their lines.

Behind, Osman Azrak, and under the great Black Flag of the Khalifa was a force of some 12,000 under Ya'qub. This was not visible to the AEA as it was positioned under the lower western slope of Jebel Surgham. Ya'qub had reformed the army but had never commanded a large force in battle. His men were mostly sword and spearmen. His task was to await events, either to support Osman Azrak's breakthrough or, if he was defeated, to attack the AEA once it had left its positions.

On the left were the combined forces of the military novice, Osman Shaykh al Din, and those of Abdullah Abu Siwar, both formed respectively around light and dark Green flags. The former commanded most of the *mulazimin* riflemen and his command numbered about 12,000 men, a force too large for his limited abilities. Abu Siwar's force actually belonged to the deputy khalifa, Ali Wad Hilu, who had remained with the Khalifa. It numbered about 4,000, mostly sword and spearmen, and he exercised much more control. The task of this large and powerful combined force was to take the Kereri hills and once there to descend on Kitchener's army wherever it happened to be, in position or moving across the plain.

Lastly, Osman Digna, the great survivor, had positioned his men, about 700 at first, in a dry water-course called Khor Abu Sunt. There it was to guard

---

17   Zulfo, *Karari*, p.151–153.
18   Zulfo, *Karari*, pp 87–88, 153.

the right and rear of the Khalifa's army in case the enemy tried to advance along the river bank and cut the road to Omdurman. Although a good tactical move, one wonders if Osman Digna did not want to sacrifice his men to the firepower of the enemy, the strength of which he was well aware.

Surprisingly, the Mahdist cavalry was interspersed among the various commands and was never concentrated in a body. The Baggara horsemen were well respected by the AEA and if massed together would have provided a formidable force. It seems that since the emirs themselves were dispersed throughout the army to help with command and control, they had wanted their mounted retainers to accompany them.[19]

The Mahdist plan, then, was either to break through the enemy line at the first attempt supported by the reserve forces in the centre and on the flanks, or to lure out Kitchener's army so that it could be ambushed from two or three sides on the Kereri plain. It was in Major Maxse's words, 'simple, comprehensive and suitable to the ground they had selected and the discipline they could enforce'. Churchill called the plan 'complex and ingenious' and it was too complex for the military minds of the Khalifa's commanders because it required a cohesive system of command and control. The plan also demanded a tactical subtlety which was lacking. The historian 'Ismat Zulfo, however, is surely right to argue that 'This challenges the notion that the Khalifa threw tens of thousands to certain death in one of the biggest massacres in history'. It was to be an ambush between two 'enormous pincers closing in on the enemy from different directions. It was an intelligent exploitation of human resources'. Why though, as Zulfo asks, did the Khalifa not simply await the advance of the enemy because he could not sit around El Egeiga forever? It was, he states, following Churchill, all to do with the Khalifa's 'fatal miscalculation of the enemy's firepower'. The Khalifa was living on past glories and did not appreciate how much warfare had changed since the victory at Shaykan in 1883.[20]

With regard to the numbers of the Mahdist army, Zulfo has refuted the number given by Wingate in his intelligence report and which has been used ever since. Wingate based his estimate of 52,000 on Ya'qub's muster books found in Omdurman after the battle, but Zulfo says these were out of date. Moreover, the organisation of the figures does not correspond to the divisions of the Mahdist army as they were on 2 September, some units had been shifted around, for example, Osman Shaykh al Din had to give men to Osman Azrak and Ibrahim al Khalil. Moreover, Churchill mentions that 6,000 men deserted on the nights of 31 August and 1 September, although Bedri remarks that to deter desertion Ya'qub had ordered that any man found in Omdurman three hours after sunrise would have his throat cut and many might have therefore returned to the army.[21] Zulfo supports some British estimates of 30-35,000 men. From those sources consulted for this present

19   Zulfo, *Karari*, pp.84–90, 111–112, 163. H. C. Jackson, *Osman Digna*, (London: Methuen & Co., Ltd, 1926), pp.152–154.

20   Maxse, *Seymour Vandeleur*, p.219; Churchill, *River War*, vol. 2, p.119–120; Zulfo, *Karari*, pp.160–163.

21   Churchill, *River War*, vol. 2, p.88–89; Bedri, *Memoirs*, p.235.

Battle of Omdurman, 2 Sept. 1898. British troops repelling the first Mahdist assault. (*Illustrated London News*)

study, the majority state that the Mahdist army totalled between 40-50,000 men and, as mentioned above, Kitchener on first inspection had calculated 50,000. Nevertheless, it is certain that the Mahdist army outnumbered the AEA.

Meanwhile, around El Egeiga, the British division had built a *zariba*, while the Egyptian division preferred to dig shelter trenches. Looking from the left to the right of the semi-circle, was firstly Lyttelton's 2nd British Brigade, with its left flank on the river, then Wauchope's 1st British Brigade; next was Maxwell's 2nd Sudanese Brigade, then MacDonald's 1st Sudanese Brigade; and then Lewis's 3rd Egyptian Brigade. Collinson's 4th Egyptian Brigade was held in reserve. Altogether, the whole AEA numbered 25,800 men. The one great fear pervading Kitchener's army was that the Khalifa would attack at night. When dawn broke on 2 September there was a collective sigh of relief; Hunter expressed this later, writing: 'When the sun rose … I never was so glad in all my born days'. Lieutenant Loch felt the Mahdists 'would have got unpleasantly close … and if they had attacked the Egyptians … I think we might have been rolled up'.[22]

Before first light, some British and Egyptian cavalry were sent to Jebel Surgham to keep watch on the Mahdists. Just before 6:00 a.m. the Mahdist army began to stir and began moving as one in dense masses, with hundreds of colourful flags flying and spearpoints glittering in the rising sun. Churchill witnessed this, as did Haig and Captain Sir Henry Rawlinson. 'It was a magnificent sight', wrote Rawlinson later, 'these thousands of wild, brave, uneducated savages advancing to their destruction.' After some skirmishing the cavalry retreated before the vast army that was moving quickly and with

---

22   LHCMA: Maurice Papers, Hunter Letters, 2/1/5, Hunter to Maurice, 14 October 1898, p.2; NAM: 1986-08-66, Loch diary, 1 September 1898, pp.30–31.

a synchronicity that was both alarming and admirable.[23] 'Long before we saw them', wrote the Senior NCO of the Warwicks, 'we heard their war cry from those thousands of throats … they must have been fully two miles away when we heard them'. The men of the British division were now standing in wait behind their *zariba*, and then at about 6:30 a.m., as they looked to the crest of high ground topping the gentle slope to their front, some 3,000 yards away, they could see the first ranks of Osman Azrak's multitude. At the same time, Ibrahim al Khalil's men appeared on Jebel Surgham, overlooking Lyttelton's brigade. 'As they came nearer', wrote Captain Dennis Granville of the Warwicks, 'they commenced their battle-cry, and all of us simply stared at them, it was a wonderful sight'.[24] Then two Mahdist guns were fired but their poor-quality shells fell 50 yards short of the *zariba*, throwing up splashes of sand. With that the Mahdists surged forward, the horsemen within the dense throng urging their men on; Ibrahim al Khalil's Kara army also fired their rifles from Jebel Surgham and moved forward in unison with Osman Azrak's men. In response, the artillery of the AEA opened fire, creating a great rolling thunder as 44 guns fired shrapnel at the approaching masses. 'It was a wonderful sight to watch our shells bursting in the air one after another from different points of the line, but you could not see that much damage was being done, though occasional gaps seemed to be refilled', wrote Lieutenant David Graeme of the Seaforths.[25] At 6:45 a.m., the British division began its rifle fire, joining the artillery guns and the Maxims. Adding to this hail of lead were the guns and Maxims of the gunboats.

The Mahdists' momentum slowed but did not stop. Granville remembered: 'We let them have it, volley after volley, right into the middle of them, simply mowing them down … Their courage was something extraordinary, as our fire, together with the artillery and maxims was simply murderous'. Captain Churcher wrote that 'I never heard such a fiendish row in all my life', as he directed his Maxims against a group on the left, 'and as far as I could tell they didn't come any further, then I turned them on the right, and kept firing away at any body of men I could see'. Captain Egerton wrote that his company 'fired 65 volleys in about three-quarters of an hour'. [26] Yet still the Mahdists continued to advance, although they were now bunching up and presenting better targets. Ibrahim al Khalil's men surged forward in spite of the fire directed at them. His horse was killed beneath him but he remounted only to be hit himself soon afterwards as he tried to direct his men into some cover. Muhammad Ishaq took over and was instantly killed as bullets, shells and shrapnel tore through the air and into the ground. A final charge of sword and spearmen was wiped out to a man. There were survivors of the Kara army and they began moving to their left to join with the depleted

---

23 NAM: 1952-01-33-4: Diary of Field Marshal Lord Rawlinson, 12 September 1898; Churchill, *River War*, vol. 2, p. 111; Douglas Scott (ed.), *Douglas Haig. The preparatory prologue 1861–1914. Diaries and Letters* (Barnsley: Pen & Sword, 2006), pp.94–95.

24 NAM: 1998-06-144, Senior NCO to Fred, 16 October 1898, p.13; NAM: 2004-03-31, Granville to his mother, 15 September 1898, p.2.

25 NAM: 2006-04-33, Graeme to his father, 6 September 1898.

26 NAM: 2004-03-31, Granville to his mother, 15 September 1898; NAM: 1978-04-53, Churcher diary, 2 September 1898, p.14; Egerton, *With the 72nd*, p.34.

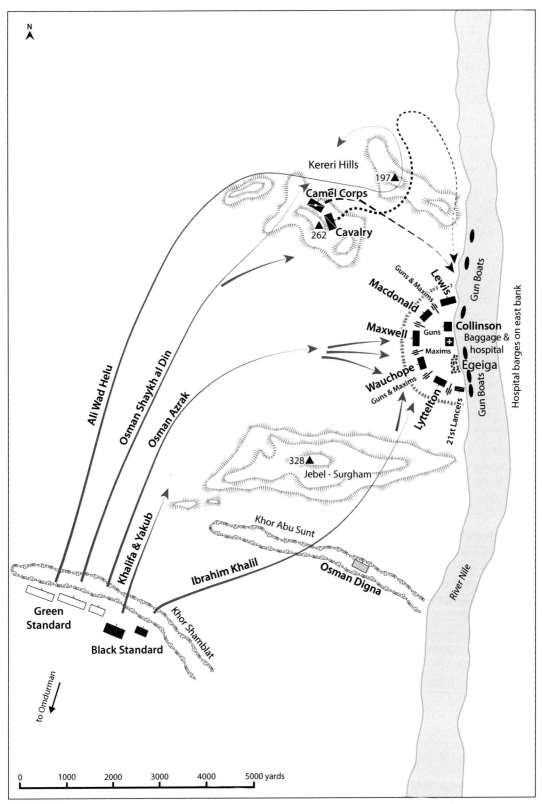

N

Kereri Hills

197 ▲

Camel Corps

262 ▲ Cavalry

Lewis

Guns & Maxims

Macdonald

Gun Boats

Maxwell

Guns

Collinson

Maxims

Baggage & hospital

Egeiga

Wauchope

Guns & Maxims

Lyttelton

21st Lancers

Gun Boats

Hospital barges on east bank

328 ▲
Jebel - Surgham

Ali Wad Helu

Osman Shaykh al Din

Osman Azrak

Khalifa & Yakub

Khor Abu Sunt

Ibrahim Khalil

Osman Digna

River Nile

Green Standard

Khor Shamblat

Black Standard

to Omdurman

| 0 | 1000 | 2000 | 3000 | 4000 | 5000 yards |

The Mahdists attack. The Battle of Omdurman, 2 September 1898.

ranks of Osman Azrak's force, now slowing to a halt amidst the hail of lead. The carnage was unrelenting, but Osman Azrak tried one last desperate expedient – a cavalry charge. British accounts suggest he gathered 200–500 Baggara horse. It is worth noting that the Kereri plain was not totally flat; the ground was cut by shallow indentations and was loosely corrugated. This, along with the mimosa bushes that dotted the area, provided some cover for men to gather, take stock and move forward again. It has been suggested that Osman Azrak had only 50 horsemen, the rest being sword and spearman, but if that was so they would hardly have been noticed by the British troops firing at them. Lieutenant Meiklejohn wrote that 500 Baggara horse charged and 'A murderous concentrated fire was turned on them and they were literally mown down, yet they never faltered, riding straight for us with wild cries and brandished weapons'. Some advanced within 300 yards of the British line and one or two came even nearer. The Senior NCO of the Warwicks felt that it was 'a cavalry charge to which Balaklava was nothing … Tons of lead went to meet them … never was such slaughter done in 2 minutes as then, it was grand, superb and something to remember, many a grim old warrior of Abdullah's [sic] force bit the dust'. Osman Azrak was killed as the attack faltered but 300 riflemen under Ibrahim Jabir found cover in a dip and for about 15 minutes managed to pepper the *zariba* with bullets, most however going high. Nevertheless, the British began to take notice: 'All our casualties were I think caused by these fellows', wrote Lieutenant Loch: 'We opened a devilish fire on them but it was sometime before we got them settled'. Captain Caldecott of the Warwicks was killed, the only British officer to die on the battlefield. Maxim fire and shrapnel accounted for Ibrahim Jabir's force and few escaped alive, those trying to retreat being shot down by marksmen from the Warwicks.[27]

Of the EA, only Maxwell's brigade was part of this fight and it was as untroubled as the British brigades, although the Mahdists managed to get slightly closer because of the Martini-Henry's slower rate of fire. Colonel Sparkes thought that 'the nearest any of them got to our trenches was 150 yards'. Major à Court felt that this was because 'the firing of the Sudanese [battalions] was wilder, especially at the longer ranges and fire discipline less than perfect'. He added, however, that the Martini's bullets were more deadly and said that wounded Mahdists who managed to retire had been hit by Lee-Metfords. One thing in the EA's favour was that it suffered fewer casualties, 'one good mark for the trench' wrote Colonel Lewis. Major Townshend ordered his battalion, the 12th Sudanese, to hold their fire until the enemy were 400 yards away. However, such was the speed and determination of the Mahdists that he was forced to give the order at 600 yards and his battalion 'opened with a heavy independent fire'. At 400 yards the enemy 'seemed to enter a rain of bullets' and were 'bundled over in heaps'. Townsend 'saw a brave man leading them on with a large flag … I have never seen a braver'. The man advanced within 150 yards 'and then he and his flag fell like a piece

---

27 Meredith (ed.), *Omdurman diaries*, p.186; NAM: 1998-06-144, Senior NCO to Fred, 16 October 1898, p.13; Zulfo, *Karari*, pp.170–179; NAM: 1986-08-66, Loch diary, 2 September 1898, p.34.

'A' Company of the Warwicks, alongside the Seaforth Highlanders, firing on the first Mahdist attack led by Osman Azrak. (*Illustrated London News*)

of crumpled white paper on the ground and lay motionless'. Townshend noticed that the enemy did not run when the attack faltered and even that 'Some of them walked off as if they were the victors'.[28]

British losses were light in spite of drawing most of the enemy's fire and the men standing ready the whole time. Lieutenant Hodgson of the Lincolns said this was why the Camerons suffered more than his own battalion because 'we ordered ours to kneel between each volley'. Captain Granville's reflections show how lucky most British soldiers were: 'One bullet went through a man's helmet, without hurting him, took the good-conduct stripe off another man's arm, and then hit a sergeant in the leg.' Captain Egerton noted that Colonel Money, the Camerons' commanding officer, had two horses shot from under him, while 'our Brigade Major, Major Snow had a bullet through his helmet'. The unlucky Caldecott was killed by a bullet from an elephant gun that severed his jugular vein.[29]

Mahdist losses have been estimated at 7,000 killed and wounded during this part of the battle. It was obvious that their tactical approach was suicidal.

28   NAM: 1966-04-44, Sparkes to Mr Turmure, 13 September 1898, p.4; Lieutenant Colonel Charles À Court Repington, *Vestigia* (London: Constable and Company Ltd., 1919), pp.151–152; NAM: 1975-03-9: Lt.-Col David Francis Lewis Journal, p.12; Nash, *Chitral Charlie*, p.111.

29   Ernest J. Martin (ed.), 'The Lincolnshires at Omdurman, September, 1898. Diary of Lieutenant Hamilton Hodgson, *Journal of the Society for Army Historical Research*, 21:82, (1942), p.77; NAM: 2004-03-31, Granville to his mother, 15 September 1898, p.2; Egerton, *With the 72nd*, p.34; Meredith (ed.), *Omdurman diaries*, p.186.

Churchill offered a cogent assessment of their tactics and noted how badly the riflemen were used, being mixed up with the sword and spearmen, rather than being utilised as a separate force to soften up the enemy before the main assault. By charging along with the rest they had little opportunity to fire properly and this explains why most Mahdist bullets flew high. The use of only two artillery pieces, and they hardly fired at all, also damns Mahdist tactics. Churchill wrote that in defeating Hicks Pasha there was 'subtlety in how the battle was approached; here on the Kereri plain there was a total lack of clear thought. In 1885, the tactics of the Arabs were very instructive. In 1898 they were imbecile and hopeless.'[30]

While the forces of Osman Azrak and Ibrahim al Khalil attacked from the centre and the right, on the left the combined force of Osman Shaykh al Din and Abu Siwar under their respective light and dark Green Flags, had moved steadily northwards towards the Kereri hills that ran north-west to south-east, the eastern end subsiding about 1,000 yards from the Nile. Numbering about 16,000 in total they soon reached the first of the high points on the southern part of the range. This feature, known as Jebel Abu Zariba, was separated from its northerly counterpart, Jebel Daham, by a depression about 1,000 yards wide. These two hills measured 300 feet high and each was a mile in length. Around them, were lesser hills and knolls, strewn with rocks and boulders that made the ground difficult to traverse. It was to this area that the Egyptian cavalry and Camel Corps had retired when the Mahdist army first began to move. The dismounted Camel Corps were on Abu Zariba, supported by some dismounted cavalry and the Horse Artillery battery. Osman Shakyh al Din was ensconced amongst his men, probably as a protective measure, and the actual command of his force had fallen to the Emir al `Arifi al Rabi', who directed his men towards Abu Zariba. They were fired upon by the Egyptians although these efforts had 'not of the slightest effect … in checking them'. Colonel Broadwood, in command, ordered the Horse Battery to withdraw to Jebel Daham and very quickly because it was facing mostly *muluzīmīn*; the Egyptians were subjected to a galling fire that caused heavy casualties. The Camel Corps had to retreat but its camels were slowed down by the ground and both men and camels fell under the enemy's fusillades. The Egyptians' right flank had been turned and they were in great danger of being cut off. Broadwood had refused to obey Kitchener's earlier order to retire to the main AEA position and instead decided to retreat further north, a move then approved by Kitchener. The Camel Corps though was ordered to retire towards the river and the main camp, which it proceeded to do pursued and fired on by the Mahdists. As the Camel Corps left the hills it looked certain to be intercepted and annihilated. But then, the gunboat *Melik* arrived on the scene and poured artillery and Maxim fire into the Mahdist ranks, the ground and rocks exploding around them. The Camel Corps' troopers, doubling up with their wounded owing to lost camels, reached the safety of Lewis's brigade. Townshend saw 'them all running as hard as they could … and we were very much interested in the way shells kept bursting

---

30   Churchill, *River War*, vol. 2, p.335; Zulfo, *Karari*, pp.179–182.

Battle of Omdurman, 2 Sept. 1898. The gunboats supporting the Anglo-Egyptian forces as the Mahdists launch their first attack. (*Illustrated London News*)

about a large green flag that was hurrying and bobbing up and down'. On Jebel Daham, the surviving cavalry and Horse Artillery vainly tried to fight off the Mahdists; Haig's trumpeter was hit 'above the right temple, the bullet embedded in the back of his head (he was still quite cheerful)'. Broadwood ordered a retreat north and two guns had to be abandoned as their crews had been badly wounded. The surviving Egyptian cavalry and Horse Artillery fled for three or four miles, followed all the way by the Mahdists, who were harassed by the gunboats. Then, exhausted, the Mahdists gave up the chase and began to move back towards the Kereri hills just as Osman Azrak's attack was petering out. Broadwood's force followed them cautiously, regaining its abandoned guns, and then moved along the river bank to rejoin the main army. It was now about 8 o'clock in the morning.[31]

---

31   Churchill, *River War*, vol. 2, pp.121–127; Scott, *Haig*, pp.94–97; Nash, *Chitral Charlie*, p.111; Zulfo, *Karari*, pp.182–188.

Chapter 8

To Omdurman: the battle continues – 2 September 1898

The Mahdist attack finally slackened at about 8:00 a.m., when the 21st Lancers were sent out of the *zariba* southwards to the eastern ridge of Jebel Surgham. Once there, through the shimmering heat, the troopers could see the apparent wreckage of the Khalifa's army streaming towards Omdurman. They could just make out the walking wounded, deserters and groups of warriors, many of whom remained atop Jebel Surgham, firing at the Lancers. The Lancers' task was to discover whether the whole Mahdist army was retreating because Kitchener feared they would rally and prepare to fight in the cramped streets and alleys of Omdurman. The suitably named Lieutenant Clerk sent back a signal to Kitchener by heliograph, explaining that 400 Mahdists were still in the vicinity. The signal did nothing to allay Kitchener's concerns and he replied: 'Annoy them as far as possible on their flank and head them off if possible from Omdurman.'[1] While this message gave Colonel Martin, the commander of the 21st Lancers, license to engage the enemy, it still required him to exercise caution. The Lancers' were meant to do nothing more than skirmish and to keep intact while at the same time trying to ensure the Mahdists did not retreat to Omdurman. For Colonel Martin and his entire command, however, this order was simply a dispensation to harass and attack the enemy, thus gaining the regiment's first major battle honour: 'Everyone expected that we were going to make a charge' remembered Winston Churchill, then in its A squadron.[2] Brigadier General Lyttelton had a poor opinion of Martin whom 'I should not class as at all above average', while the regiment was 'disappointing. It is a very fine lot of men … & the squadron leaders are good, but the NCOs are very

---

1 NAM: 1963-10-27: Wyndham Papers, Sirdar to Colonel Martin, 2 Sept. 1898, Photographic Facsimile; Terry Brighton, *Winston's Charge. Lieutenant Churchill in the British Army's Last Cavalry Charge* (Hard Corps Books, 2020, Kindle e-book). Chapter 5, unpaginated (text search required); Granville Egerton, *With the 72nd Highlanders in the Sudan Campaign* (London: Eden Fisher & Co. Ltd, 1909), p.36.
2 Winston S. Churchill, *My Early Life. A Roving Commission* (London: The Reprint Society, 1944), p.200.

indifferent & I fancy the other officers not over good.'³ Colonel Martin was to show his indifference as a commander very soon after receiving the message.

The 320 Lancers, who had survived the campaign so far, moved off the eastern ridge of Jebel Surgham faced west and then south trotting along in column or long line of troops. At the head of the column was C Squadron under Captain Doyne, then behind this was D Squadron under Captain Eadon, next came B Squadron under Major Fowle, and then finally A Squadron, under Major Finn. Ordinarily, each squadron had four troops of 110 men each and the penultimate troop in A Squadron was the one commanded by Churchill. On the Mahdists' side, Osman Digna had originally placed his own men, about 700 strong, in the dried depression known as Khor Abu Sunt, in order to guard the road west to Omdurman. While the Lancers had been watched throughout by the Mahdists, they had not been able to see the ground ahead clearly from Jebel Surgham. A Lancer patrol had taken a cursory look at Osman Digna's men and had estimated their numbers at around 400. It had then headed back to the high ground. What the Lancers then missed was a reinforcement of some 2,000 men sent by the Khalifa to Osman Digna, whose movement had been hidden by the high ground jutting south and from the depression of the khor. Moreover, the Lancers from their vantage point could not even see Ya'qub's thousands huddling around the end of the western ridge of Jebel Surgham. Thus, by the time Colonel Martin led the regiment southwards he had no idea of the real numbers positioned to the right of the Lancers' line. They could see a few hundred men positioned in the open but the Lancers had not perceived that they stood on the edge of a depression, that there was low ground behind them.

At first, Martin sought to outflank the men who were in view, to move around to their right flank and engage them, 'to attack them from a more advantageous quarter' in Churchill's words.⁴ This would have been in keeping with Kitchener's order to 'annoy' the enemy and would have put the Lancers between the Mahdists and Omdurman, thus 'heading them off'. By now, the Lancers' long column was about 250 yards from the enemy, it was some 15 minutes since Kitchener's order had been received, and now the Mahdists began to open fire. 'Such a target at such a distance could scarcely be missed', wrote Churchill 'and along the column here and there horses bounded and a few men fell.'⁵ Martin did not hesitate and he gave the order. The bugle sounded and the whole column swung right into line, C Squadron now on the left, D Squadron and B Squadrons in the centre and A Squadron on the right.

Without any further orders, the regiment began to charge, with Churchill soon sheathing his sword in favour of his Mauser pistol. Likewise, Major Finn carried his revolver instead of his sword. The officers were now out in front and Finn later told his wife: 'the men rode straight and well, a couple

---

3   QM: NL/1: General Sir Neville Lyttelton Papers, NL/1/6/NGL/FAM/379, Lyttelton to Talbot, 14 September 1898.

4   Churchill, *My Early Life*, p.201; 'Ismat Hasan Zulfo, *Karari. The Sudanese Account of the Battle of Omdurman* (London: Frederick Warne (Publishers) Ltd, 1980), pp.190–195.

5   Churchill, *My Early Life*, p.201.

of horses were shot dead before the squadron reached the dervishes', while Lieutenant Smyth remembered that 'My right hand man drops, his horse shot under him. Bullets seem to be whistling and splashing all around.' As the Lancers picked up speed their horses and the bullets threw up clouds of dust and stinging stones forcing the men to bow their heads as they gripped their lances. It became clear to Finn that his squadron overlapped the Mahdist left and so he swung it to his left in order to hit the enemy rather than air. At about 150 yards, the Lancers could see other men behind the Mahdist firing line. Private Hewitt of B Squadron thought 'We were in a fine line and worked up a good speed before the shock, fit to take anything in front, so it would have been something solid to stop us.' At 50 yards, the officers in front could now see the unexpected, a deep khor lined ranks deep by enemy spear and swordsmen, with, as Lieutenant Montmorency remembered, 'their upturned faces grinning hate and defiance at us'.[6] As the Lancers saw the enemy masses, their lances tilted to take the first line which they did with an audible crash as man and horse smashed into the Mahdists, many of whom were knocked back, sometimes into the air, among their shouting comrades who rose to meet the enemy. Churchill was astounded to see that 'A score of horsemen and dozen bright flags rose as if by magic from the earth'. Some of the Lancers now found the solid mass that could stop them; hundreds of Mahdists were knocked over but up to 30 Lancers were dismounted by the impact. The lucky ones were able to remount their horses quickly, but the khor was at some points six to seven feet deep and the drop was enough to disable horses. The khor was also wide, hence the unseen numbers concealed within it. Now began desperate hand-to-hand combat, amid the noise of the shouting and screams of both men and horses. Those Lancers on the right having rode into the Mahdists diagonally, managed to avoid a thick part of the enemy ranks. The 'decreasing slope' wrote Churchill to General Sir Ian Hamilton, 'enabled us to gallop through not jump it. Result we struck – faster and more formed than the centre troops', although he and others were then engaged by Mahdists while at the other side.[7]

The centre troops hit the thickest part of the enemy and some horses were stopped dead in the crush. Lieutenant Grenfell's troop, which should have been commanded by Churchill but for his late arrival in Egypt, was swamped by Mahdists. Grenfell, unhorsed, was soon cut down, first by a sword cut and then by spears, one of which stopped his wrist watch at the moment of his death. His body was then liberally hacked about. Lancers were now fighting for their lives or helping to save others. Privates Varley and Rowlett were pulled out of the khor at different times by Private Brown. Lieutenant Wormald's sword bent double after hitting the chainmail of a Mahdist horseman. Luckily for Wormald a Lancer following up skewered the man with his lance. Private Byrne, wounded in the right arm, flailed painfully

---

6   Peter Harrington and Frederic A. Sharif (eds.), *Omdurman 1898: The Eyewitnesses Speak* (London: Greenhill Books, 1998), pp.116, 127–128; Brighton, *Winston's Charge*, Chapter 5, unpaginated (text search required).

7   Randolph S. Churchill, *Youth. Winston S. Churchill 1874–1900* (London: Mandarin Paperbacks, Minerva Paperback, 1991), p.417.

Battle of Omdurman, 2 Sept.
1898. The charge of the
21st Lancers as depicted by
Lieutenant Angus McNeill
of the Seaforth Highlanders.
(*Illustrated London News*)

with his sword but got through to the other side. He then went back in to rescue Lieutenant Molyneux who was unhorsed. Byrne, unable to use his arm effectively, used his horse to keep back four assailants but was then hit in the chest by a spear and dropped his sword. Nevertheless, both he and Molyneux escaped. Grenfell's troop eventually suffered 10 killed and 11 wounded with only four fit men lining up on the other side. Major Wyndham, the second in command, was unhorsed but fought back with revolver and sword. Captain Kenna managed to seat him on his horse but both men were then thrown. Wyndham disappeared in the mayhem but got out the other side only to be attacked by a Mahdist horseman, who was shot dead by Lieutenant Montmorency. Meanwhile, Montmorency tried to recover Grenfell's body by dismounting and putting it over his horse, but the horse bolted and threw it off. The horse was recovered by Corporal Swarbrick, while Captain Kenna rode to Montmorency's rescue enabling him to remount.[8]

Churchill provides a vivid first-hand impression of what he felt during the fighting. 'The whole scene flickered like a cinematograph picture ... I remembered no sound. The event seemed to pass in absolute silence. The yells of the enemy, the shouts of the soldiers, the firing of many shots, the clashing of sword and spear, were unnoticed by the senses, unregistered by the brain. Several others say the same.' [9] Lieutenant Smyth's impressions were written down like a 'flickering cinematograph picture'. 'Am met by swordsman on foot', he wrote, 'Cuts at my right front. I guard it with sword. Next man, fat face ... having fired, missed me, throws up both hands. I cut him across the face. He drops. Large bearded man in blue, with two-edged sword and two hands, cuts at me ... my guard carries it off. Duck my head to spear thrown which just misses me.' He survived another sword cut which scraped him

---

8   Brighton, *Winston's Charge*, Chapter 6, unpaginated (text search required); Philip Ziegler, *Omdurman* (London: Collins, 1973), pp.152–154. Churchill, *My Early Life*, p.180.

9   Winston Spencer Churchill, *River War. An Historical Account of the Reconquest of the Soudan* (London: Longmans, Green, And Co., 1899), vol. 2, p.142.

and his horse and then he was on the other side of the khor. Rallying his men, Smyth saw 'horrible sights. Everyone seems to be bleeding ... It seems to be blood, blood, blood, everywhere. Horses and men smothered with their own or other peoples.' Smyth saw the youngest officer, Lieutenant Nesham, 'led away with left hand hanging down'. Nesham was lucky to be alive because at one point each of his legs were held by Mahdists, but who then pushed his spurs into his horse's flanks which surged forward out of the khor. A trooper was given a crash course in how to tie a tourniquet to Nesham's wrist by the wounded Lieutenant Brunton.[10]

Time slowed down during the mayhem and as the regiment rallied some 150 yards outside the khor those with watches learned that they had been fighting for only two minutes. Some Lancers, including Churchill, wanted to charge again but Colonel Martin, who had ridden through both the khor and the Mahdists without drawing either his sword or revolver, thought better of it. The men dismounted, drew their carbines and began to fire at the advancing enemy. Their shooting was effective and gradually the Mahdists retired towards Omdurman. The Lancers let them go and began to take stock of what had happened. The regiment had lost 21 killed and 50 wounded out of 320, the highest loss of any unit in the AEA on 2 September. Some 119 horses had also been killed or wounded.[11] The wounded Lancers, and the extent of their wounds, were now all too evident. Sergeant Freeman tried to rally Grenfell's troop but Churchill remembers that 'His face was cut to pieces, and as he called his men to rally, the whole of his nose, cheeks and lips flapped amid red bubbles. Surely some place might have been found on any roll of honour for such a man!' He then continues, 'From the direction of the enemy there came a succession of grisly apparitions; horses spouting blood, struggling on three legs, men staggering on foot, men bleeding from terrible wounds, fish-hook spears stuck right through them, arms and faces cut to pieces, bowels protruding, men gasping, crying, collapsing, expiring.'[12] Smyth was told to collect the dead: 'The less said or written about that the better. It was ghastly. The tears streamed down my cheeks and I was physically sick.'[13]

The dead Lancers had been horribly mutilated and 20 of them were buried in the khor. Grenfell's remains were sent by his friends with the wounded to El Egeiga. Lieutenant Brunton was despatched to Kitchener to relate what had happened: it was now 9:30 a.m. Seventy dead Mahdists were left where they fell, while most of their wounded had been carried off by their retreating comrades. What had been the result of the charge? Major à Court thought 'it had neither frightened nor hurt the dervishes much, and it practically ruined the Lancers'. Captain Haig wrote that the 21st had 'got their charge, but at what cost? I trust for the sake of the British Cavalry that more tactical knowledge exists in the higher ranks of the average regiment than we have

10 Brighton, *Winston's Charge*, Chapter 6, unpaginated, (text search required); Harrington & Sharif (eds), *Omdurman 1898*, p.128; Churchill, *River War*, vol. 2, pp.141–142.
11 Churchill, *Youth*, p.418; SAD: SIR: Main Sequence, 'Intelligence Report, Egypt', No. 60, 25 May to 31 December 1898, p.41 2020 <https://www.dur.ac.uk/library/asc/sudan/sirs; http://palimpsest.dur.ac.uk/slp/sirs1.html>, accessed 12 December.
12 Churchill, *River War*, vol. 2, p.139; Churchill, *My Early Life*, p.205.
13 Harrington & Sharif, *Omdurman 1898*, pp.128–129.

seen displayed in this one'. Major Maxse pointed out that the charge had the 'disadvantage of incapacitating the regiment' thus preventing it from capturing the Khalifa later. 'The fact that both officers and men behaved with great gallantry in a nasty place is no excuse for a blunder.'[14] However, once accounts of the charge began to appear in the press in October, many derived from the Lancers themselves, the charge became to be seen as the most important event of the battle. And much ink has been spilt describing it ever since, including here, because it remains, particularly thanks to Churchill, the one part of the battle where the fighting was not done at a distance, where the British engaged their enemy in the most dramatic fashion, in hand-to-hand combat and where technology played little part. Colonel Martin remained unrepentant telling the *Hampshire Chronicle*, 'If cavalry are going to wait first to calculate the strength of the foe, and are only to attack if they find him weak enough, what is the use of them on the field of battle?'[15] One retort might be that it should perform the task demanded of it, in this case to harass the enemy and push him away from Omdurman and to act as light cavalry. The 21st Lancers had failed in this task because it did not detect Ya'qub's huge force readying to attack and the fact that Kitchener's army was going to blunder straight into it.

At 9:00 a.m., the AEA had begun to march across the Kereri plain, most of it heading south west towards Jebel Surgham. The plan had been hastily arranged because Kitchener wanted to reach Omdurman quickly. Thus, the army marched in echelon with Lyttelton's brigade leading on the left, followed behind but to its right by Wauchope's brigade, then similarly came Maxwell's brigade. The next brigade should have been MacDonald's, but Hunter placed it last in order to secure the army's right flank. Instead, Lewis's 3rd Egyptian Brigade, considered to be rather unsteady, was placed here, but had to march across MacDonald's front to reach its position and ended up some way behind Maxwell's brigade as a result. By the time MacDonald's troops began their march, they were well behind the other brigades and seemingly isolated on the dusty plain. Hunter, though, had provided MacDonald with three batteries of artillery (18 guns) and eight Maxim machine guns. The Camel Corps and Egyptian cavalry were also following on. Collinson's 4th Egyptian Brigade had been left to guard the camp and to bring the transport to Omdurman. The army was now strung out and as à Court later wrote, the 'muddle' was because 'there was no distance named between the brigade echelons when we were ordered to advance. What K. then needed was a good infantry drill man, and he did not happen to have one.' À Court was with Lyttelton's brigade and found Wauchope's marching 'upon our heels in spite of my protests'. A competition was in process between the two British brigades to reach Omdurman first and march discipline consequently

---

14 Lieutenant Colonel Charles À Court Repington, *Vestigia* (London: Constable and Company Ltd., 1919), pp.152–153; Douglas Scott (ed.), *Douglas Haig. The preparatory prologue 1861–1914. Diaries and Letters* (Barnsley: Pen & Sword, 2006), p.102; Colonel F. I. Maxse, *Seymour Vandeleur* (London: The *National Review* Office, 1906. Reprinted: London: Forgotten Books, 2015), pp.227–228.

15 Quoted in Edward M. Spiers, 'Campaigning Under Kitchener', in Edward M. Spiers (ed.) *Sudan. The Reconquest Reappraised* (London: Frank Cass, 1998), p.72.

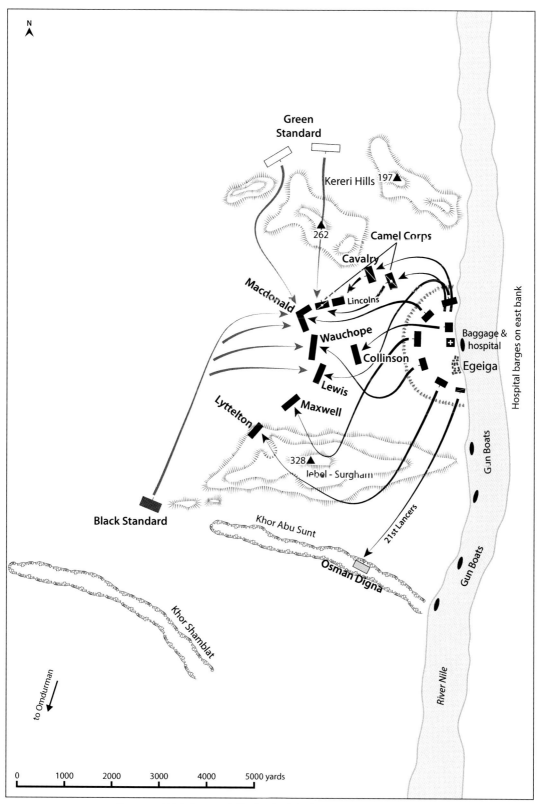

N

Green
Standard

Kereri Hills 197 ▲

262 ▲

Camel Corps

Cavalry

Macdonald

Lincolns

Wauchope

Collinson

Baggage &
hospital

Egeiga

Lewis

Lyttelton

Maxwell

328 ▲

Jebel - Surgham

Hospital barges on east bank

Black Standard

Khor Abu Sunt

21st Lancers

Osman Digna

Gun Boats

Gun Boats

Khor Shamblat

River Nile

to Omdurman

| 0 | 1000 | 2000 | 3000 | 4000 | 5000 yards |

The second Mahdists attack. The Battle of Omdurman, 2 September 1898.

foundered. As the troops marched they came under occasional attack from Mahdist wounded: Captain Egerton wrote that 'a seemingly dead man rose to his feet and began slashing with a large two-handed sword at the men nearest him. In a moment four or five of my men were round like wasps, and he fell bayoneted to rise no more.' Lyttelton wrote that 'There was some work in bayonetting the wounded but it had to be done. They hold up their hands for mercy & when the men passes on they fire at them. I am afraid some of the men thoroughly enjoyed their work.' Indeed, as one private admitted: 'We finished them off, and the Sudanese finished them off too.'[16] Nevertheless, as Captain Churcher recalled, 'crowds of prisoners and deserters came in from all directions', attesting that the killing was not totally indiscriminate.[17]

As they headed for the eastern ridge of Jebel Surgham, the British brigades were soon far ahead of Maxwell's Egyptian brigade.[18] Colonel Lewis, from his position in the plain, heading more towards the western ridge of Jebel Surgham, now saw 'Dervishes under a large Black Flag … on my right, but though I pointed them out was ordered to march on and catch up my place in the echelon.'[19] None of the three brigades ahead of Lewis could see Ya'qub's force moving around the western end of Jebel Surgham. Lyttelton's brigade was heading towards the scene of the 21st Lancers' charge from where it would swing west expecting to intercept fleeing Mahdists and cut them off from Omdurman. Wauchope's brigade would have followed but was stopped as events began to change dramatically after Maxwell's brigade was ordered to clear Mahdist riflemen from the top of Jebel Surgham. Major Smith-Dorrien's 13th Sudanese Battalion accomplished this task, climbing and firing some 200 feet to the top. Once there, they began to engage Mahdists on the western slope and realised that another huge force of the enemy was deployed below the western ridge.[20] By then, Ya'qub's force was on the move, mostly towards MacDonald's isolated brigade, although one group split off to attack Maxwell's men on top of Jebel Surgham. This was led by Muhammad al Mahdi, a son of the Mahdi himself, and included Muhammad Wad Bishara, the former governor of Dongola, both of whom were killed as were many of their men. Maxwell's troops now began firing on Ya'qub's main force and this compelled him to launch his attack against MacDonald's brigade. Goaded by the sight of Ibrahim al Khalil's body being brought down from the slopes of Jebel Surgham, Ya'qub raised his spear, rode along the front line of his men exhorting them to action and led the charge himself. His thousands rose up, banners flying and surged towards the isolated enemy.[21] MacDonald was aware that Mahdist forces were to his front and had deployed his 3,000 men

16 Egerton, *With the 72nd*, p.38; QM: Lyttelton Papers, NL/2/9/NGL/KL/507, Lyttelton to his wife, 5 September 1898. Edward M. Spiers, *The Scottish Soldier and Empire, 1854–1902* (Edinburgh: Edinburgh University Press), p.145.

17 NAM: 1978-04-53, Churcher Diary, 2 September 1898, p.15.

18 À Court, *Vestigia*, p.169.

19 NAM: 1975-03-9, Lewis Journal, 2 September 1898, p.13.

20 General Sir Horace Smith-Dorrien, *Memories of Forty-Eight Years' Service* (London: John Murray, 1925; Kindle e-book, Pickle Partners Publishing, 2013), Chapter 6, unpaginated, (text search required).

21 Zulfo, *Karari*, pp.212–213.

accordingly. His artillery opened fire at 1,100 yards and MacDonald noted that 'No sooner had we opened fire than up went innumerable standards amongst them a prominent black one, the Khalifas [*sic*] and they opened a furious fusillade and at once bore down upon us.'[22] Luckily for MacDonald, Ya'qub's force had only 1,000 firearms, the rest of the force, some 12,000, were armed with sword and spear and their only chance was to get close to the enemy. MacDonald requested help from Lewis's brigade but Lewis was unaware of his predicament and refused because of his explicit instructions to advance on Omdurman. One of Lewis's officers, Brevet Major Sparkes, described Lewis as a 'gallant little chap' but felt that 'he now lost the chance of his life' and should have gone to MacDonald's aid: 'we should have shared the whole fight and made their casualties considerably greater.'[23]

By now, the 9th Sudanese, the brigade's right-flank battalion, began to fire without orders and this was taken up by the other battalions to its left, the 10th Sudanese, the 2nd Egyptians, and the 11th Sudanese. The artillery and Maxims were deployed between the 9th and 10th Battalions. The men were so excited that MacDonald and other officers rode out in front knocking up their rifles. After a reprimand from MacDonald, the brigade calmed down and then, when ordered, delivered a series of devastating volleys, followed by independent fire. Still the ranks of the Mahdists came forward and the artillery changed to case shot, becoming in effect massive shotguns. 'So rapid was our fire', wrote one officer, 'that above the sound of the explosions could be heard the swish of our bullets going through the air just like the swish of water.' Mahdist riflemen lay down to fire on the enemy and despite the inferiority of their weapons, they were not armed with Remingtons but the leftovers from the arsenal, 'kept up a pretty hot fire'. [24] The Mahdists had advanced to within 400 yards of MacDonald's line and then began to waver. They were now under severe fire from Lewis's brigade, which had come up on their right flank and also were being fired upon by Maxwell's men, the Maxims and the 32nd Field Battery on Jebel Surgham. 'I do not claim that we helped much', wrote Lewis, 'but we were a great moral support.'[25]

Ya'qub had been killed, spear in hand, and his force was now disintegrating under the fire of Kitchener's army. Many began fleeing westwards into the desert. The great Black Flag was planted by its guards as an act of defiance and a rallying point. By the time it was captured 100 men lay dead around it with another 200 wounded. The flag was taken by Brevet Major Hickman of the 15th Sudanese to Kitchener, who had watched the action from Jebel Surgham. Some 2,000 Mahdists were captured while 4,500 were killed or wounded.[26] Many Mahdists had sought martyrdom, driven by their religious devotion or fanaticism, while others had not. Babikr Badri and his friends belie the former image of the religious fanatic. They had kept their heads

22   'Fighting Mac 1898. Page 2 of an original letter by Major General Sir Hector Macdonald,' *Soldiers of the Queen*, 94, (1998), p.24.
23   NAM: 1966-04-44, Sparkes Papers, Sparkes to Mr Turmure, 13 September 1898.
24   An Officer, (Lieutenant H. L. Pritchard), *The Sudan Campaign, 1896-1899* (London: Chapman & Hall Ltd., 1899), p.208.
25   NAM: 1975-03-9, Lewis Journal, 2 September 1898, p.13.
26   Zulfo, *Karari*, pp.216–217.

down throughout the attack, lying behind a small sand hill. 'I rubbed my face into the sand trying to bury my head in it, thoughtless of suffocation, so distracted was I by the fear of death,' wrote Bedri. Pretending to be wounded by tying a bloodied bandage around his left arm, the blood coming from his friend who had suffered a minor wound, Bedri allowed his friends the customary right to take him off the battlefield, after which they managed to return to Omdurman safely.[27]

Meanwhile, MacDonald's brigade had no time to reflect on their victory because just as the Black Flag's attack faltered, the Camel Corps reported that the Green Flags of Shaykh al Din and Abu Siwa were now streaming down from the Kereri hills and readying to attack. MacDonald did not hesitate and he told his officers what they would do next: he would disengage the brigade from fighting Ya'qub's forces, leaving them to Lewis, and then swing the brigade to face north to meet the oncoming enemy. He swung round the 9th Sudanese, who for the time being became the left-hand battalion, while the 2nd Egyptians covered their left rear from the survivors of the Black Flag. Major Laurie's artillery battery was placed on the right of the 9th; on the artillery's right came the 11th Sudanese battalion, then came the artillery battery of Captain Peak. Soon, the 10th Sudanese rushed to take up its position on Peak's right, followed by the artillery battery of Captain De Rougemont. His open right flank was then covered by the Camel Corps. The Maxim guns were placed at various points within the new line. While this manoeuvre was being undertaken, splendidly disciplined though it was, the brigade was coming under heavy fire from the *mulazimin* of Shaykh al Din's force and had no time to get smartly into order. Indeed, MacDonald's brigade suffered 120 casualties in 20 minutes, while the Camel Corps suffered 40 losses.[28] The Mahdists advanced steadily, firing all the time, being continually reinforced by hundreds still pouring over the hills. But when they were 700 yards away from MacDonald's brigade, the Mahdists were met by devastating salvoes from its artillery, coupled with the withering fire of the Maxims. Abu Siwar was killed but still the Mahdists advanced through the dust and smoke. At 500 yards, the *mulazimin* ran out of ammunition; they drew their swords and spears and advanced in 16 successive waves but each one was shot down. According to Steevens, being one who was there, the Mahdists 'were superb, beyond perfection. A dusky line got up stormed forward: it bent, broke up, fell apart, and disappeared. Before the smoke had cleared, another line was bending and storming forward in the same attack.'[29] Finally, several hundred Dighaim horsemen tried to charge MacDonald's left flank but all were annihilated. In defeating Ya'qub's force and those of the Green Flags, the troops of MacDonald's brigade had expended 160,000 rounds of ammunition and were down to two bullets apiece by the time the Mahdists broke. A few Mahdists had managed to get to the firing line but were killed by bayonets before they could inflict any losses themselves. By

27   Babikr Bedri, *The Memoirs of Babikr Bedri* (London: Oxford University Press, 1969), pp.236–240.

28   Ziegler, *Omdurman*, p.173; An Officer, *Sudan Campaign*, p.212.

29   G. W. Steevens, *With Kitchener to Khartum* (Edinburgh and London: William Blackwood and Sons, 1898), p.282.

this time, ensuring the Mahdists did not rally, MacDonald had been joined on his left first by Wauchope's men, and then to Wauchope's left by Lewis's brigade, whose combined fire shot down many of those retreating. When the attack of the Green Flags came on, Kitchener was now well aware of the situation having received a request from Hunter for a British brigade to help MacDonald. Although Wauchope was directly ordered by Kitchener promptly to head to the left, Wauchope instead detached the Lincolns to the right in support of the Camel Corps. By the time the Lincolns arrived and began firing, the Mahdists were already breaking, allowing MacDonald to bring the 2nd Egyptians into the line as he ordered the whole brigade to advance. Mahdist survivors were unable to rally even if they had wanted to, as the whole AEA, now including Collinson's 4th Egyptians, pivoted westwards and began to march towards the desert, driving the Mahdists before them. The Egyptian cavalry and Camel Corps swept forward to cut down the few who resisted. Around 11:30 a.m., or possibly slightly later, Kitchener ordered the infantry to halt. Hunter had been impressed by MacDonald's brigade and later told Rundle: 'But chief and foremost in the incidents of the 2nd of Sept. up to noon … was the action of MacDonald's brigade in its final grapple with the enemy. One is also compelled to offer a tribute of admiration to the desperate gallantry of the foe.'[30]

'Desperate gallantry' was all that could be said of the Mahdist performance during the battle. The Khalifa's plan, such as it was, had been smashed by the firepower of the British and Egyptian divisions. Where the plan had worked, as the AEA emerged from the *zariba* and had left MacDonald's brigade isolated, the Khalifa's lack of command and control over his scattered forces had meant that they could not be brought to the crucial point quickly enough, leaving the units of the Black Flag and the Green Flags to be defeated in detail. The lack of proper leadership among the Mahdist generals also played its part. Ya'qub had never commanded a large force and his inexperience meant he missed the opportunity to attack MacDonald's brigade sooner. Shaykh al Din's lack of leadership was evident when he made a fatal error and allowed his *mulazimin* to go chasing after Broadwood. Moreover, Abu Siwar, who had kept his force in check, not going beyond the Kereri hills, could have helped Ya'qub. Instead, he and his men sat watching the latter's defeat, awaiting the return of Shaykh al Din's exhausted warriors. If all had gone to plan MacDonald's brigade might have been annihilated, and his supporting EA artillery lost along with the eight Maxims as well as the Camel Corps. Might Kitchener's army have broken afterwards? Lewis's brigade certainly contained one unreliable battalion, the 7th Egyptians, which had wobbled when confronting Ya'qub's masses. Hunter said its performance had 'left much to be desired and their bad example might have had a disastrous effect'.[31] It was also possible that Collinson's isolated and inexperienced brigade might

30   SAD: SAD 964: General Sir Archibald Hunter Papers. Sudan Campaigns: May-October 1898, 964/4/15, Hunter to Rundle, 7 September 1898, p.50; Archie Hunter, *Kitchener's sword-arm. The Life and Campaigns of General Sir Archibald Hunter* (Staplehurst: Spellmount, 1996), pp.97–100; Ziegler, *Omdurman*, pp.168, 172–173; An Officer, *Sudan Campaign*, pp.212–214.
31   SAD: Hunter Papers, Sudan Campaigns, 964/4/30, Hunter to Rundle, 7 September 1898, p.65.

have succumbed to panic too, although he could have retreated back to the *zariba*, to be supported by the gunboats. Nevertheless, the remaining AEA units held the high ground and were supported by the 32nd Field Battery with them. The Egyptian cavalry had remained intact too. The brigades of Wauchope, Lyttelton and Maxwell, would have been able to deploy significant firepower. If there were to be hand-to-hand fighting, they might still have won but with significant losses. The damage to Kitchener's career of such losses would have been mortal. But MacDonald was not defeated and Kitchener's career was in the ascendant. The AEA's task had been helped by the Mahdist's failure to appreciate who or what they were fighting against.[32]

The Khalifa by this time was in Omdurman having fled with survivors such as Osman Digna and the wounded deputy khalifa, Ali Wad Helu; Shaykh al Din joined them later. The Khalifa tried to rally others by having the great drum, the *Noggara*, beaten and the huge elephant tusk, the *ummbaya*, blown, but to no avail. Eventually, he went to pray in the wreckage of the Mahdi's tomb. Sometime in the late afternoon, the Khalifa, his family and followers fled the city, first going south and then turning west, reaching Umm Ghunaym on 5 September.[33]

After a short halt, Kitchener also began the march south to Omdurman, his right flank covered by the Egyptian cavalry and Camel Corps, who continued to hassle the Mahdist survivors in the desert. The troops passed many wounded and dying Mahdists. One showed his wound to the journalist Ernest Bennett: 'A shell splinter had struck the miserable man full in front, and literally ripped his body open from side to side. Another man lay face downward upon the sand, breathing bubbles through a pool of gore, and actually drowning in his own blood.'[34] Again, little mercy was shown to wounded Mahdists, especially those who continued to resist. Major Townshend recounted that some 'were getting up and firing at us as we passed, and our men were shooting them dead'. Bennett would afterwards censure Kitchener and the army for deliberately killing the wounded; even Churchill, writing to his mother, spoke of the 'inhuman slaughter of the wounded and that Kitchener was responsible for this'.[35] In response, Gatacre wrote that if the wounded tried to kill a British soldier he 'would be excused for shooting at his disabled enemy; in principle it would be wrong, but in practice it becomes a necessity'. The Anglican chaplain, Owen S. Watkins, later took issue with Bennett but admitted that some wounded had indeed been killed but only if they were deemed armed and therefore dangerous. 'In no single instance did I see an unarmed man slain; those who were killed were all showing fight and in many cases were bayoneted in the act of firing

32   Churchill, *River War*, vol. 2, pp.153, 335; Zulfo, *Karari*, pp.218-221 & 230; Henry Keown Boyd, *A Good Dusting. A Centenary Review of the Sudan campaigns 1883-1899* (London: Guild Publishing, 1986), p.235.

33   Zulfo, *Karari*, pp.222–223, 232–233, 238–239; Bedri, *Memoirs*, pp.238–239, 242.

34   Ernest N. Bennett, *The Downfall of the Dervishes* (London: Methuen & Co. 1898. Reprinted: London: Forgotten Books, 2012), pp.190–191.

35   N. S. Nash. *Chitral Charlie. The rise and fall of Major General Charles Townshend* (Barnsley: Pen & Sword Military, 2010), p.114; E. N. Bennett, 'After Omdurman', *Contemporary Review*, 75, (Jan. 1899), pp.18–33; Churchill, *Youth*, p.424. Ziegler, *Omdurman*, pp.185–186.

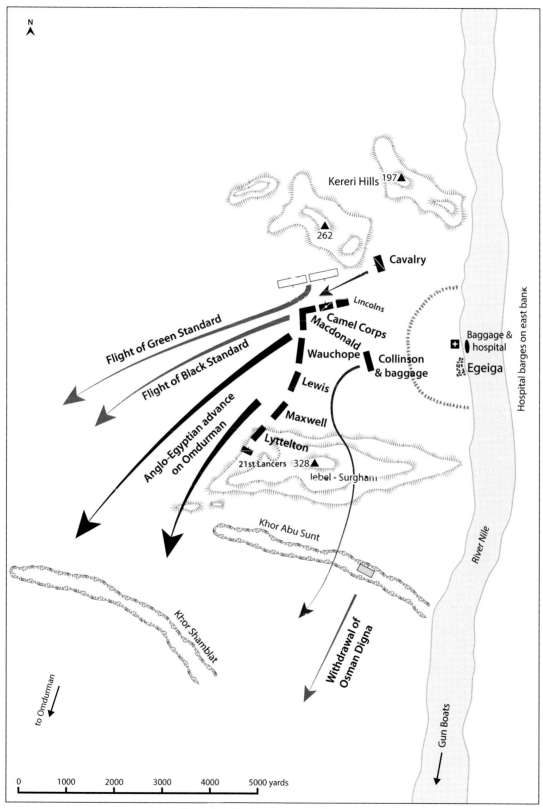

N

Kereri Hills 197 ▲

262 ▲

Cavalry

Lincolns

Camel Corps
Macdonald

Flight of Green Standard

Flight of Black Standard

Wauchope

Collinson
& baggage

Baggage &
hospital

Egeiga

Lewis

Anglo-Egyptian advance
on Omdurman

Maxwell

Lyttelton

21st Lancers 328 ▲

Jebel - Surgham

Khor Abu Sunt

Khor Shamblat

Withdrawal of
Osman Digna

to Omdurman

River Nile

Hospital barges on east bank

Gun Boats

0   1000   2000   3000   4000   5000 yards

Onwards to Omdurman, 2 September 1898.

on our men.'[36] This was an issue that was later ignored by the Victorian public and it did no harm to Kitchener's reputation or his career.

The AEA stopped at the Khor Shambat for some rest but many British soldiers drank from the filthy pools within it. Captain Granville, for example, told his mother, 'At 4 p.m., we got to a filthy Khor … of stagnant water, simply liquid manure, which my thirst compelled me to drink about a gallon of.' Bennett's account mentions that in some 'shallower parts', dead horses, mules and donkeys could be seen. 'The want of self-control and common sense at this *khor* may quite well be partly responsible for the large numbers of typhoid cases which subsequently occurred.'[37]

Leaving most of the army behind, Kitchener moved off with Maxwell's brigade and the 32nd Field Battery at about 2:30 p.m. and entered Omdurman. The population warily watched the troops wondering whether they would be massacred, but when the keys of the town were presented to Kitchener and he affirmed that nothing would happen if there was no resistance, the population rejoiced and started greeting the troops as liberators. Kitchener's affirmation was the crucial point, as one officer related: 'In this way the Sirdar obtained possession of the town with practically no house-to-house fighting, and so saved the many lives which such fighting would have cost.'[38] Eventually, Kitchener and the 13th Sudanese under Major Smith-Dorrien came to the Khalifa's walled enclosure but as there was no obvious way in they skirted the wall to their left towards the river bank and once reaching it they turned right heading south, looking for an opening. There was some skirmishing as the 13th had to deal with the survivors of the wrecked forts and all had to cross a deep, filthy, drainage channel. The first smashed gate they came to led to the *Bait al mal*, the treasury which was full of food and other taxes paid in kind. Later, Kitchener would open the grain stores to the population and as Bedri remarks, 'this was the first good action of Lord Kitchener to the poor and hungry.'[39]

Then, they came to a second gate which the men opened and the 13th were soon inside the Khalifa's compound. They led the way along an avenue that stretched to the Mahdi's tomb. Smith-Dorrien and Major Maxse kicked open one door that led to an empty courtyard, while another was opened and led to the open area around the mosque. This space was crammed with wounded who were being tended by their families. As they moved towards the southern end of the enclosure, two Baggara, one horseman, the other on foot, dashed out and speared a Sudanese corporal through the head: 'it took off the top', wrote Maxse, 'just like the top of a boiled egg': both Baggara were killed.[40] Kitchener and his staff, including Hunter, arrived at the Mahdi's tomb, where they were fired on four times by the 32nd Field Battery

---

36   W. Gatacre, 'After the Atbara and Omdurman', *Contemporary Review*, 75, (Feb.1900), pp.299–304; Owen S. Watkins, *With Kitchener's Army* (London: S. W. Partridge & Co., 1899), pp.189–190.

37   NAM: 2004-03-31, Granville to his mother, 15th September 1898; Bennett, *Downfall*, p.194.

38   An Officer, *Sudan Campaign*, pp.217–218; Ziegler, *Omdurman*, pp.193–194.

39   Bedri, *Memoirs*, p.240.

40   An Officer, *Sudan Campaign*, p.218; WSRO: Maxse Mss 219, F. I. Maxse Papers, Maxse to his father, 13 September 1898, pp.18–22.

positioned further north. The gunners had seen the Black Flag that was being carried behind Kitchener and thought the Khalifa was preparing to fight. This friendly fire killed the journalist Hubert Howard, who had taken part in the charge of the 21st Lancers. Kitchener then moved on to the prison and ordered the release of those within, especially the Europeans who had been held there since Khartoum fell in 1885.

Now realising that the Khalifa had escaped, the AEA, after marching into Omdurman with bands playing, settled down for the night. 'But in the tortuous, sweltering lanes and enclosures of the wicked city there was no rest or sleep', wrote Egerton, 'murder, rapine, and every devilment stalked the streets, and I imagine there is little doubt that therein some of the soldiers of the Soudanese troops took a very free hand.'[41] Indeed, many of the Sudanese had scores to settle. Bedri records that one soldier turned up at a house where he had been a slave since childhood. He was welcomed but then shot the owner dead and stamped on the corpse's stomach. Bedri saw an incident where a soldier was dragging away a slave-girl and then shot her owner when he remonstrated; both soldier and girl went off laughing, they were brother and sister and had known their former owner since birth.[42] Moreover, the Sudanese soldiers had been joined by the Ja'alins attached to Stuart-Wortley's force who had crossed the river to seek their revenge on those who had massacred their tribe in 1897.

One of Ernest Bennett's criticisms of Kitchener was that nothing was done for the Mahdist wounded. Wingate explained that 'To attempt the medical treatment of so vast a number was manifestly beyond the capabilities of the military field hospitals.' One field hospital was established at Khor Shambat for any who could crawl to it; while another was established in Omdurman for those who had managed to get back. This was supervised by a former prisoner, an Egyptian doctor, Hassan Effendi Zaki and the help provided evidently 'elicited their [the wounded] gratitude and surprise.'[43] For those left on the battlefield nothing was done until 3 September when food and water was sent out to them. Hundreds had survived their terrible wounds, some would linger for days: 'These wretched creatures', wrote Burleigh, 'had been seen crawling or dragging themselves for miles to get to the Nile for water or into villages for succour.'[44] It seems those wounded who had no friends or relatives in Omdurman were left to the tender mercies of fate, the sun, vultures, jackals, and marauders.

Bennett also condemned the destruction of the Mahdi's tomb and the desecration of his remains which were thrown into the river. The skull was kept back, Kitchener toying with ideas about what to do with it. Eventually, it was buried at Wadi Halfa following a missive from an outraged Queen Victoria. Kitchener justified the destruction as necessary for 'political

---

41 Egerton, *With the 72nd*, p.44.
42 Bedri, *Memoirs*, p.241.
43 TNA: Kitchener Papers, PRO 30/57/14/M11, (No.2), Sir F. R. Wingate, 'Note on the Dervish wounded at Omdurman', 3 March 1899; Bennett, 'After Omdurman', p.26. Ziegler, *Omdurman*, p.217.
44 Burleigh, *Khartoum*, p.233.

A depiction of the memorial
service to General Gordon
amidst the ruins of Khartoum.
(*Illustrated London News*)

considerations', a view that was backed up by Cromer as 'justifiable, but very necessary'. While some voices in Britain supported Bennett, the public did not and Kitchener's reputation, perhaps strengthened by his apparent ruthlessness, was instead enhanced further.[45]

Then, on 4 September 1898, the campaign to take Omdurman was completed by a ceremony across the river in the ruins of Khartoum, at the place where Gordon had been killed. The flags of Britain and Egypt were hoisted, hymns were sung and Kitchener was seen to cry.[46] Gordon had been avenged, but the job had not been completed – the Khalifa was still at large and a French force had arrived on the Nile.

---

45   TNA: Kitchener Papers, PRO 30/57/14//M11, Nos 1 & 2: Kitchener to Cromer, 1 February 1899; Cromer to Salisbury, 17 February, 4, 12 March 1899, pp.2–3; Ziegler, *Omdurman*, pp.220–221.

46   Ziegler, *Omdurman*, pp.224–229.

Chapter 9

To Fashoda, the Blue Nile and Kordofan 1898-1899

On 3 September 1898, Kitchener opened secret orders that revealed the British government suspected the presence either of the French or the Abyssinians at Fashoda, about 500 miles south of Khartoum. If the intruders were French troops, Kitchener was to deny that they had any right to be at that location and was given a free-hand to deal with the intrusion. He was also to impress on the French that their presence generally 'in the Nile Valley is an infringement of the rights both of Great Britain and of the Khedive'.[1]

By the time Kitchener sailed up the Nile on 10 September it was known that the intruders were indeed French. Five days earlier, a damaged Mahdist gunboat had arrived in Omdurman from Fashoda, unaware of the Khalifa's defeat. The gunboat's captain confirmed he had fought Europeans and was able to describe their flag. Armed with this knowledge, Kitchener took Wingate and an Egyptian artillery battery with him in the gunboat, *Dal*, while the *Nasir* and the *Fateh* carried the 11th and 13th Sudanese Battalions and 100 Cameron Highlanders. Accompanying them was the *Sultan* and on 14 September the flotilla was joined by the *Abu Klea*.

On 15 September, at Dem el Zeki, the Mahdists who had attacked the French weeks earlier were engaged by Kitchener's flotilla. Most of the Mahdists fled into the bush, while their last remaining gunboat, the *Safia*, was badly damaged. Apart from this action, the journey south was without incident and for Wingate something of a tonic. 'I have made up some sleep', he told his wife, 'I feel a different creature and am really enjoying the journey which is most interesting and the scenery in parts quite beautiful'. To his son, Wingate was more jovial: 'At all the villages we stop at we are welcomed with shouts and yells of delight but I expect our Froggy friends at Fashoda won't appreciate our visit.'[2]

---

1   Quoted in Darrell Bates, *The Fashoda Incident of 1898. Encounter on the Nile* (Oxford: Oxford University Press, 1984), p.127.

2   M. W. Daley (ed.), 'Omdurman and Fashoda 1898. Edited and annotated letters of F. R. Wingate', *Bulletin (British Society for Middle Eastern Studies)*, 10:1 (1983), pp.24–25; SAD: SAD 233: Wingate Papers, 233/5/95, to Ronald, 13 September 1898.

One important advantage held by Kitchener was the presence among his Sudanese soldiers of men from the Shilluk and Dinka tribes, through whose country the flotilla was now sailing. These local soldiers would be vital in cementing British and Egyptian authority in the area and undermining that of the French. On 14 September, for example, Shilluk tribesmen became agitated as the flotilla passed by and Wingate related that 'our soldier-Shilluks made them understand that we were friends'.[3] Some villagers were brought along and then sent to Kaka to inform the Shilluk king, (the Mek or *reth*), one Nur Nyidok, also known as Kur Abd al Fadil, of Kitchener's arrival. Later, on 18 September, local Shilluks accompanied two Shilluk soldiers who carried Kitchener's letter protesting against the French presence, to Captain Marchand, the French commander at Fashoda,[4]

Marchand's reply, which came the next day, 'staggered' Kitchener with its presumption. Marchand had boldly asserted that he had fulfilled the orders of his government to occupy Fashoda and lay claim to the Bahr al Ghazal region. He had taken the Shilluk country under his protection after having signed a treaty with the Mek. Kitchener, stated Marchand in his note, was welcome to visit 'in the name of France'. The size of Kitchener's flotilla had not, it seemed, overawed the French force of about 120 officers and men. On 20 September, Marchand and one of his officers, Captain Germain, came aboard the *Dal* to meet Kitchener and Wingate. The upshot of the meeting, which was cordial, was that Marchand insisted he would stick to his position unless ordered to leave by the French government. He raised no objection, however, to the raising of the Egyptian flag nearby, a demand that Kitchener and Wingate had argued over the night before because Kitchener had initially wanted the British flag raised as well. It was agreed that the whole matter should be referred to the governments in London and Paris. After toasting this compromise, Wingate went ashore to select a spot for the Egyptian flag, which was done at 1:00 p.m. Two hours later, Kitchener himself came ashore with his officers and visited the French position, where more drinks were consumed amidst a convivial atmosphere. As he was leaving, the French presented Kitchener with a gift of flowers and vegetables; Kitchener, in return, presented Marchand with a formal letter of protest, returned to the *Dal*, and set off with most of his force to the point where the Sobat river joined the Nile.[5]

To keep a watch on the French, Kitchener left behind the *Abu Klea*, while Major H. W. Jackson, his 11th Sudanese Battalion and four artillery pieces were established about 300 yards south of the French post, which occupied the only high ground in the area. Jackson's command was soon made miserable when heavy rain fell every evening, saturating the ground

3   Daly (ed.), 'Omdurman and Fashoda', Wingate to his wife, 14 September 1898, p.27.
4   David Levering Lewis, *The Race to Fashoda* (New York: Weidenfeld & Nicolson, 1987), pp.206–209; Ronald M. Lamothe, *Slaves of Fortune. Sudanese soldiers & the River War 1896–1898* (Woodbridge: James Currey, 2011), pp.179–180.
5   Daly (ed.), 'Omdurman and Fashoda', Wingate to his wife, 18 and 23 September 1898, pp.29-32; General Sir Horace Smith-Dorrien, *Memories of Forty–Eight Years' Service (Illustrated Edition)* (London: John Murray, 1925; Kindle e-book, Pickle Partners Publishing, 2013), Chapter 7, unpaginated (text search required). Bates, *Fashoda Incident*, pp.130–134.

and giving rise to swarms of mosquitos. Having come from the desert, Jackson's command was not prepared for tropical weather and all their equipment and supplies were soaked. They had brought no comforts and had only blankets and hastily constructed *tukls* (huts) for shelter, which collapsed under the wind and downpours. The French, meanwhile, were well protected, having set out from Africa's west coast and marched across the central tropical zone, a journey of some 2796 miles.[6]

On leaving Fashoda. Kitchener and his flotilla sailed south up the Nile for over 60 miles until they reached the river Sobat. The flotilla then sailed south-east up the Sobat looking for any Abyssinian outposts, but found none. Returning to the Nile, Kitchener left behind at the junction three companies of the 13th Sudanese, under two British officers, the remaining two artillery pieces and two Maxims. Major H. Smith-Dorrien was ordered to ensure the post was properly established and then to return forthwith in the *Fatteh*. Thankfully for Smith-Dorrien he did not have to stay long because the area contained 'heavy rank vegetation and the largest mosquitoes I have ever seen'.[7] Meanwhile, Kitchener and Wingate in the *Dal*, sailed past Fashoda on 21 September and at that moment, Lieutenant Cowan, commanding the *Sultan*, delivered Kitchener's second letter of protest to Marchand, and received in return Marchand's own protest note for Kitchener. Cowan could not do anything with this note because the *Sultan* had been detailed to remain behind. He tried to pass it on to Smith-Dorrien as he returned in the *Fatteh*, but he refused to accept it. Marchand's letter was instead handed back and Fashoda, with its French occupants, was effectively cut off from the rest of the world.[8]

While sailing away up the Nile to the Sobat river, Kitchener and Wingate composed their

CAPTAIN J. B. MARCHAND,
In Command of the French Expedition to Fashoda.

CAPTAIN J. M. GERMAIN.

Captains J. B. Marchand and J. M. Germain, who by occupying Fashoda with their small force of French officers and Senegalese soldiers, nearly caused a war with Britain. (*Illustrated London News*)

6   H. W. Jackson, 'Fashoda 1898', *Sudan Notes and Records*, 3:1 (1920), pp.1–3.

7   Smith-Dorrien, *Memories*, (Kindle e-book), Chapter 7, unpaginated (text search required).

8   G. N. Sanderson, *England, Europe & the Upper Nile 1882–1899* (Edinburgh: Edinburgh University Press, 1965), pp.336–337; Smith-Dorrien, *Memories*, (Kindle e-book), Chapter 7, unpaginated (text search required).

own version of events and their opinions of Marchand's position now that the latter was isolated. Kitchener's telegrams and his despatch told of Marchand's desperate plight, and the tale of a small, brave band of intrepid soldier-explorers who were now in a hopeless position. Wingate certainly felt this, as he explained to his wife: 'Thus the poor Froggies are virtually our prisoners ... shut up in a position hundreds of miles distant from their nearest support, and with which it will take months to communicate, with scarcely any ammunition and supplies ... though one cannot help feeling pity for the poor wretches, [for] they fully realize the futility of all their efforts and will be glad to be recalled as we shall be to get rid of them.'[9]

On 24 and 25 September 1898, Kitchener sent two telegrams to London with the first news of the 'incident'. These gave a flavour of what was written in the despatch, which did not arrive in Britain until October. Meanwhile, an abridged version was telegraphed from Cairo to London on 29 September.[10] 'For all its value as propaganda', according to one historian, 'Kitchener's account was grossly misleading as a factual appreciation.' Indeed, the French force was certainly much better off than Jackson's command and when Marchand arrived in Cairo in November to communicate with his government, he was incensed on reading Kitchener's version of the discussions at Fashoda.[11]

Nevertheless, while Marchand was away, relations between his deputy, Captain Germain, and Jackson deteriorated owing to Germain's hostility. He broke the earlier agreement between Kitchener and Marchand that they sit still and await events and instead sought to communicate with the Abyssinians, and also began to build a fortification. Jackson's response was to withdraw 300 yards further south, to persuade the Shilluks to stop sending the French food supplies and to send a gunboat up the Sobat to prevent any French and Abyssinian discussions. The agreement with the Shilluks was particularly effective. Jackson handled the matter with some care, not wishing to start a war. Thankfully, the newly-promoted Major Marchand returned in December and relations eased because Marchand had received orders to withdraw from Fashoda.[12]

In Europe, France had backed down after the British government had told the French that before any talks could take place, Marchand's expedition would have to be withdrawn; the British had also begun to make war preparations by mobilising elements of the Royal Navy. French public opinion was divided over whether Fashoda was worth fighting for, and was already riven by the Dreyfus case, while French politics were generally febrile. The French navy was not in a position to confront the Royal Navy, while France's ally, Russia, was not interested in the possibility of war with Britain over an area of the world that was of no interest. Thus, on 3 November 1898, just as he had arrived in Cairo, Marchand had received his orders to withdraw

9   Daly (ed.), 'Omdurman and Fashoda', Wingate to his wife, 23 September 1898, p.31.
10   Bates, *Fashoda Incident*, pp.136–137.
11   Sanderson, *England* p.339; Lewis, *Race to Fashoda*, p.226.
12   Jackson, 'Fashoda 1898', pp.5–7; Sanderson, *England*, pp.343–344.

from Fashoda, which he and his men did on 11 December 1898.[13] They reached Djibouti in French Somaliland on the east coast on 16 May 1899, thus completing a full west to east transit of Africa.

While Kitchener's account of Marchand's position had been exaggerated, it nevertheless fulfilled the function that both he and Wingate had intended. It had also given the French a reason to order Marchand's withdrawal, enabling them to save face. As no conflict had taken place at Fashoda, which the British had renamed Kodok to spare French susceptibilities, relations between the two countries remained cordial and would lead to diplomatic discussions that culminated in the 1904 *Entente Cordiale*. Together, Kitchener and Wingate had played an astute diplomatic game.[14] Britain was left in control of the whole Nile valley and the territory of Bahr al Gazal and all that was left for them to do now was to eliminate the last vestiges of Mahdism.

Smith-Dorrien arrived back at Omdurman on 25 September but his stay was to be short-lived. On 7 October, he, along with the 13th Sudanese Battalion, were sent up the Blue Nile to take part in operations against a Mahdist emir, Ahmed Fedil, who was based at Gedaref to the east of Khartoum.

Ahmed Fedil was a devoted follower of the Khalifa and had been summoned by his master to join him at Omdurman for the great battle. But as he had approached the White Nile, Ahmed Fedil had heard of the Khalifa's defeat. He had then hoped to join the Khalifa in Kordofan but his men had demanded that they first return to Gedaref to gather their families before setting off once again to cross the White Nile. On nearing Gedaref they learned that the town had already fallen to the EA.

Earlier, on 5 September, Lieutenant Colonel C. Parsons, whose force had occupied Kassala in late-1897, had heard about the battle of Omdurman and the next day had received a note from the War Office instructing him to capture Gedaref, a feat thought possible owing to Ahmed Fedil's absence. On 7 September, Parsons set off with a small force and reached the swollen, fast-flowing Atbara river two days later. It took a week for Parsons' force to cross because the men had to construct their own boats. Once across, a brisk march brought Parsons to Gedaref and as his small army approached the town on 22 September, it was confronted by the 3,000 men of the garrison, under Emir Saadulla. Parsons commanded 500 men of the 16th Egyptian Battalion, 450 men of an Arab Battalion that had formerly belonged to the Italians, 350 Sudanese irregulars, and 80 men of the Sudanese Slavery Department, mounted on camels, a combined total of just 1,380 men. Parsons quickly positioned his troops on some high ground. The Mahdists attacked, but were soon stopped by rapid rifle fire. As the Mahdists wavered, Parsons ordered the Arab battalion to counter-attack, followed by the Egyptian battalion. But as they began to move down the slope in front, firing was heard from behind because a Mahdist force had outflanked the EA position and began to attack the camels comprising the

---

13   Sanderson, *England*, pp.339–362; Bates, *Fashoda Incident*, pp.151–168; Jackson, 'Fashoda 1898', pp.7–9.

14   Bates, *Fashoda Incident*, pp.140–141.

baggage train. The irregulars fled, but the Slavery Department men held off the Mahdists long enough for Parsons to bring up the Egyptian battalion in support, who then drove off the enemy. Parsons and his plucky force entered Gedaref and received the surrender of the 200 Mahdists who had been left behind and who promptly joined Parsons' command. Two small cannons were also surrendered. Parsons then prepared the town for defence because he had heard that Ahmed Fedil was in the vicinity. On 28 September, Ahmed Fedil's force launched two unsuccessful attacks on Gedaref and were driven back with heavy losses. Leaving behind some 500 dead, they retreated eight miles to the south and began to pillage the local inhabitants. Parsons later lamented that: 'Owing to the small force at my disposal I was unable to prevent looting and the cruel treatment of the natives.'[15] Parsons, however, was now trapped in Gedaref and in need of relief.

Meanwhile, on 19 September, Major General Hunter, commanding the 16th Sudanese Battalion, two Maxim guns, and 20 men of the Royal Irish Fusiliers, had advanced up the Blue Nile in the gunboat, *Tamai*, along with two other gunboats, the *Sheikh* and the *Hafir* – ostensibly to look for Abyssinian incursions. Hunter had also been instructed to offer Ahmed Fedil terms of surrender, but one messenger was shot dead by Ahmed Fedil himself, while he whipped the other and sent him back with a message of defiance.

Hunter's flotilla reached Rosaires on 29 September, about 400 miles south of Khartoum, but a cataract prevented any further advance. Thereafter, Hunter returned down the Blue Nile, having left garrisons at Rosaires, Sennar, and Karkoj. Most of the local chiefs came to Hunter to pledge their loyalty to the new government. Having achieved all he could, Hunter sailed back to Omdurman, arriving there on 2 October 1898. Smith-Dorrien had been left in charge at Abu Harez, which became the EA's main base. Egypt's authority had been re-established and the Abyssinians denied the chance to encroach on Sudanese territory.

It was from Abu Harez that Major General Rundle, Kitchener's chief-of-staff and his deputy now that the Sirdar had returned to Britain for a rest, despatched a relief column under Lieutenant Colonel Collinson to help Parsons at Gedaref. Collinson's column arrived on 21 October, without mishap, but after a gruelling march owing to a lack of water. Nevertheless, Collinson's arrival was timely because Amed Fedil had earlier launched an assault, albeit half-hearted, on Gedaref. Repulsed yet again, Ahmed Fedil retreated towards Karkoj with his men and their families.[16]

From this time until December, Ahmed Fedil dodged and weaved trying to cross the Blue Nile, but he and his army were constantly thwarted by the gunboats. Eventually, the Mahdists moved 20 miles south of Rosaires to Daikhila, knowing that the gunboats could not sail beyond the cataract, and began to cross over to the west bank of the Blue Nile. Lieutenant Colonel

15   TNA: WO 32/6143: Sudan. Nile Expedition. 'Report on recent operations of Kassala troops.' Parsons to chief-of-staff, 12 October 1898, pp.1–5.
16   TNA: WO 32/6143/7700/8976: Sudan. Nile Expedition. Kitchener to the Under-Secretary of State for War, 6 December 1898, pp.3–5.

Lewis was now in charge of the pursuit and on 26 December 1898, he found Ahmed Fedil's force still in the process of crossing the river. The Mahdists were using a large island as a stepping-stone because the river's flow on the eastern side was fairly slow, but on the western side it ran much faster and this was holding up the crossing. Consequently, most of Ahmed Fedil's army was still on the island when Lewis found it. The Mahdists, numbering nearly 3,000 men, prepared for battle by deploying on some sand hills on the island's western side, covered from the river's west-bank heights by Ahmed Fedil and over 300 men, many of whom had rifles. Lewis had at his disposal about 1,000 men, made up of half the 10th Sudanese Battalion, 30 men from the 9th Sudanese, and 400 irregulars under the former Mahdist, Sheik Bakr Mustaja.

After failing to dislodge the Mahdists from the sand hills using long-range fire from his two Maxim guns, Lewis resolved on a two-pronged attack. The irregulars crossed to the southern end of the island, while Lewis led his Sudanese infantry from the north. Lewis's men advanced under heavy fire over open ground and stopped to recover at another line of sand hills. Thinking the battle was over, the Mahdist commander, Emir Saadulla, whom Parsons had defeated at Gedaref, led the Mahdists from their vantage point in a wild attack against Lewis's position. Cheered on by their comrades on the west bank, the Mahdists attacked with their usual abandon and paid the price. Lining their own sand hills, Lewis's men poured rapid rifle fire at short-range into the Mahdist masses, who soon broke and fled and were then attacked by the irregulars coming up from the south. Eventually, about 2,000 men surrendered, along with hundreds of women and children. The Mahdists had lost about 600 killed, many of whom drowned trying to swim to the west bank, including Emir Saadulla. Lewis's force suffered about 180 casualties, some 30 being killed. Lewis had gained a stunning victory, which had once again demonstrated the fighting qualities of the EA's Sudanese soldiers. The Mahdists had forsaken a good defensive position in order to launch an ill-considered attack.

Later, Ahmed Fedil with a small band of loyal adherents managed to cross the White Nile and reach the Khalifa in Kordofan, but without most of his surviving force which had already surrendered after being intercepted at the White Nile by the gunboat, *Metemma* [17]

In Kordofan, Ahmed Fedil was able to join the Khalifa at Jebel Qadir, where the latter had been camped for many weeks. Since fleeing Omdurman in September, the Khalifa had moved around southern Kordofan gathering loyal followers. In January 1899, Colonel Walter Kitchener, the Sirdar's brother, was sent with a small force to kill or capture the Khalifa. At Shirkayla, Colonel Kitchener found the Khalifa with a substantial following, which was much larger than he had been led to believe. Heavily outnumbered and short of water, Walter Kitchener turned and retreated back to the Nile.

---

17 TNA: WO 32/6143: Sudan. Nile Expedition. 'Report on the defeat of Ahmed Fedil' by Lt. Col. D. F. Lewis, 29 December 1898, pp.1–5. Winston Spencer Churchill, *River War. An Historical Account of the Reconquest of the Soudan* (London: Longmans, Green, And Co., 1899), vol. 2, pp.252–287.

Over the following months, famine hit the Kordofan region and no help was given to the inhabitants in the hope that this would undermine support for the Khalifa. Cromer criticised this policy as inhuman, but the Sirdar refused to budge.[18] The famine did affect the Khalifa's following because many deserted him to seek aid. When Walter Kitchener had discovered the Khalifa's encampment in January, the Mahdist host had comprised about 10,000 men; by November, it had dwindled to about half that number.

In November 1899, Wingate received information that the Khalifa was marching towards Omdurman and that Ahmed Fedil was raiding along the west bank of the river Nile in search of food for his master's army. On 21 November, Wingate set out with 3,700 men to the wells at Gedid. The following day, he caught up with Ahmed Fedil's force and sent Colonel Mahon ahead with one company of Egyptian cavalry, two companies of the Camel Corps, four Maxim guns, two artillery pieces, and some unmounted irregulars. Wingate himself brought up the slower-moving infantry comprising the 9th and 13th Sudanese Battalions and one company of the 2nd Egyptian Battalion. Ahmed Fedil's force launched a determined attack on Mahon's men, but were finally defeated when Wingate's sweating infantry finally arrived. Ahmed Fedil escaped to the Khalifa leaving behind 400 dead and numerous women and children.

Wingate's men were exhausted and short of water but were granted little rest because they now had to secure the wells at Gedid. Having learned that the Khalifa's army was heading to the same place, Wingate marched his tired troops through the night, nearly breaking them in the process, but reached the wells just before the Khalifa arrived. At Gedid, Wingate was told by a Mahdist deserter that the Khalifa was encamped about seven miles away at Um Dibaykarat. In the early hours of 24 November, Wingate marched to engage the enemy, in the expectation it would stand and fight because it had no other option. At 3:40 a m., the EA reached some high ground overlooking the Khalifa's camp.

At about 5:10 a.m., dawn broke and the battle of Um Dibaykarat began when the Mahdists attacked and attempted to turn the EA's left flank. They lacked the numbers to perform this movement and Wingate, by extending the left of his line, was able to repel the assault. The Mahdists charged with all their usual ferocity but were shot down by the EA's firepower. As the attack faltered, Wingate ordered his men to advance. They chased the fleeing Mahdists for over a mile and stopped once they had taken their camp. By 6:25 a.m., the battle was over. In the camp, Mahdist survivors surrendered in their hundreds, while thousands of women and children were rounded up. The light was now better and Wingate and his officers were able to inspect the battlefield. Opposite the 9th Sudanese Battalion's former position they found the bodies of the Khalifa, of Ahmed Fedil, of the deputy khalifa, Ali Wad Helu, and those of two of the Khalifa's brothers and one of the Mahdi's sons. Wingate learned that having seen his attacks fail, the Khalifa had decided that his loyal emirs and their bodyguards should join him in martyrdom. Seated on the ground

---

18   Philip Magnus, *Kitchener. Portrait of an Imperialist* (London: John Murray, 1958), pp.151–152.

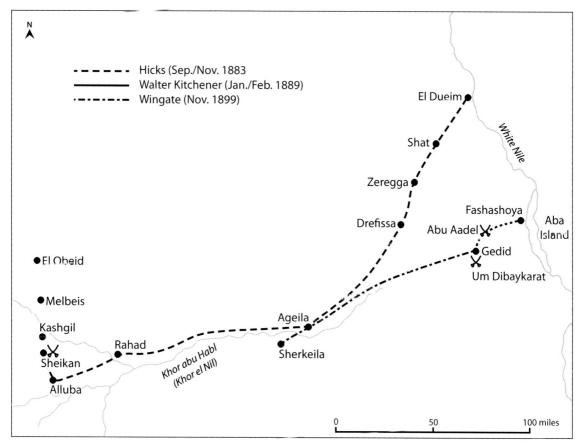

N

- – – – – Hicks (Sep./Nov. 1883
- ——— Walter Kitchener (Jan./Feb. 1889)
- ·–·–·– Wingate (Nov. 1899)

El Dueim

Shat

White Nile

Zeregga

Drefissa

Fashashoya

Abu Aadel ✗

Aba Island

El Obeid

Gedid

Um Dibaykarat

Melbeis

Kashgil

Ageila

Rahad

Sherkeila

Khor abu Habl (Khor el Nil)

Sheikan ✗

Alluba

0   50   100 miles

Marching into Kordofan, from Hicks to Wingate.

and facing towards Mecca, the Khalifa and his loyal band, as Wingate reported, 'unflinchingly met their death' as the group were shot by heavy fire from the EA. All were buried with due ceremony by 'the surviving members of their own tribesmen'. Once all was over, Wingate's force collected 3,000 men and 6,000 women and children. Among the captives was the wounded Osman Shaykh al Din. Osman Digna, however, had once again escaped.

Wingate's own losses were trivial: three men had been killed and 23 had been wounded. Mahdist losses were estimated at 1,000 killed and wounded. Wingate pointed out proudly in his despatch that 'From 4 p.m. on the 21st to 7 a.m. on the 24th, a period of 63 hours the troops had covered a distance of 57 miles and fought two successful actions.' Lord Kitchener could now report that 'The country has been finally relieved of the military tyranny which started in a movement of wild religious fanaticism upwards of 19 years ago. Mahdism is now a thing of the past, and I hope that a brighter era has at length opened for the Sudan.'[19]

19   TNA: WO 32/6143: Sudan. Nile Expedition. 'Despatch from Col. Sir Reginald Wingate to Major General Lord Kitchener of Khartoum, 25 November 1899, pp.1–12; Kitchener to the Under-Secretary of State for War, 25 November 1899, pp.3–4; 'Ismat Hasan Zulfo, *Karari. The Sudanese Account of the Battle of Omdurman* (London: Frederick Warne (Publishers) Ltd, 1980), pp.243–246; Churchill, *River War*, vol. 2, pp.287–300.

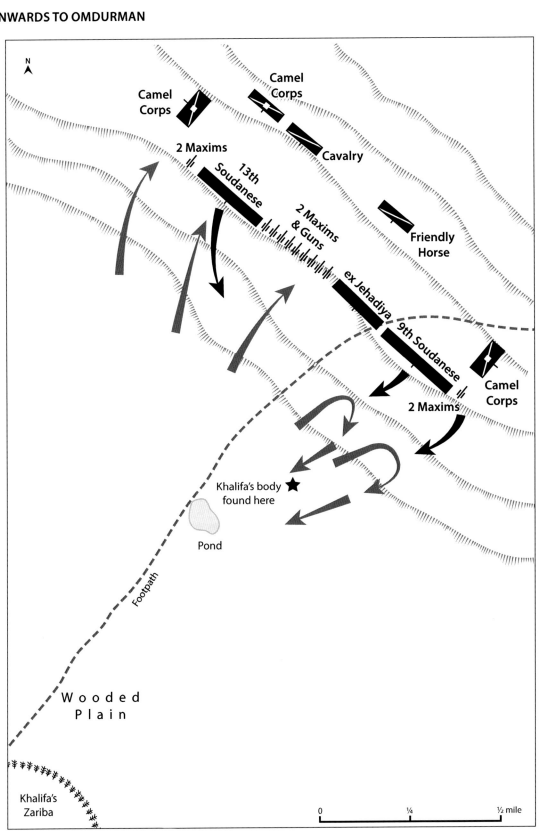

The Battle of Um Dibaykarat, 24 November 1899.

Conclusion

Even before the Khalifa's last battle, Britain and Egypt had settled the future government of the Sudan. On 19 January 1899, an agreement was signed that established the Anglo-Egyptian Condominium, a fiction that suggested Egypt had an equal say in the governance of the restored province of the Sudan. Britain, however, would rule the Sudan without the interference of the Egyptians or the European powers that controlled the Caisse de la Dette.[1] Kitchener, ennobled on 1 November 1898 as Baron Kitchener of Khartoum, of Aspall in the County of Suffolk, for securing the Sudan, became the first British governor general before resigning in December 1899 in order to serve in South Africa. He was succeeded by Reginald Wingate, who also became the Sirdar of the Egyptian Army. The last British governor general would be Sir Alexander Knox Helm, who served between 29 March 1954 and 12 December 1955.

The Anglo–Egyptian victory at Omdurman had avenged the 1885 death of General Charles Gordon, had settled the fate of the Sudan and had cemented Britain's control of the Nile Valley. The campaign had been Kitchener's victory, as many acknowledged; Hunter, for example, wrote that 'Kitchener deserves all he gets. He has run the show himself. His has been the responsibility.' Lieutenant Pritchard, writing later as 'An Officer', felt that victory was owed to the 'genius and untiring perseverance of our commander'.[2] Indeed, Kitchener had carried the plan of the campaign in his head throughout and had seen it through to maturation. Not only had the responsibility been great, but until early 1898 the pressure had been intensified by Kitchener's fear of being replaced, not as Sirdar, but as overall commander by a British Army general backed by the War Office.

Nevertheless, in the end, all obstacles were overcome, both man-made and natural. Firstly, Kitchener had ensured the campaign had been cheap, a necessity owing to Egypt's precarious finances. The overall bill had come to £[Egyptian]2,354,354, of which £[Egyptian]780,488 (about £800,000)

---

1   G. N. Sanderson, *England, Europe & the Upper Nile.1882–1899* (Edinburgh: Edinburgh University Press, 1965), pp.366–367.

2   LHCMA: Maurice Papers, Hunter Letters, 2/1/5, Hunter to Maurice, 14 October 1898, p.5; An Officer, (Lieutenant H.L. Pritchard), *The Sudan Campaign 1896–1899* (London: Chapman & Hall Ltd., 1899), p.261.

had been a gift of the British government. For this outlay, Egypt had, in theory, regained a territory of about one million square miles. Secondly, the logistical arrangements had been excellent, helped by the fact that Kitchener and many of his officers in the EA had experience of fighting in the Sudan or on the border with Egypt. The usual desert supply transport – camels – had been expertly organised by the Sirdar's brother, Colonel Walter Kitchener, throughout the campaign, and had been complemented by the numerous sailing craft plying the Nile. But it had been the appliance of science, so to speak, that had made a real difference. The construction of about 600 miles of railway, first along the banks of the Nile and then across the Nubian desert, thanks to the discovery of a water supply, helped convey both the Egyptian and British forces into the heart of the Mahdist empire. Thirdly, the gunboats had been crucial in sweeping the Mahdists from the river and enabling the safe passage of men and supplies: at Omdurman, the firepower of the gunboats proved crucial to the success of Kitchener's army. Fourthly, the ability of the Egyptian and British forces to communicate with the other and with Cairo and London was eased by the laying of about 900 miles of telegraph wires. Kitchener had rightly appreciated that to achieve victory logistical arrangements had to be near perfect. Indeed, in this regard, the campaign stands out as an exemplar of the Victorian army's way of warfare, demonstrating that the AEA became, in the words of one historian, 'a highly effective and economical instrument of imperialism … because the logistical difficulties had been mastered beforehand'.[3]

The cost in lives for the Anglo-Egyptian forces was relatively small. It has been estimated that altogether 1,200 men died in action or from their wounds or sickness. The exact number of Mahdists who were killed or wounded will never be known, although a contemporary British source estimated the figure at about 36,000. This probably did not include the Sudanese civilians who died, most at the hands of the Mahdists themselves, such as the members of the Ja'alin tribe in 1897.[4]

After the conclusion of the campaign, Kitchener and his officers, particularly Hunter and MacDonald, were lauded as heroes of the British empire. Hunter would serve with some success in the South African War of 1899-1902 before returning home in late-1900 because of his health. He never had an active command again. MacDonald, the hero of Omdurman, also fought in South Africa, but his career ended in disgrace because of a homosexual scandal and he committed suicide in 1903. Kitchener's career, however, continued on its upward trajectory. As commander-in-chief of the British forces in South Africa between 1900 and 1902, he defeated the Boers and finished this war. He then became commander-in-chief in India until 1909 and was promoted to field marshal after his departure. In 1911,

3   Winston Spencer Churchill, *The River War. An Historical Account of the Reconquest of the Soudan* (London: Longmans, Green and Co., 1899), vol. 2, pp.386–387; H. Bailes, 'Technology and Imperialism. A case study of the Victorian army in Africa', *Victorian Studies* 24:1, (Autumn, 1980), p.87.
4   Henry S. L. Alford & W. Dennistoun Sword, *The Egyptian Soudan. Its Loss and Recovery* (London: Macmillan and Co., Limited, 1898. Reprinted Dallington: The Naval & Military Press, 1992), pp.290–291.

Kitchener succeeded Cromer as the British Agent and Consul General of Egypt. Following the outbreak of the First World War in 1914, he was appointed secretary of state for war and remained in that office until his death at sea in June 1916. His famous image on one of this war's recruiting posters reminds us still of his importance as a national figure.

Of the surviving Mahdists, the deputy, or third, khalifa Muhammad al Sharif, was executed, along with two sons of the Mahdi, in August 1899 on the orders of Colonel Lewis, for allegedly plotting to join the Khalifa in Kordofan. Osman Shakyh al Din died in captivity in 1900 from the wound received during his father's last battle. Osman Digna was captured near Suakin in January 1900 and was imprisoned at Wadi Halfa. Eventually, he was allowed to reside there freely and even went on a pilgrimage to Mecca. He died in 1924.[5]

With the destruction of the Mahdist state the British hoped that Mahdism itself would be crushed forever. In this hope, they were to be disappointed. Mahdism did not simply disappear, it evolved into a more secular form, especially with the foundation of the Umma party in 1945 which still plays a role in Sudanese politics to this day. Whatever the British had hoped after the battle of Omdurman in 1898, the influence of the Mahdi and his beliefs have never gone away.[6]

---

5   For two contrasting views relating to the legitimacy of these executions, see 'Ismat Hasan Zulfo, *Karari. The Sudanese Account of the Battle of Omdurman* (London: Frederick Warne (Publishers) Ltd., 1980), p.247; Richard Hill, *Slatin Pasha*, (London: Oxford University Press, 1965), pp.68–69. H. C. Jackson, *Osman Digna* (London: Methuen & Co. Ltd., 1926), pp.160–167.

6   For a summary of Mahdist politics until 1998 see Peter Clark, 'Omdurman in the context of Sudanese History' in Edward M. Spiers (ed.), *Sudan. The Reconquest Reappraised* (London: Frank Cass, 1998), pp.217–220.

Glossary

'amil	provincial governor of an *'imala*
amir	commander or officer
ansar	helpers or followers of the *Mahdi*
ashraf	members of the *Mahdi's* family
bait al amana	the arsenal in Omdurman
bait al mal	treasury in Omdurman; provincial towns also had one.
fellahin	Egyptian peasant
ghanima	a tax on (or plundering of) the enemies of Islam
'imala	province governed by an *'amil*
jebel	hill, mountain
jibbah	patched shirt or smock worn by the *Mahdi's* followers
jihadiya	riflemen who were formerly slaves
Khalifa	successor to the *Mahdi*
khashkhasan	men of the Khalifa's bodyguard armed with obsolete firearms
khor	riverbed that is dry until the Nile rises
Mahdi	'chosen guide' or 'expected messenger'
Mahdiya	the Mahdist state 1885–1898
mulazimin	the Khalifa's rifle armed bodyguard
muqaddam	commander of a *muqaddamiya*, a section of the Khalifa's army
mushammaratiya	spearmen of the Khalifa's bodyguard
qadi al Islam	chief judge
qadi	judge
rub'	the principal unit of the Mahdist army
Turkiyya	the period of Turco-Egyptian rule of the Sudan 1820–1885
tukl	basic hut
ushr	tax on one-tenth of a merchant's imported goods
zaka	alms-giving; the third pillar of Islam
zariba	fortification made from thorn bushes

Bibliography

Primary Sources

British Library (BL)
Lansdowne Papers, 88906

Durham University, Sudan Archives (SAD)
General Sir Archibald Hunter. Sudan Campaigns, 964
Sir Reginald Wingate Papers, 231, 233, 266, 267
Sudan Intelligence Reports (SIR): Main Sequence, Intelligence Report, Egypt, No. 49,
    22 June – 18 August 1896, supplementary to 27 August 1895(6), <https://www.dur.
    ac.uk/library/asc/sudan/sirs; http://palimpsest.dur.ac.uk/slp/sirs1.html>, accessed 1
    Sept. 2020
SIR: Main Sequence, Intelligence Report, Egypt, No. 54, 1 June – 17 July, 1897, <https://
    www.dur.ac.uk/library/asc/sudan/sirs; http://palimpsest.dur.ac.uk/slp/sirs1.html>,
    accessed 5 Sept. 2020.
SIR: Main Sequence Intelligence Report, Egypt, No. 55, 18 July – 30 September 1897,
    <https://www.dur.ac.uk/library/asc/sudan/sirs; http://palimpsest.dur.ac.uk/slp/sirs1.
    html>, accessed 5 Sept. 2020
SIR: Main Sequence, Intelligence Report, Egypt, No. 59, 13 February – 23 May 1898
    <https://www.dur.ac.uk/library/asc/sudan/sirs; http://palimpsest.dur.ac.uk/slp/sirs1.
    html>, accessed 15 Sept. 2020.
SIR: Main Sequence, Intelligence Report, Egypt, Report, No. 60, 25 May to 31 December
    1898, p.2, <https://www.dur.ac.uk/library/asc/sudan/sirs; http://palimpsest.dur.
    ac.uk/slp/sirs1.html>, accessed 12 December 2020.

**King's College, University of London, Liddell Hart Centre for Military Archives
    (LHCMA)**
Major General Sir J. Frederick Maurice Papers, General Sir Archibald Hunter Letters:
    2/1/2

The National Archives (TNA)
Cabinet Papers, CAB 37
Kitchener Papers, PRO/30/57
War Office (WO) 32 Papers Relating to the Sudan Campaign: 6142, Operations; 6143,
    Sudan. Nile Expedition; 6380, Sudan Campaign

National Army Museum (NAM):
Cameron Letters, 1983-05-55
Churcher Diary 1978-04-53
Fitton Letters 1994-10-42

Fraser Letters 1979-06-139
Gore Anley Papers 1984-12-50
Granville Letter 2004-03-31
Graeme Letter 2006-04-33
Hodgson Letters 2003-08-8
Kitchener-Wood Letters, 1968-07-234
Lewis Journal, 1975-03-9
Loch Diary 1986-08-66
Lloyd Letters 1977-09-43
Rawlinson Diary 1952-01-33-4
Ready Diary 1966-09-142
Robinson Papers 1993-07-55
Sandelands Letters 1996-08-384
Senior NCO of the Royal Warwickshire Regiment Letter 1998-06-144
Sparkes Letter 1966-04-44
Watson Letters 1983-04-112
Watson Papers 1984-12-4
Wyndham Papers, 1963-10-27

Queen Mary, University of London [QM]
Sir Neville Lyttelton Papers NL/2

West Sussex Record Office (WSRO)
Frederick Ivor Maxse Papers, 219, 327, 367

Contemporary accounts and published primary sources

Alford, Henry S. L. and Sword, W. Dennistoun, *The Egyptian Soudan. Its loss and recovery* (London: Macmillan and Co., Ltd., 1898. Reprinted Dallington: The Naval & Military Press, 1992)

An Officer (Lieutenant H. L. Pritchard), *The Sudan Campaign 1896-1899* (London: Chapman & Hall Ltd., 1899)

Atteridge, A. Hilliard, *Towards Khartoum. The Story of the Soudan War of 1896* (London: A. D. Innes & Co., 1897)

Burleigh, Bennet, *Khartoum Campaign*, (London: Chapman Hall Ltd., 1899)

Bennett, Ernest N., *The Downfall of the Dervishes* (London: Methuen & Co. 1898. Reprinted: London: Forgotten Books, 2012)

Bennett, Ernest N., 'After Omdurman', *Contemporary Review*, 75 (January 1899), pp.18–33

Churchill, Randolph S., *Youth. Winston S. Churchill 1874–1900* (London: Mandarin Paperbacks, Minerva Paperback, 1991)

Churchill, Winston Spencer, *River War. An Historical Account of the Reconquest of the Soudan* (London: Longmans, Green, And Co., 1899), 2 volumes

Colvile, Colonel H. E., *History of the Sudan Campaign* (London: Intelligence Division of the War Office, 1889), Part 1

Daley, M. W., (ed.), 'Omdurman and Fashoda 1898. Edited and annotated letters of F. R. Wingate', *Bulletin (British Society for Middle Eastern Studies)*, 10:1 (1983), pp.21–37

Egerton, Granville, *With the 72nd Highlanders in the Sudan Campaign* (London: Eden Fisher & Co. Ltd, 1909)

'Fighting Mac 1898. Page 2 of an original letter by Major General Sir Hector Macdonald,' *Soldiers of the Queen*, 94, (1998)

Gatacre, Major General W., 'After the Atbara and Omdurman', *The Contemporary Review*, 75, (Feb. 1899), pp.299–304

Haggard, Lieutenant Colonel Andrew, *Under Crescent and Star* (Edinburgh and London: William Blackwood and Sons, 1895)

Harrington, Peter and Sharif, Frederic A., (eds.), *Omdurman 1898: The Eyewitnesses Speak* (London: Greenhill Books, 1998)

Knight, E. F., *Letters from the Soudan* (London: Macmillan & Co., 1897)

Martin Ernest J., (ed.), 'The Lincolnshires at Omdurman, September, 1898. Diary of Lieutenant Hamilton Hodgson, *Journal of the Society for Army Historical Research*, 21:82, (1942) pp.70–82

Harris, John., (ed.), The Nile Expedition of 1898 and Omdurman – The Diary of Sergeant S. W. Harris, Grenadier Guards, *Journal of the Society for Army Historical Research*, 78:313, (Spring 2000), pp.11–28

Montague-Stuart-Wortley, E. J., My Reminiscences of Egypt and the Sudan (from 1882 to 1899), *Sudan Notes and Records*, 34:2 (December 1953), pp.172–188

Maurice, Colonel J. F., *The Campaign of 1882 in Egypt* (London: J. B. Hayward & Son, 1887. Reprinted: Portsmouth: Eyre & Spottiswood, Grosvenor Press, 1973)

Maurice, Major General Sir Frederick (ed.), *The Life of General Lord Rawlinson of Trent. From His Journals and Letters* (London: Cassell & Co. Ltd, 1928),

Maxse, Colonel F. I., *Seymour Vandeleur* (London: The *National Review* Office, 1906. Reprinted: London: Forgotten Books, 2015)

Meredith, John (ed.), *Omdurman Diaries 1898. Eyewitness Accounts of the Legendary Campaign* (Barnsley: Leo Cooper, 1998)

Milner, Alfred, *England in Egypt* (London: Edward Arnold, 1894)

Scott, Douglas (ed.), *Douglas Haig. The Preparatory Prologue 1861–1914. Diaries and Letters* (Barnsley: Pen & Sword Military, 2006)

Slatin Pasha, Colonel Sir R., *Fire and Sword in the Sudan. A Personal Narrative of Fighting and Serving the Dervishes* (London: Edward Arnold, 1896. Reprinted: London: The Long Riders' Guild Press, nd.)

Stanton, E. A. E., 'The Peoples of the Anglo–Egyptian Sudan', *Journal of the Royal African Society*, 2:6 (January, 1903), pp.121–131

Steevens, G. W., *With Kitchener to Khartum*, (Edinburgh & London: William Blackwood & Sons, 1898)

Watkins, Owen S., *With Kitchener's Army* (London: S. W. Partridge & Co., 1899),

Woods, Frederick (ed.), *Young Winston's Wars. The Original Despatches of Winston Churchill* (London: Sphere Books Ltd., 1972)

Autobiographies, biographies and memoirs

Arthur, Sir George, *Life of Lord Kitchener* (London: Macmillan & Co., 1920), vol. 1

Arthur, Sir George. *General Sir John Maxwell*, (London: John Murray, 1932)

Atwood, Rodney, *General Lord Rawlinson. From Tragedy to Triumph* (London: Bloomsbury Academic, 2018)

Beckett, Ian F. W. *Johnnie Gough V. C.* (London: Tom Donovan Publishing Ltd., 1989)

Bedri, Babikr, *The Memoirs of Babikr Bedri* (London: Oxford University Press, 1969)

Cecil, Lord Edward, *The Leisure of An Egyptian Official* (London: Hodder & Stoughton, 1921)

Churchill, Winston S., *My Early Life. A Roving Commission* (London: The Reprint Society, 1944)

Cromer, The Earl of, *Modern Egypt*, (London: Macmillan, 1908), vol. 2

Daly, M. W., *The Sirdar. Sir Reginald Wingate and the British Empire in the Middle East* (Philadelphia: American Philosophical Society, 1997)

Gatacre, Beatrice, *General Gatacre. The Story of the Life and Services of Sir William Forbes Gatacre 1843–1906* (London: John Murray, 1910)

Grenfell, Field Marshal Lord, *Memoirs* (London: Hodder & Stoughton, 1925)

Hicks Beach, Lady Victoria, *Life of Sir Michael Hicks Beach (Earl St. Aldwyn)* (London: Macmillan & Co. Ltd., 1932), vol. 2

Hill, Richard, *Slatin Pasha* (London: Oxford University Press, 1965)

Hunter, Archie, *Kitchener's Sword-arm. The Life and Campaigns of General Sir Archibald Hunter* (Staplehurst: Spellmount, 1996)

Jackson, H. C., *Osman Digna*, (London: Methuen & Co., Ltd, 1926)

Jackson, Sir Herbert W., Fashoda 1898, *Sudan Notes and Records*, 3:1 (January 1920), pp.1–11

James, Lionel Colonel, *High Pressure* (London: John Murray, 1929)

Magnus, Philip, *Kitchener. Portrait of an Imperialist* (London: John Murray, 1958)

Manning, Stephen, *Evelyn Wood VC. Pillar of Empire* (Barnsley: Pen & Sword, 2007)

Nash, N. S., *Chitral Charlie. The rise and fall of Major General Charles Townshend* (Barnsley: Pen & Sword Military, 2010)

Newton, Lord, *Lord Lansdowne: A Biography* (London: Macmillan, 1929)

Owen, Roger, *Lord Cromer* (Oxford: Oxford University Press, 2004)

Pollock, John, *Kitchener* (Combined paperback edition, London: Robinson, 2002), vol. 1

Pugh, R. J. M., *Wingate Pasha* (Barnsley: Pen & Sword Military, 2011)

Repington, Lieutenant Colonel Charles à Court *Vestigia* (London: Constable and Company Ltd., 1919)

Roberts, Andrew, *Salisbury. Victorian Titan* (London: Weidenfeld & Nicholson, 1999)

Royle, Trevor, *Fighting Mac. The Downfall of Major-General Sir Hector Macdonald* (Edinburgh: Mainstream Publishing, 1982.

Royle, Trevor, *The Kitchener Enigma* (London: Michael Joseph, 1985)

Scudamore, Frank, *A Sheaf of Memories*, (New York: E. P. Dutton & Company, 1925)

Wingate, Sir Ronald *Wingate of the Sudan. The Life and Times of Sir Reginald Wingate* (London: John Murray, 1955)

Secondary Sources

Barczewski, Stephanie, *Heroic Failure and the British* (New Haven: Yale University Press, 2016)

Bates, Darrell, *The Fashoda Incident of 1898. Encounter on the Nile* (Oxford: Oxford University Press, 1984)

Baynes, John, *Far from a donkey. The Life of General Sir Ivor Maxse KCB, CVO, DSO.* (London: Brasseys, 1995)

Beaver, William, *Under Every Leaf* (London: Biteback Publishing, 2012)

Beckett, Ian F. W., *A British Profession of Arms. The Politics of Command in the Late Victorian Army* (Norman: University of Oklahoma Press, 2018)

Boot, Max, *War Made New. Technology, Warfare, and the Course of History, 1500 to Today* (New York: Gotham Books, 2006)

Curtin, Philip D., *Disease and Empire. The Health of European Troops in the Conquest of Africa* (Cambridge: Cambridge University Press, 1998)

Featherstone, Donald, *Omdurman 1898. Kitchener's Victory in the Sudan* (Westport, CT and London: Praeger, 2005)

Featherstone, Donald, *Weapons & Equipment of the Victorian Soldier* (London: Arms and Armour Press, 1978; 1996)

Finkel, Caroline, *Osman's Dream. The Story of the Ottoman Empire 1300–1923* (London: John Murray, 2006)

Green, Dominic, *Three Empires on the Nile. The Victorian Jihad 1869–1899* (New York: Free Press, 2007)

Holt, P. M., and Daly M. W., *A History of the Sudan. From the Coming of Islam to the present day* (London: Longman 1988)

Keown-Boyd, Henry, *A Good Dusting. A Centenary Review of the Sudan Campaigns 1883–1899* (London: Book Club Associates, 1986)

Konstam, Angus, *Nile River Gunboats 1882–1918*, (Oxford: Osprey Publishing, 2016),

Lamothe, Ronald M., *Slaves of Fortune. Sudanese soldiers and the River War 1896-1898*, (James Currey: Woodbridge, 2011)

Lewis, David L., *The Race to Fashoda* (New York: Weidenfeld & Nicolson, 1987)

Miller, Stephen M. (ed.), *Queen Victoria's Wars. British Military Campaigns, 1857–1902* (Cambridge: Cambridge University Press, 2021)

Moore–Harell, Alice, *Gordon and the Sudan. Prologue to the Mahdiyya 1877–1880* (London: Frank Cass, 2011)

Robinson, R. & Gallagher, J. with Denny Alice, *Africa and the Victorians* (London: Macmillan, 1981)

Sanderson, G. N., *England, Europe and the Upper Nile* (Edinburgh: Edinburgh University Press, 1965)

Sanderson, G. N., 'The Nile Basin and the Eastern Horn, 1870–1908', in Roland Oliver and G. N. Sanderson (eds), *The Cambridge History of Africa 1870–1905* (Cambridge: Cambridge University Press, 1985), vol. 6, pp.592–679

Sandes, Lieutenant Colonel E. W. C., *The Royal Engineers in Egypt and the Sudan*, (Chatham: Institution of Royal Engineers, 1937)

Sèby, Berny, *Heroic Imperialists in Africa. The Promotion of British and French Colonial Heroes, 1870–1939* (Manchester: Manchester University Press, 2013)

Snook, Colonel Mike, *Beyond the Reach of Empire. Wolseley's Failed Campaign to Save Gordon and Khartoum* (London: Frontline Books, 2013)

Spiers, Edward (ed.), *Sudan. The conquest reappraised*, (London: Frank Cass, 1998)

Spiers, Edward M., *The Scottish Soldier and Empire, 1854–1902* (Edinburgh: Edinburgh University Press, 2006)

Spiers, Edward M., *The Victorian solider in Africa* (Manchester: Manchester University Press, 2004)

Theobald, A. B., *The Mahdiya. A History of the Anglo–Egyptian Sudan 1881–1899* (London: Longmans, Green & Co., Ltd., 1951)

Vandervort, Bruce, *Wars of Imperial Conquest in Africa 1830–1914* (London: UCL Press, 1998)

Wesseling, H. L., *Divide and Rule. The Partition of Africa 1880–1914* (Wesport, CT: Praeger Publishers, 1996)

Wright, William, *Omdurman 1898*, (Stroud: Spellmount, 2012)

Ziegler Philip, *Omdurman* (London: Collins, 1973)

Zulfo, 'Ismat Hasan, *Karari*, (London, Frederick Warne (Publishers), 1980)

Articles and Chapters

Bailes, H., 'Technology and Imperialism. A case study of the Victorian army in Africa', *Victorian Studies* 24:1, (Autumn, 1980), pp.83–104

Beckett, Ian F. W., 'Kitchener and the Politics of Command' in Edward M. Spiers (ed.), *Sudan. The Reconquest Reappraised* (London: Frank Cass, 1998), pp.35–53

Clark, Peter, 'The Battle of Omdurman in the Context of Sudanese History', in Edward M. Spiers, (ed.), *Sudan. The Reconquest Reappraised* (London: Frank Cass Publishers, 1998), pp.202–222

Daly, M. W., 'The Soldier as Historian: F. R. Wingate and the Sudanese Mahdia', *Journal of Imperial and Commonwealth History*, 17:1 (1988), pp.99–106

Dighton, Adam, 'Race, Masculinity and Imperialism: The British Officer and the Egyptian Army (1882–1899)', *War & Society*, 35:1 (2016), pp.1–18

Gooch, John, 'Italy, Abyssinia and the Sudan 1885-98', in Edward M. Spiers (ed.), *Sudan. The Reconquest Reappraised* (London: Frank Cass, 1998), pp.128–145

Spiers, Edward M., 'Campaigning Under Kitchener', in Edward M. Spiers (ed.), *Sudan. The Reconquest Reappraised* (London: Frank Cass, 1998), pp.54–81

Spiers, Edward M., 'Intelligence and Command in Britain's Small Colonial Wars of the 1890s', *Intelligence and National Security*, 22:5 (2007), pp.661–681

Spiers, Edward M., 'Reconquest of the Sudan, 1896–1898', in Stephen M. Miller (ed.), *Queen Victoria's Wars. British Military Campaigns, 1857–1902* (Cambridge: Cambridge University Press, 2021), pp.260–280

Stearn, Roger T., 'G. W. Steevens and the message of empire', *Journal of Imperial and Commonwealth History*, 17:2 (1989), pp.210–231

Stearn, Roger T., 'War correspondents and colonial war, c. 1870–1900', in John Mackenzie (ed.), *Popular Imperialism and the Military 1850–1950* (Manchester: Manchester University Press, 1992)

Surridge, Keith, 'Herbert Kitchener' in Steven J. Corvi & Ian F. W. Beckett (eds), *Victoria's Generals* (Barnsley: Pen & Sword Military, 2009)

G. Tylden, 'Egyptian Army Uniforms, 1882–1898' *Journal of the Society for Army Historical Research*, 20:77, (Spring, 1941), pp.56–57

Unpublished theses

Mahaffey, Corinne, 'The Fighting Profession. The Professionalisation of the British Line Officer Corps, 1870–1902', (unpublished PhD thesis, University of Glasgow, 2004)

e-Books

Brighton, Terry, *Winston's Charge. Lieutenant Churchill in the British Army's Last Cavalry Charge* (Hard Corps Books, 2020, Kindle e-book)

Lyttelton, General Sir Neville, *Eighty Years: Soldiering, Politics, Games* (London: Hodder & Stoughton, 1927, Borodino Books, 2017, Kindle e-book)

Smith-Dorrien, General Sir Horace, *Memories of Forty-Eight Years' Service* (London: John Murray, 1925, Pickle Partners Publishing, 2013, Kindle e-book)

Websites

Flaherty, Chris, '1883 Till 1914 Army of Egypt Infantry', <http://www.ottoman-uniforms-.com/1883-till-1914-army-of-egypt-infantry/>, accessed 29 June 2020

<http://www.uniformology.com/LANCERS-11,html>, accessed 30 October 2020

Index